LOST
IN THE SACRED

LOST
IN THE SACRED

Why

the

Muslim

World

Stood

Still

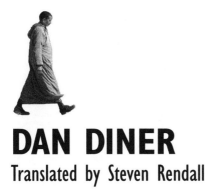

DAN DINER
Translated by Steven Rendall

Princeton University Press
Princeton and Oxford

First published in Germany by Ullstein Buchverlage GmbH under the title *Versiegelte Zeit* © by

Ullstein Buchverlage GmbH, Berlin. Published in 2005 by Propyläen Verlag

English edition copyright © 2009 by Princeton University Press

Published by Princeton University Press, 41 William Street, Princeton, New Jersey 08540

In the United Kingdom: Princeton University Press, 6 Oxford Street, Woodstock,

Oxfordshire OX20 1TW

Library of Congress Cataloging-in-Publication Data

Diner, Dan, 1946–

[Versiegelte Zeit. English]

Lost in the sacred : why the Muslim world stood still / Dan Diner ; translated by Steven Rendall.

p.   cm.

Includes bibliographical references and index.

ISBN 978-0-691-12911-2 (hardcover : alk. paper)   1. Islamic countries—Civilization.

2. Islamic countries—History.   I. Rendall, Steven.   II. Title.

DS35.62.D5613   2009

909'.09767—dc22   2008035413

British Library Cataloging-in-Publication Data is available

This book has been composed in Adobe Garamond Pro

Printed on acid-free paper. ∞

press.princeton.edu

Printed in the United States of America

1 3 5 7 9 10 8 6 4 2

Maxime Rodinson
1915–2004

In memoriam

CONTENTS

PREFACE

Discourse about the Muslim World in general and the Arab Middle East in particular is an ambiguous undertaking, generally evoking strong reactions. Two postures informing such discourse are at loggerheads. One claims that the lamentable state of the region is the result of the religion and the culture of Islam impeding modernity. The other blames Western domination—if it admits that there is a crisis at all. Delving into the heart of the debate reveals a profound controversy about the very underpinnings of Western culture—the trinity of secularization, enlightenment, and modernity—and their legacy and legitimacy. How far is their reach? Are they indeed universal, as they claim to be? Or are they just dubious means and modes of Western supremacy and dominance imposed on others?

For about a generation a postmodern and postcolonial discourse in the humanities and social sciences has successfully challenged the traditional canon on which Western supremacy is alleged to have established itself. This enterprise has had accomplishments. Customary worldviews have been revised substantially. It seems, however, that the tide is turning—not backward into old and refuted perceptions of knowledge and meaning, but rather toward a post-postcolonial interpretation that transcends the binary juxtaposition of modernity and modernity in reverse. Such a comprehension of the world preserves the universal advantages of secularization, enlightenment, and modernity. Any intention to undermine the prestige and standing of those three pillars, entailing enchantment, knowledge, and change, gives cause for concern. Although they are Western in origin, their validity is universal. Their universality, however, may be realized in a multitude of forms, according to the specific cultures and religions involved.

This book was originally written and published in German. For the translation into English I thank Steven Rendall. Thanks go as well to Bruce Allen, Mark Bellis, and especially to Madeleine Adams, who copyedited the text with great skill. Also, I would like to thank Robert Zwarg for his support in the final preparation of the manuscript. Last, but not least, I would like to express my gratitude to Brigitta van Rheinberg of Princeton University Press, who from the very beginning was enthusiastic about having the book published by her press.

*limadha ta'akhkhara al-muslimun wa-taqaddama
ghayruhum?*

Why have Muslims fallen behind,
and why have others forged ahead?
(Shakib Arslan, 1930)

SOME SEVENTY-FIVE YEARS AGO, a book bearing the title *Why
Have Muslims Fallen Behind, and Why Have Others Forged Ahead?* was
published in Cairo.[1] At the time, the Syrian Lebanese journalist, writer,
and politician Shakib Arslan (1869–1946) was addressing a Muslim and
Arab public—but his question has lost none of its sting today. It has, if
anything, grown more acute and pressing because the situation in the
Arab world, and in many parts of the wider Muslim domain, shows not
much improvement compared with the West, but also compared with
non-Western cultures—in Asia, for instance, especially in the Far East.
In the Middle East, time seems to stand still. Indeed, in light of the development now sweeping other parts of the world, it seems to be falling
behind.

How did it come to this? How could this occur in the Arab-Muslim
world? Is this lamentable situation exogenous, arising because of Western
culture's dominance and its subversive effects on the region? Or is it endogenous? Does it come down to economics or to politics? Or is it a result
of religion or of culture? And is there a remedy? What needs to be done?

These questions, pressing as they are for the Middle East and for the
wider Muslim world, cannot be answered adequately, much less conclu-
sively, here or indeed anywhere. They are too complex to yield simple or

facile answers. Still, these questions continue to be raised, not always openly, often hesitantly, sometimes even shamefacedly. Questions about the condition of the Arab-Muslim world, especially when posed by Westerners, are liable to be deemed offensive, as if, right from the outset, they imply an unspoken, disparaging judgment of Islam—a civilization that for centuries was anathema to Christendom and the wider West.[2]

Any concern about the Middle East and its inhabitants' lived experience arouses suspicion—suspicion, as it happens, that is quite uncalled for, despite being deeply ingrained today in the West. For far too long, Christendom and the West as its secular garb generally have regarded the religion, culture, and civilization of Islam as constituting the ultimate Other. At best, East and West have been familiar aliens: simultaneously close and far apart. Over time, this relationship of constant proximity engendered its own set of images, which depicted the Orient, Islam, and Arabs in an unfavorable light. It was important for Muslims to repudiate such images of themselves that had been formatted by others, especially when these had evidently hardened into a canon.

The Palestinian American literary scholar Edward Said outlined what this canon entailed in his book *Orientalism*, published in the late 1970s. In it, Said took on the body of Western scholarship concerning the "Orient" and Islam, addressing himself to specialists and the general public alike. Since then, the term *Orientalism* has been deemed derogatory, referring to an academically shaped attitude toward the East in general and toward Islam in particular, in which Westerners rewrite the "Orient" (and Islam) in light of their image of the Other, only to disparage what they have rewritten. Said argued that the scholarship amassed in this dubious undertaking had, in effect, advanced the West's dominance and penetration of the region. In essence, he was mounting a critique of the notion of a canon of Oriental scholarship as a necessary first step toward intellectual and cultural decolonization.[3]

With his thesis of a Western "Orientalizing" canon—a thesis that, however accurate in certain respects, is nevertheless questionable overall— Said put his finger on a fatal weakness in the traditional academic representation of the Other. To be sure, much in the arsenal of scholarship on the Orient and Islam was in need of critical overhaul and revision. But in the years since Said wrote his seminal work, this has largely happened;

indeed, it has at times overshot the mark. So the problem Said bequeathed to posterity is now situated elsewhere: his critique of the West's mode of imaging the Orient has succeeded all too well, and this success has not always benefited the people of the region. One can go further: Said's views have abetted an unholy alliance between *premodern* conditions still prevalent in the Middle East and an apologetic *postmodern* discourse that has established itself in the West.

The unfortunate effect of this alliance has been to withhold from Middle Easterners the fruits of modernity, which is to say their experience of the present. It is this present lost that prompts the painful question about the state of affairs in which the Arab and Muslim world finds itself entangled. This is the question that Shakib Arslan has spelled out so explicitly in the title of his book.

This book is something of an intervention, designed to transcend contemporary fault lines and to see the Muslim world's predicament with fresh eyes. It seeks to clarify the state of the Arab-Muslim East but not to genuflect to the pieties of postmodern discourse. The questions it raises are chiefly related to the past, although their implications resonate in the present.

My concern with the Middle East is both historical and political. It grows out of my involvement with the region over many years, out of my intellectual participation in its fate. My aim is to revisit questions linked to an earlier interest of mine: the fate and the social fabric of the people living there. I do not deny that interest in this subject has been related to political projects that have sought to induce radical change. And yet those projects, even in their day, generated the very questions that now perplex us: questions of development, modernity, secularization, and emancipation.[4]

These radical political inclinations are no more. Their proponents spoke in the then not yet discredited categories of the great worldviews of the late nineteenth and early twentieth centuries—freedom and equality, socialism and communism, Marxism and psychoanalysis. The traditions urged with such radical intent and in such multiple guises were indeed those of the West, especially the Enlightenment. Cloaked in a seemingly anti-Western rhetoric, the project of radical change indeed sought to inject these traditions into the Middle East. Nothing came of it, however. But the traditions they represented—and this beyond all time-bound ideological distortions—still supply a useful compass for navigating the present crisis in the region.

Prompted by pressing political issues, two areas suggested themselves for close scrutiny. One was the Palestinian conflict; the other was the continuity of the prevailing central state power in the Arab Middle East and the striking weaknesses of everything related to civil institutions. The first area of study fed into the second by asking how it came about that the legal guarantees regarding possession of land in the Middle East were so poorly articulated. Control of land, as well as the legal and institutional arrangements put in place to ensure that control, was in flux.[5]

The second area of study was the role of state, society, and property in the Middle East. Framing it in terms of the history of institutions and social structures, I sought to explain the striking preponderance of the power of the central state. Paradoxically, because of its autonomous character, the state, for all its capacity to be the stronghold of power, is structurally weak because it is insulated from any changes or transformations society potentially might create. When changes *are* instigated, they are top-down, decreed and enforced by state power. They are administrative and by nature authoritarian, and they involve subordinating the population.[6]

Some of the language used in this book is drawn from a different time, which is not a bad thing. Even if current thought has shifted away from "society" to "culture," the old categories have not lost their explanatory power, especially with regard to cultures and societies that are struggling to cope with modernity or (as in the case of Muslim countries, particularly in the Middle East) have not performed up to the expectations modernity demands. It is instructive to try to explore such questions without instantly and automatically invoking religion as the cause.

Culture, however, gets its due in this undertaking—culture in the sense of "soft" phenomena such as belief and ethics, law and conscience. Concerning our subject, there is no way to evade these questions. They must be raised either covertly or overtly, because in the Muslim world, the question of culture seems thoroughly imbued with the sacred.

The presence of the sacred as studied in this book is less related to the religious sphere in the narrow sense (that is, theology, dogma, or liturgy) than with the burning omnipresence of transcendence in all aspects of life—and precisely where Western thinking would least expect it. Thus the sacred, as construed here, is an anthropological energy of sorts that needs to be culturally differentiated, temporally delimited, and institutionally regulated if it is to be rendered bearable. Such delimitations of the sacred, including even its partial profanation, are resorted to in a lengthy process of disenchanting the world, a process embodied in secularization.

Secularization is a process of partitioning and diversifying a social order that once happened to be an integral whole and from whose core the sacred radiated. In the process of secularization, that whole dissolves into discrete spheres of inner and outer, private and public, holy and profane. In this process, the divine sovereign is transformed into worldly procedures; multiple separate powers replace the absolute integrity of the sacred in meaning as well as in function.

Secularization delimits the sacred. Without the constraints of secularization, the sacred is omnipresent in daily life and in all its routines: in the world of work, in the sphere of ethics and morals—and in politics, too. When the sacred is ubiquitous, the distinction between the inner and the outer worlds is transcended. In the domain of violence and the use of force, the energy of the sacred transgresses the human drive to preserve one's own biological existence. The distinction between worldly and heavenly is transgressed.

The violence particular to sacred time is not intrinsic to the religion of Islam. It is much more the result of a traumatic collision between two modes of life: the Western secular mode, based on the acceleration of time (that is to say modernity), and Muslim lifeworlds, which, while reflecting a traditional self-image of superiority, are characteristically impregnated with the sacred and therefore based on the deceleration of time.

My aim is not to write a history of Arabs and Muslims, or, for that matter, of the Middle East. Instead, I explore questions of development (or, more precisely, of why it has been hampered) in the domain of Muslim culture and civilization. Moreover, this phenomenon became visible in the early modern period, when massive transformations were discernible in the West. The emerging contrast between the West and the Muslim world is diagnosed as the foundational cause of the present crisis. Although analytical in its approach, this historical perspective is infused with empathy for its subject. This is not a contradiction because empathy is a means of understanding.

This book is composed of six chapters. They follow a timeline, inducting the reader into issues central to the malaise with which I began. Chapter 1 deals with the present. It examines a recent review of this hampered development in the Arab world. The document in question is the *Arab Human Development Report*, issued by the United Nations for the first time in 2002. This picture of the Arab world sketched in dry statistics may serve as a stimulus to tackle historical questions from the more distant past.

Moving from the present day to the recent past, chapter 2 foregrounds 1924, the year when the Turkish Republic, arisen from the ashes of the Ottoman Empire, abolished Islamic institutions of long standing, notably the caliphate. The deepening crisis into which this plunged the Muslim world spread to adjoining areas such as India, which, prior to that subcontinent's partitioning in 1947, had the largest concentration of Muslims in the world. The situation in British India after the 1920s matters for our inquiry, since the relationship between the Hindu and the Muslim population became increasingly troubled as independence approached. From this fertile soil sprang the first shoots of an interpretation of Islam that would later be characterized as radical. Moreover, the topography—the matrix of time and space—of the crisis that struck the Muslim world in the 1920s and 1930s yields insight into even earlier events. I will show how deeply this crisis was rooted in the circumstances of the nineteenth century and how it was aggravated by the rivalries of the Great Powers, playing the "Great Game" in the area encompassing the North-West Frontier and Central Asia, and also by the "Eastern Question," which sealed the fate of the Ottoman Empire.

The causes of this crisis lie in the different trajectories taken in the early modern era by the West and the Muslim world. We will explore this in chapter 3, which raises the question of secularization and modernity in relation to one of its core aspects—language and printing—and pursues this issue down to the present. The mechanical reproduction of texts marks, as much as anything does, the advent of the modern era. We will ask why, in the Muslim world, the introduction of the printing press was delayed for about three hundred years. Did this delay impede the spread of knowledge, and thus development? What role did the sacred play in this? And what kind of profanation was wrought by the mechanical reproduction of writing? At issue is the presence of the sacred in the very pores and interstices of Arabic writing, and in the language itself, especially in the Muslim's holy book, the Koran. The presence of the sacred is glossed here as a barrier to the kind of reform of language and usage that is the sine qua non of modern development. We go on to ask whether reform is being hampered today by some sacred taboo analogous to the earlier Muslim resistance to printing.

The early modern era was a time of radical change, as medieval Christendom evolved into what we now recognize as Western culture. The Renaissance, the invention of printing, the Reformation, and the "discovery" of the New World—these upended the entire medieval worldview. Chapter 4 discusses how little this process was remarked upon in the Muslim world. That this was so may be linked to the massive expansion of the Ottoman Empire then under way and its unquestioned domination of the trade routes in the Old World. Meanwhile, in the West the riches of the New World, in the form of gold and silver, had amplified the emerging new economic order of mercantilism. The dynamic unleashed by the mercantile spirit crafted a work ethic that would be fully developed only in the later industrial age. If the Ottoman Empire, and with it the Muslim world, managed to remain untouched by this early development, it would be drawn into this whirl at a later date and under unequal terms. Whether the Ottoman Empire was drifting into decline or stagnation, or was even on the brink of collapse—a question prompted by an emerging gap, then becoming increasingly evident, between the institutional, technological, and scientific cultures of East and West—was repeatedly debated from the late sixteenth century onward, especially among Ottoman intellectuals and bureaucrats.

Chapter 5 shows why and how the central government regulated "society" in the Middle East. The form and processes of the worlds of work and social life were generally determined by institutions and legal ordinances imbued with the sacred. From the beginnings of Islam to the end of the Middle Ages (that is, Islam's classical era), the conjoining of political power and economic benefit was pursued by means of institutions whose purpose was to extract riches in the form of booty, taxes, and rents; in a later age, there were also ground rents for oil resources. The accumulation of prop-erty, the limits that were applied to the use of capital, and, in particular, the form of labor and its temporal regulation are discussed in this chapter with reference to the Arab-Muslim Middle Ages. The point of thus fram-ing our discussion is that Muslim civilization was then unquestionably su-perior to Western Christendom. So why did this scenario not yield what we now recognize as development? Why did the high culture of the classi-cal age of Islam not lead, as analogous historical tendencies later would in the West, to an era of Muslim protomodernity—despite the fact that in that earlier Muslim world, elements of "bourgeois society" were not hard to find? Was this due to external factors, such as the incursions of the Mongols or the Black Death? Or did it result rather from the characteristic unmediated domination of the fabric of social life by central rule?

Chapter 6 concludes the study by asking how time and history are represented in Muslim civilization. What reading of history did the Arab-Muslim world develop? How did it see itself in relation to the flow of time? Quite unlike the historical thought developed in the West—namely, as something tied inextricably to movement and development—within the context of Islam, the concept of time has been "sealed off," as it were, by the sacred. Does the phenomenon of decelerated time express material circumstances or perhaps a cultural anthropology particular to the Mid-dle East? Or does the key lie in Islam as a religion? And just how do the material and the cultural worlds relate to each other? Does sacred time simply mirror stasis, the absence of change? Or does a historical perspec-tive on time have an impact on social change? It is interesting that the core of historical thought in Islam is characterized by the understanding of time not as a linear development directed to the future, but rather as a return to an idealized, utopian past. Representations of ideal time, of the good and the righteous, are imbued with elements of divine law, for it is by obeying divine law that one is assured of leading a righteous life and, thus, fulfilling "history." Hence the juxtaposition of divine law and pro-fane historical thought as arrested versus dynamic time.

Judaism, Christianity, and Islam are revealed religions; Islam and Judaism are religions of the law. Because both hark back to divine law, they are more in affinity with each other than with the third monotheistic religion of revelation, Christianity. Indeed, so pronounced is this affinity that Judaism and Islam are virtually interchangeable. This common ground serves as an epistemic yardstick, especially when comparisons, inferences, or analogies hold out the promise of enhanced insight. If, however, there is a core difference between these two religions of the law, it is that two thousand years of Diaspora life have equipped Jews to live in two temporal orders: Jewish time and that of the local culture in whose midst Jews happen to be. Having to live in, and between, different times enabled Jews to develop a dual modus vivendi analogous to separated spheres of life that later evolved with secularization. This strategy of separation was not available to Islam. As a religion embracing law, power, and domination, Islam is an intrinsically political religion.[7]

The meaning of terms and concepts applied here is ambiguous and manifold. Take, for example, the term *Islam*. When it is used as a noun, the emphasis is on the sacred. Its adjectival form (*Islamic*), and even more the related adjective *Muslim*, both show a semantic shift toward more worldly meanings, whereas the noun *Muslim*, especially when used in its plural form (*Muslims*), again carries greater religious weight. But *Islam* can also stand for a civilization and culture, with the sacred held firmly at arm's length. This is chiefly the case when used in combination with other words and meanings—as, for example, in the title of Bernard Lewis's book on Middle Eastern Jews, *The Jews of Islam*. What *Islam* means here is less a religion than a social order, including a way of life, an art, a culture, a civilization in the widest sense.

The use of *Muslim* and *Arab* as attributions requires comment as well. Not all Muslims are Arabs, just as not all Arabs are Muslims. During the high tide of Arab nationalism in the twentieth century, however, homage was paid to an "ethnifying" (or even entirely ethnic) notion of Arabness. When *Arabs and Muslims* was put forward as a conjoined term, it related to those who belong both to the Arab nation and to the Islamic *umma*, the universal community of believers, drawing ethnic Arabness closer to the Muslim faith. As we can see, the differences are fluid, and this fluidity inclines sometimes more to the Muslim, or the religious, pole, and sometimes more to the national, or the ethnic, pole. Attributions often so closely approximate as to fuse: thus the terms *Arab* and *Muslim* may be used in the same context as synonyms.

The adjective *Arabic* can also describe different affiliations, or even be dissociated from *Arabs* as an ethnic term of belonging. For example, Middle Eastern Jews who have a strong sense of affiliation with Arabic language, literature, and culture can be referred to as *Arabic Jews* or even as *Arab Jews*, but not as *Jewish Arabs*.[8]

This book is not intended to be an academic treatise; rather it is an essay and, as such, is aimed at a broad readership. This is reflected in its manner of presentation. Thus the reference notes do not aspire to even approximate completeness. They are mere indications; only in exceptional cases do I make explicit reference to the scholarly literature.

I would like to express my gratitude to the academic and nonacademic staff of the Simon Dubnow Institute for Jewish History and Culture at the University of Leipzig, who aided me in many ways as I put the finishing touches on the text. I also thank my students in the History Department of the Hebrew University of Jerusalem for many inspiring discussions, chiefly on the question of secularization, and also the Institute for Advanced Study in Princeton, where I spent the academic year 2004–2005 as a member writing this book.

1 KNOWLEDGE AND DEVELOPMENT

The State of the Arab World

"Orientalism" and Its Adversaries—Rifa'ah at-Tahtawi and the *Arab Human Development Report*—Language and Social Lifeworlds—Knowledge and Technology—Freedom and Prosperity—Power and Benefit—Military and Politics—Mehmed Ali and Gamal Abdel Nasser—Ground Rent and Productivity—Oil Wealth and Stasis

IN 2002 *TIME* MAGAZINE SURPRISED ITS READERS by naming as Book of the Year a work hardly likely to appeal to their taste or meet their expectations. Neither a work of fiction nor a nonfictional study addressed to a broad readership, it was, in fact, a dry report, larded with statistics and other data, concerning the state of the Arab world. Its style, drawn from the social sciences, suggested that it would be a dull read. It was the first in a series issued by the United Nations under the title *Arab Human Development Report* (AHDR). *Time* had made a shrewd choice: within a short time everyone was talking about the AHDR. In the meantime, it has been downloaded from the Internet more than a million times. It was, one might say, a big success.[1]

And yet the AHDR itself was about a failure. It provided a meticulous, unsparing, and comprehensive account of the lamentable state of the Arab world: chronically stagnant economies, restricted freedoms everywhere, declining levels of education, hampered scientific and technological development—not to mention the deplorable situation of women. The AHDR lists in great detail everything that belongs to a serious diagnostic inventory of a political community. And every twelve months, a new assessment is made. And so it will be, year after year.[2]

Compiled by Arab sociologists, political scientists, economists, and cultural scholars on behalf of the United Nations and the Arab Fund for Economic and Social Development, the AHDR holds a mirror up to the Arab world. The image it shows is not appealing, and stomaching it is no easy task—chiefly because it pitilessly reveals an ongoing hiatus in the Arab world: the wide gap between, on the one hand, an elevated feeling of self-esteem based on an alleged superiority in religion and civilization, and, on the other hand, the constant denial of this superiority by reality. The AHDR uses this irreconcilable conflict between self-image and reality to call on Arabs to undertake self-examination as a precondition for fundamental change. The document does not just take stock of the Arab world; it is also appeals for action.

When turning the pages of the AHDR, the historically informed observer is reminded of an Arab document from an earlier time—a document that, although it deploys less radical language in pointing out deficiencies of development and modernization, is similar in recommending change. This is a diary by an Egyptian scholar and imam at the prestigious al-Azhar University, Rifa'ah at-Tahtawi (1801–1873), published in Cairo in 1834.[3] It relates Tahtawi's experiences and observations as the spiritual advisor to a group of students dispatched to study in Paris. The Egyptian pasha Mehmed Ali (1769–1849) had sent the group to France, then the leader in technological progress. The pasha, who first learned to read and write late in his long life, had set in motion a process of accelerated modernization in his country. To him, Tahtawi's diary seemed so important that he made the book, which appeared under the ornate title *The Purification of Gold in the Comprehensive Description of Paris*, compulsory reading for state officials and civil servants. Tahtawi's observations and impressions would, he hoped, spur Muslims to imitate Western culture and its way of life.[4]

Tahtawi's diary, which became very well known among the literate public in his native land, emerged from his experiences during the Egyptian study group's stay in Paris. The students in the group were supposed to learn French, and to begin then and there the translation into Arabic and Turkish of textbooks and encyclopedias in the areas of philosophy, linguistics, geography, natural science, and technology. By making these translations, the group, which consisted of about forty scholars, helped to create a new Arabic terminology in tune with modern demands. The foundations of what was to become known in the late nineteenth century as the Arab Renaissance, the *nahda*, were laid at that time.[5]

Mentioning Tahtawi and his diary in connection with the publication of the AHDR is symbolic insofar as Tahtawi's name has become an icon of memory, standing for concrete efforts at reform in the Arab world. As a document related to Mehmed Ali's attempts at modernization, the diary was reprinted in Egypt, especially when reforms were about to be introduced.[6] So in 1958 when a new edition was published to accompany the modernizing course adopted by Gamal Abdel Nasser (1918–1970). Because of the time that has passed and changed conditions, Tahtawi's diary of 1834 may have little in common with the *Arab Human Development Report* of 2002, yet both documents, using the language of their times, issue calls to change. And the point of comparison in both is the West.[7]

The conclusions drawn in the AHDR concerning the state of development in the Arab world are far-reaching. So far-reaching, in fact, that the implications can hardly be concealed by the strictly technocratic language used throughout. On close inspection, we can see that the recommendations formulated in such a restrained yet urgent tone are radical in their significance. In truth, the AHDR is a plea for deep transformation. To be sure, change is supposed to come from within and be carried out by the ruling elites, for whose eyes the report is ultimately intended. Both its diagnosis and its recommendations, however, are so sweeping that it is barely conceivable that the change demanded could proceed without great upheavals. Thus, this document prepared under UN auspices must be considered a revolutionary manifesto.

The authors' unsparing examination is new in its compelling and self-critical openness. Above all, it is new because it implicitly opposes a ubiquitous discourse, spawned in recent decades in the heart of the West and its academic citadels, that traces the infirmity afflicting the Arab lands and the broader Middle East primarily, if not exclusively, back to foreign, to alien dominance. For this Western discourse, causes operating in the countries themselves are of secondary importance. The argument goes like this: The "Orient" as such is said to be a figment of Western imagination, fantasies, and desires. According to this argument—showing the extent of the distortion—Muslims were perceived as having adopted a self-image constructed by others. That made it all the easier to subjugate and control them.[8]

This interpretation has had consequences. Because it attributed the inequality between East and West less to forms of dependency and their diverse causes than to a textual interpretation that had come to be taken as reality, this recent Western interpretation strengthened an attitude that was already widespread in the Middle East, which ascribed the unfortunate condition of Muslims mostly to external causes. Written statements can influence conditions on the ground, however, just as a change in interpretation can help transform reality. But for the most part such statements serve to embellish reality, rather than to encourage investigation of the causes of one's own affliction. If reality is perceived as text and actuality as representation, there is no incentive to shake up material living conditions. It suffices to interpret them differently.

Both the "Orientalism" thesis and the postcolonial discourse that followed hard on its heels affected how the conditions of underdevelopment were perceived—so much so as to substitute textual for social criticism.[9] The epistemological worlds associated with Karl Marx and Max Weber were largely forgotten. The thesis of the Orient as text and colonialism as the source of all evil may, in reality, have wrought less havoc than some of its more notorious critics have assumed, but that intellectual damage has resulted is beyond question.[10] It will take some effort to turn the tide by going back to a social, rather than textual, interpretation of social reality.

There is general agreement that from a certain time on the Orient was in no position to resist the West—militarily, economically, or culturally. In the nineteenth and especially in the first half of the twentieth century, Arabs and other Muslims were at the mercy of Western power.[11] The fact that foreign, indeed Christian, powers were able to do as they pleased in the region became lodged firmly in Muslim consciousness as a collective trauma. The humiliation experienced at that time is omnipresent in the area. It is part of the canon of memory and of people's own self-conception. And so it is passed down from one generation to the next.[12]

Yet invoking colonial machinations to explain one's own deficiency proves on closer inspection to be less exonerating than at first glance—because then the question arises as to how it was that the European powers

were able to seize control of the Middle East in the first place. Was it because of Western advantage, established much earlier on, or because of
some inherent disadvantage on the part of the Middle East? However we
answer this question, it points to the fact that the relationship between
East and West was based on inequality even *before* the colonial period.
This unequal relationship can be understood only by clarifying its causes.

So the trauma of colonialism is real, but so is the fact that its constant
invocation serves to prolong the humiliation rather than cure it. Viewing
oneself as chronically victimized cripples any inclination toward change.
At the same time, it impedes a well-grounded understanding of how
things came to this pass.

In contrast, the authors of the *Arab Human Development Report* sought to
sharpen Arabs' perception of their own share of responsibility for stasis
and hampered development. They did so prudently and with due cau-
tion. So prudently, in fact, that they sometimes seem to deviate from
their goal of unvarnished stocktaking, as when the apex of medieval Islamic civilization, which was shaped by Arabs, is contrasted with the lamentable present—as if the many intervening centuries never existed.

It is no accident that this kind of narrative, marked as it is by a major
ellipsis, ignores the circumstances of the early decline of the Arab-Muslim
realm, not to mention the rise of the subsequent, and no less Muslim,
high culture of the Ottomans, which led to a major unleashing of power
and cultural attainment in the Middle East and beyond. Contrasting
the peak of Arab-Muslim civilization of the Middle Ages with the unfortunate state of Arabs today, while ignoring the civilizing achievements
of the Ottomans' four centuries of control over the Arab heartlands of
Islam, culminates in the perception of Muslim rule as a form of foreign
domination.[13]

Interpretations of history do not determine the weal and woe of peoples, but they can cloud, or even distort, people's collective image of their
own reality. Ottoman rule as a reason for Arab culture's decline strength-
ens the foundational argument that underdevelopment was caused by
external forces, that is, by "outsiders"—especially since this period of supposed decline gave way to the intrusion of colonialism—a period relatively
short in duration, but all the richer in humiliations seared into memory.

Thus the afflictions of the Arabs are interpreted as being caused primarily, if not exclusively, from the outside—by plots, cabals, conspiracies, and other machinations set in motion against the East. This mode of self-interpretation reveals a significant deficit in secularization, because images of plots and conspiracies substitute for explanations offered by the social sciences bearing on socially complex phenomena.[14]

In this way of seeing things, the Jewish state of Israel, deemed to have been implanted by the West in the heart of the Arab world, is held responsible for the deplorable state of the Arabs. Even the authors of the AHDR think themselves obliged to refer, in their opening pages, to the Arab-Israeli conflict. This is said to have exhausted the Arabs. No matter how skeptical one may be about common Arab interpretations of history, *this* perception cannot simply be denied: the century-long conflict draws off enormous amounts of energy and erodes significant social reserves. Moreover, the very existence of the Jewish state symbolizes to Arabs, beyond the tribulations of the present conflict, a continuation of the historical domination by the colonial powers.

Doubtless, the Palestinian question stands in the way of development. But did it *cause* the state of the Arab world? No causal connection is discernible, which is not to deny that a settlement between Israelis and Palestinians is urgently needed.

The authors of the AHDR focus only on the present. As diagnosticians of the deplorable present, it is not their task to inquire into causes, which is as much as to say into the past, the domain of historians. But it is from just such a perspective that we must now discuss the statements made in the AHDR.

The AHDR describes problems and shortcomings in the Arab world with which historians and scholars in the humanities and social sciences focusing on the Middle East have always been concerned: the obvious deficiencies in social mobilization, the obstacles to technological and scientific development, the continuing omnipresence of the state, the weaknesses of political institutions, the chronic lack of democracy, and the deliberate exclusion of women.[15] The report evades, however, one all-enveloping issue: that of secularization. This omission is not to be held against the authors. In the Arab and Muslim East, one needs to be very prudent in critiquing religion. So the problem of secularization is not raised as a strategic issue. It is at most indirectly touched on, as when it is explained that, in Islam, science and belief are not mutually exclusive. By referring to the Islamic Middle Ages as a period when science and belief both flourished, the AHDR thinks itself absolved of any need to probe further.

The question of secularization cannot be reduced to religion, however; it far transcends religion. Ultimately, secularization is a drive to transformation that affects all areas of life. The rather modest part of the AHDR devoted to belief in the narrower sense points, instead, to the religious pluralism within Islam, to differences among the various legal schools and how open these were to questions of science, society, and culture—nor does it omit the problematic impact of approaches to exegesis ranging from conservative to radical.[16]

But there is no mention of secularization in the sense of a separation of spheres of life and social intercourse—the spheres of the intimate, the private, and the public. Secularization implies an endless process of definition, interpretation, negotiation, transformation, and conversion of the boundary between the modes of inner life and the outer world. It also means the decoding and appropriation of the world by human reason. Religion as a system of belief impregnating societies hampers this process. This is especially true in the case of Islam, a religion of law that claims to regulate all spheres of life. The arrested development in the Muslim world can be diagnosed, then, as a deficit of secularization.

The question of the historical causes of the Arab world's current plight is not specifically raised in the AHDR's assessment, but it dogs the reader throughout. Yet the question is not exactly new; diagnosticians of the past have repeatedly tried to explain how it is that from a certain point in history social time in the West accelerated, whereas in the Middle East a retrogression fraught with consequences set in. Might there be a causal connection between progress in the West and stasis in the East?

In the search for the causes of the different outcomes of modernity for East and West, a conceptual complex for social diagnosis insinuates itself, which claims to be universal but actually is aligned with the Western path of development. When this conceptual complex is trained on the social experience of other cultures, we get an unavoidable teleological perspective from which history seems to be fulfilled in the direction preordained by Western development—or else not to occur at all.

Western historians and scholars in the social sciences and humanities dealing with the Middle East, the Arab countries, and Muslim civilization generally are wary of drawing such conclusions, however. After all, for many years they have been accused of "Orientalism," simply because their research constantly contributed to amassing a canon of knowledge about a civilization that can be seen as the Other.[17]

Culturally conditioned forms of blindness are never impossible; in fact, they are probable—more probable, in any event, than their so often invoked contrary. But to conclude this is not to instantly condemn to outer darkness the question, overt or covert, of the lack of development in the East. It is, after all, a question asked by the people of that region; even if it is not always openly expressed, it is always in their hearts. Despite all the rhetoric to the contrary, the West embodies the very question the Orient asks about itself. Seen in this way, the interest guiding the authors of the AHDR, their epistemic compass, as it were, does not lack a sense of direction. They want to help change the conditions in the Arab world, to change these in such a way that they deliver a modernity that meets the needs of the people living there. The dynamic that the authors of the AHDR want to set in motion by this stocktaking of theirs—objective in tone, alarming in substance—would conduce to a development guided by Western standards.[18]

The *Arab Human Development Report* for 2003 concerns development of a knowledge-based society in the Arab world—or rather with the limits to such development. The current state and steady growth of knowledge are the capital of each society. Knowledge offers options for productivity and growth; it represents social wealth in the process of being created. Whether communities amass such capital or are condemned to hampered development is determined by their capacity to generate knowledge. A civilization's future hangs on whether it is able to fulfill the requirements to create and sustain a mature culture of knowledge.

The authors of the AHDR adhere to this prognosis. In order to weigh future prospects, they use qualitative and quantitative parameters to assess the conditions and guidelines for production of knowledge in the

Arab world. They concentrate, first, on one condition that is indispensable to the spread and dissemination of knowledge. This can be called "qualitative literacy," in contradistinction to "quantitative" or "primary" literacy, which means the spread of the ability to read and write. It is not as if in the Arab world primary literacy is as universal as it might be. Certainly, the educational system in the Middle East is seriously deficient in everything that has to do with teachers, or teaching materials, or classroom spaces without which there can be no proper education. But more important, putative instruction in reading and writing fails to train students in skills that are even remotely related to a modern way of dealing with knowledge. At issue here is a society's ability to absorb knowledge in a written form designed for optimal dissemination, to process the texts produced at a speed conducive to the spread of knowledge, and to pass these on in a suitably enriched form. Data presented in the AHDR reveal that the Arab world's ability to meet these criteria is poor to very poor.

This begins with the problem of translation into Arabic of texts from other languages, that is, the transmission of knowledge produced outside the domain of Arabic language and culture. The AHDR informs the astonished reader that in the 1970s in the whole of the Arab world the number of books translated from other languages was only about one-fifth as many as in a rather small country such as Greece. In the 1980s over a period of five years, only 4.4 books per million inhabitants of the Arab world were translated. In Hungary, over the same period, 519 books were translated per million inhabitants, and in Spain the number was 920.[19]

Things are no better with overall Arab book production. Whereas in North America there were 102,000 new publications in 1991, the Arab book market had to make do with 6,500—according to the AHDR, 1.1 percent of the world's book production for 5 percent of the world's population. And the trend is downward. In 1996, no more than 1,945 books were published in all Arab countries put together, which amounted to 0.8 percent of the world's book production. Seventeen percent of the titles were religion-specific, compared with a global average of 5 percent.[20] Moreover, printing runs of books in Arabic are extremely low. With a market—because of the high rate of illiteracy admittedly an abstract one—of some 300 million inhabitants in twenty-two Arab countries, works of fiction were printed in runs of between one thousand and two thousand copies. A printing of five thousand copies would be considered a bestseller.

The reasons for such a dramatic situation with regard to the means of communicating knowledge are manifold. The AHDR mentions the still widespread prevalence of illiteracy and harsh government censorship, which forces authors and publishers to run the administrative gauntlet. One comparative statistic cited by the AHDR points to a circumstance that relates more to illiteracy than to obstacles such as censorship or government embargos on paper supply. As if it were a mere detail, the authors mention that in Turkey, with a population barely one-quarter that of the Arab world, far more books are produced than in all Arab lands combined.

The reference to Turkey gives us pause—and furnishes a lead. Both the Arab countries and Turkey were formerly part of the Ottoman Empire. So we can assume that they started out from similar, or even identical, conditions for development. But Turkey, whose population is no less Muslim than in the Arab countries, is an avowedly secular polity. Emblematic of this secularism is the fact that ever since Atatürk abolished the Arabic alphabet in 1928, Turkish has been written and printed using the Latin alphabet.

Later on, we will examine the correspondence between secularism and the introduction of romanized script in a broader historical context. Suffice it now to note the link, at once enlightening and disturbing, between the sacred imprint of the Arabic language and the inherent restrictions for final profanation.

Language in its various domains of usage is becoming steadily more important in today's knowledge-based cultures—especially where technology produces rapid change. The Arabic language, however, seems to hamper this accelerated development. On this issue, the AHDR refers to a crisis affecting the Arabic language. The crisis finds its cause in the diglossic tension of Arabic, that is, its division into high Arabic on the one hand, and the various vernaculars, the so-called dialects, on the other. The difference between these two levels of Arabic consists chiefly in their flexibility. Whereas colloquial Arabic is a supple means of expression, adapted to all domains of everyday life and mirroring the general feeling about language, high Arabic, essentially a written language hardly used by the common people, is far less flexible. The rigidity of high Arabic stands in the way of social and technological changes gaining public recognition, simply by hampering their expression and thus entrance into the linguistic canon.[21]

Against this background, the AHDR refers to the immense demands made on language and linguistic competence in today's knowledge-based societies. The tasks of language are no longer limited to interpersonal communication, education, and, if you will, literary edification. Languages are also becoming means of production. This holds not only for the domains of sociolinguistics, psycholinguistics, and neurolinguistics, but also for brain research. It holds too for the technological demands of language engineering in software development and other areas of language use that are being spun off. In order to adapt Arabic to these demands, the AHDR suggests, it needs to be fundamentally reformed. In particular, the chronic deficit in translations from foreign languages makes electronic translation into Arabic all the more urgent. But if this is to happen, adaptability in the linguistic medium is essential.

So the preconditions for a functionally adequate use of Arabic in today's knowledge-based societies are fundamental renewal and modernization of language, involving a simplified grammar, a formalized opening up to colloquial Arabic, and the elaboration of a serviceable linguistic apparatus. This would help break open the hermetic structure of Arabic and free it for unlimited use. What needs to be done can be compared with the qualitative changes undertaken by Tahtawi—with the difference that Tahtawi was attempting to adapt Arabic to the age of the machine, whereas today the needs of electronic and biomolecular technology make a far more complex adaptation of the language essential. In Tahtawi's day, it was a matter of creating words and concepts, whereas now a change in the structure of the language is required.

It would make little sense to bypass Arabic altogether in the sciences and resort to English as the international scientific language. Introducing English as a third language alongside high Arabic and the various vernaculars is not a suitable response to the imperatives of knowledge and education. After all, the goal is not to restrict knowledge to the high culture of an educated elite, but to disseminate it comprehensively and widely. Moreover, the AHDR explains in its relentless way, knowledge of English in the Arab world, despite the Internet and satellite TV, is not advancing, but retreating.

Knowledge is supposed to permeate society by osmosis. Like a vascular system in the social body, language's role is to keep knowledge in constant flux. If this system is no longer functioning, the society risks cardiac arrest. Hence the high language has to reflect changes going on in the colloquial world; it must be constantly reinvigorated. Only thus can it respond adequately to changing demands.

Whereas in Tahtawi's time a developed linguistic capability could still be confined to a relatively small part of the population, in a society based on the dissemination and progress of knowledge, whose mediating communication extends to all social milieus, nothing but a fundamental linguistic reform will do. But who is to undertake such a reform? Who owns or controls Arabic? As the language of the Koran, Arabic is sealed off by the sacred. Changing the modalities of language would mean raising the question of religion and secularization in a much more radical way than the authors of the AHDR deem tenable.

So a reform of Arabic binding on all Arabs would not only strain the bond unifying the Arab nation, a bond that, in any case, can endure only minimal pressure. It would also mean revisiting the still unresolved problem of secularization. The call for reform of Arabic therefore touches on basic issues of Arab-Muslim self-understanding. Such an assault on a tradition thus immersed in the sacred would be tantamount to the kind of revolution triggered by Martin Luther's translation of the Bible.

The barrier erected by high Arabic is only one expression—albeit an important one—of what the AHDR describes as a decreasing capacity in the region for objective processing of knowledge. Compared with other emerging countries such as Brazil, China, or South Korea, the trend is nothing short of dramatic, especially since it reveals a massive gap. If one considers basic data in the area of scientific and technological progress—patents and investment in research and development, always an indicator of long-term growth—a stasis of the social fabric is evident.

Whereas the number of research findings produced in Arab countries and published in international scientific journals rose from 465 in 1967 to some 7,000 in 1995—an annual increase of around 10 percent—during the same period China was able to increase its production elevenfold annually and South Korea no less than twenty-four-fold. Measured by output, Arab research efforts during the period trailed far behind at 2.4 percent of the worldwide total. This situation is reflected in the number of patents applied for, especially as patents indicate the state of research aligned to practical applications. Thus in the United States between 1980 and 2000, about 370 patent applications came from all Arab countries combined, whereas the figures for Israel and South Korea were 8,000 and 16,000, respectively. Moreover, the majority of patent applications issuing from Arab countries were filed by foreigners working and living there.[22]

But for a knowledge-based society in today's world, applied research is less critical than basic research. This is the true wellspring of innovation. In fields rich in future promise—information technology and molecular biology, for instance—virtually no research is carried out in Arab countries. Of all published and internationally recognized research projects in Arab countries, some 90 percent were in the applied sciences. Of some 280 research centers operating outside universities in the Arab world, the bulk are devoted to research in agriculture, the food sector, public health, the environment, and the water supply. Less than 3 percent of these centers specialize in information technology or molecular biology.

The situation is no different in the field that drives future development: investing in the interface between scientific and technological research and its economic implementation. Whereas developed countries invest as much as 5 percent of their gross national product in this field, in the entire Arab world such investments are a paltry 0.2 percent. Here the AHDR's reference to how state and private investment correlate in the critical field of research and development is significant. In the Arab world, more than 90 percent of investments are made by the state, with only some 3 percent stemming from private investors. In developed countries, the ratio is about fifty-fifty.[23] From this we can conclude that in the Arab world private investors shy away from long-term investments. Predictability of private property rights and calculability of long-term economic returns therefore seem at a low ebb, a point to which we will return later when we address the question of good governance.

The question of administratively decreed imports of industrial goods and knowledge brings us to governmental order and the political system.

In this connection, the AHDR mentions two failed modernization projects in the past. One we have already mentioned: Mehmed Ali's top-down attempt in the first half of the nineteenth century to modernize Egypt industrially along French lines.[24] The second was the Soviet-influenced and equally centralist effort made by Gamal Abdel Nasser in the 1950s and 1960s to lead his country into the modern age.[25] In both cases, the authors of the AHDR note, knowledge was brought in and mechanically communicated, but not adapted to Egypt's own needs to the point where it could be further reproduced within the country. Such direct transfer of knowledge may yield short-term successes, but it is not apt to generate a process of inexorable, self-propelling innovation.[26]

A tradition of carrying out basic research and so anchoring science, construed as thought and action in line with society's requirements, cannot be founded in this way. The fact that Mehmed Ali and Nasser imported available knowledge and the matching technologies and forms of organization may have to do with their own military backgrounds: their zeal for reform was initially connected with their desire to modernize their armed forces, and therefore to instigate development in areas of the economy and society that could be useful to the army.[27]

The factories set up by Mehmed Ali were intended as facilities for producing weapons and materiel for his military. The army he raised and the fleet he built were soon the most modern in the Middle East, commanding respect on all sides.[28] Compelling proof was provided by the successful campaigns of Mehmed Ali and his stepson Ibrahim Pasha (1789–1848): in Sudan, in the Arabian peninsula, and in Greece, but also against the troops of his overlord, the sultan in Istanbul. Nasser followed in Mehmed Ali's footsteps, though with scant military success, as witnessed in the inter-Arab coalition war in Yemen in the mid-1960s—not to mention his poor showing against Israel.

Nasser's Egypt has been justly described as a military society.[29] Societies ruled by the military generally have weak social fabrics. A society primarily built on military prestige tends to associate governmental stability with the reputation of its armed forces. Hence it is that military prestige trumps all other social categories. The pressure to achieve visible successes as quickly as possible causes the transfer and integration of foreign technology to take priority over autonomous, long-term production of knowledge.[30]

The authors of the AHDR point out that intellectually innovative and technologically creative thinking is not unknown in Muslim civilization. Again they refer to the distant period of the Arab-Muslim Middle Ages. At the height of the Abbasid caliphate from the eighth to the tenth centuries, but also afterward, up to the destruction of Baghdad by Mongol invaders in 1256, there were major achievements. Moreover, the results of research were put to practical use. The sciences were not confined to an ivory tower of mere theory, but their practical applications suffused everyday life. The same was true of the broad-based translation projects, chiefly from the Greek, that were then embarked on. The flurry of translation into Arabic is thought to have fed into the process of knowledge production. Rationality based on mathematical analysis was not confined to a small circle of initiates, but was widely diffused and so could be put to general use. Thus—to speak in present-day language—a knowledge-processing culture was achieved. The wide-ranging unfolding of Arab-Muslim civilization at the time can be compared, the authors claim, with that of the West since the seventeenth century.

Some eight centuries separate the heyday of the Arab-Muslim Middle Ages from Mehmed Ali's attempts to modernize Egypt, however. By taking as their yardstick such a distant period, the authors of the AHDR again ignore a far more proximate past, the "other" Muslim civilization of the Ottomans. Closer examination of the social fabric of the Ottoman Empire and its reaction to the rise of the West in the historically relevant phase (between the end of the sixteenth and the beginning of the nineteenth century) could provide many insights into the enigma of Western accelerated development, on the one hand, and Middle Eastern hampered development, on the other—an enigma to which we will return later.[31]

Mehmed Ali's modernization project in the first half of the nineteenth century is an example of merely importing technology without providing for its indigenous renewal and expansion. The extent to which local efforts to conduct research were forgone can be seen from the way in which knowledge was obtained in the East at the time. It seemed sufficient to send young scholars to France (considered the Mecca of technological knowledge), to have them learn French, and then to set them to translating technical handbooks and other publications, chiefly those concerned with practical applications. As we mentioned earlier, this kind of reproductive transfer of technological knowledge, focused entirely on practical uses, may have served the ruler's short-term interests, but it yielded little of benefit to society as a whole.

The historical example of Mehmed Ali in Egypt allows us to study the fundamental but problematic relationship between reproductive technology, the extension of personal power, and unsustained economic development.[32] While the group of scholars working under Tahtawi's spiritual supervision was translating technical handbooks and other literature in France, he witnessed the 1830 July Revolution in Paris.[33] This experience provided him with enlightening discoveries that he noted in his diary: for example, the fact that without the checks and balances provided by the separation of powers in a body politic—which is as much as to say, without freedom, without the rule of law, without democratic procedures—no prosperity can be achieved.

By observing the situation in France and studying the French constitution, Tahtawi grasped the complex linkage between politics and economics—a relationship that is still of interest with regard to the Middle East.[34] This insight remained hidden from his master Mehmed Ali, or to put it the other way around, Ali seems to have understood it all too well. After inspecting the translation of Machiavelli's *The Prince* the pasha had commissioned in 1825, he suppressed its publication.[35] As an autocratic ruler, he hardly wanted his subjects to be instructed in the techniques of rule and domination. Egypt's process of modernization from above—decreed and enforced by the state—would bypass the question of rule and therefore political involvement on the part of the population. The prospects of success were not great, because from a certain level of development of the means of production economic progress without political participation is hard to come by.

The people of the Middle East were not allowed to gain insight into the mechanics of rule and its application. To understand these matters requires an understanding of the interweaving of what makes society work. The task of amassing a canon of knowledge concerning society falls to the social sciences, whose rise is accompanied by the notorious process of "disenchanting" the world. Disenchantment is a consequence of secularization. In fact, it is its very essence.

The AHDR informs the reader that with a few exceptions, such as Egypt, research in the social sciences in the Arab world began in the 1960s.[36] Furthermore, research into other cultures was traditionally rare. There is no department of humanities or social sciences dedicated to researching the West and its unique character—if you will, a kind of scholarly "Occidentalism."[37] Widespread ignorance regarding the West leads people in the Middle East to imagine conspiracies or to misconstrue alleged realities.[38]

Not that the introduction of the social sciences was urgently needed for development to proceed. Here the natural sciences and technology unquestionably take priority. But a better understanding of the social environment helps in efforts to decipher the natural world as well. Thus the social sciences conduce to accelerating a development whose true breeding ground is secularization. According to the AHDR, the brain drain afflicting the Arab world proves that those with intellect and expertise do not think they have a future there. Thus it is estimated that since 1976, 23 percent of all Arab engineers, 50 percent of all Arab physicians, and 15 percent of all qualified scientists have emigrated. About 25 percent of the three hundred thousand students who completed their degrees in the academic year 1995/96 emigrated. Between 1998 and 2000, more than fifteen thousand physicians left their countries in the Arab world.

The abilities of educated people in the Arab world are no less than elsewhere. On the individual level, they may meet the highest standards. This is shown by what they have accomplished outside the Arab world. But on the home front, their achievements are less impressive. Their own material culture lacks the necessary conditions anchored in an orchestrated division of labor encompassing society as a whole. In other words, the pace of social rationalization as a precondition of further development is hampered.[39] A sufficient generalization of scientific and technical standards is lacking.

The AHDR draws attention to this festering wound: individually, Arabs can achieve great things, but collectively they do not inhabit a cultural space that is closely integrated horizontally and well as vertically, such that it engenders a creative community based on a high degree of division of labor. As the AHDR puts it: that an Arab writer might be considered for the Nobel Prize for literature is within the bounds of possibility and has in fact occurred; in the end, a writer's work is individual in nature. But that a scientist working exclusively in an Arab country might be awarded the Nobel Prize is less likely. For that to happen, a foundation of social support for constantly communicated knowledge is required.[40] And that, in turn, requires a secular material culture.

Strengthening the individual is a task for secular culture. Ultimately, the development and broadening of knowledge requires that the individual be given room to maneuver—the blessings of personal freedom. The first AHDR emphasized that freedom is one of the most important resources for development.[41] We can add categorically that in an age of knowledge-based societies, freedom increasingly proves a productive force in its own right. If the Soviet Union collapsed as a result of state-imposed restrictions on freedom, it was not only because it kept intellectuals and others pushing for civil liberties under close supervision; it collapsed also because evolving new technologies in a knowledge-based society necessitates, among other things, generalized conditions of procedural openness, accessibility, and permeability. What is called for is a culture that aspires to openness everywhere, with a transparency protected from interventions on the part of state and other agencies of authority and power. Science needs such a culture in order to thrive as much as people need air in order to breathe. This social oxygen is freedom. Limitations placed on thought and communication hinder development; in extreme cases, they block development entirely. A climate of political bullying and administrative restriction has consequences for creativity and competitiveness.

The AHDR's criticisms are more modest. The restricted freedom in the Arab world lies far below the threshold of what new technologies require by way of unfettered imagination and individual autonomy if they are to take off. The AHDR's criticisms invoke the prerequisites for what is commonly called bourgeois or civil society: the rule of law, guarantees and protections of private property that allow predictions to be made and enable long-term calculations in the realm of economics. Only with reliable protection of private property can private owners, and especially investors from one's own country, plan long-term investments involving more or less calculable and generally acceptable risk.

Tahtawi drew attention to this connection in his diary, as when he emphasized the importance of the French constitution's underwriting of private property, which protects "the rich," as he calls them, against uncertainty and bribery.[42] After all, capital avoids countries thought to be politically problematic, because they cannot guarantee stability. And it is political stability that promises progress and growth in the research and development area. It is to be distinguished from the kind of stability that used to seem sufficient in the area of raw materials extraction. Today what matters is not the stability of the regime, but trust in good governance— to be construed as the rational management of resources and procedures, including the consent and even the participation of the governed.

A regulated, let alone a democratically regulated, acquisition of power in the Arab world is not evident. If there are parliaments at all, they serve at the ruler's pleasure. The latter's power is almost unchecked; if there are any checks, it is only because he has consented to them. They were not wrested from him—at least not as the further separation of powers was that Tahtawi described during the July Revolution in Paris.

Since no significant separation of the spheres of public and the private, state and society, politics and economy can be presupposed, power tends, if not overtly then informally and covertly, to intervene in all areas of community life. The sciences and academia are not free to operate in line with professional guidelines and attendant standards of quality. Academics and intellectuals are expected to meet the ruler's expectations. The control, domination, and omnipresence of the state's security apparatus, of nepotism and corruption, are the consequences of the notorious role that rule plays in all spheres of social and political life. Such penetration of society by the state—and not, as it should be, of the state by society— hinders the emergence of the preconditions of transparency and the rule of law, as these can only be provided by an advanced separation of powers. Moreover, the omnipresence of the state erodes the independence of the justice system, which is therefore little respected by the population.[43]

The AHDR constantly circles around the phenomenon of the public arena. Its authors lament the fact that such an arena, which is indispensable for critiquing and monitoring the state, has not emerged in Arab countries.[44] And without a developed public arena, no public opinion that reflects society and thus monitors power is possible. Hindering criticism and bullying the press are therefore endemic. In any case, media such as radio and television, which are run by the state, are required to disseminate the government's views. Recently, an Arab public arena worthy of the name has begun to appear as a result of satellite TV and the Internet. Entirely free it is not. It *has* opened pathways for critique, but it is still quick to defer—especially to the rulers of the countries in which the broadcasts originate.[45] The fact that the July Revolution witnessed by Tahtawi was triggered by the French king's attempt to restrict freedom of the press—government forces had attacked newspaper offices and destroyed their printing presses—is not an ironic commentary on history, but rather a necessary civilizing component of what is involved in the struggle for freedom. According to the findings of the AHDR, Arab countries have the lowest share of what we would call freedom, that is, the political cultures of the Arab world bring up the rear in a global comparison.[46] Whereas the broad global trend in the 1990s was toward increased freedom, the Arab world regressed. Five Arab states are listed among the least free countries.

But can we simply apply concepts developed in the West, especially the concept of freedom, to the political cultures of the Middle East, shaped as these have been by Islam? The question is not easy to dismiss. Traditionally within Western culture too there are various ideas, differing in significance and scope, of what freedom means, especially when there is a need to set limits to it.[47] In his diary, Tahtawi reviews the individual articles of the French constitution, only to balk at the magnitude of the task when it comes to translating the word *freedom* into Arabic. For this semantic element of the European store of experience, Arabic has, in his view, no suitable word. It is not that Arabic has no word for freedom, but the original meaning of the Arabic *hurriyya* is merely the opposite of slavery, not at all what is associated with *libertas* in the Western tradition— the right to participate in governmental affairs.[48]

Tahtawi resorted to translation by analogy. What the French mean by the term *freedom* and also strive to achieve he transcribed with the Arabic terms for *justice* and *moderation*. So in attempting to translate the word *freedom*, Tahtawi was thinking not of freedom or specific freedoms fought for and attained, but rather of the blessings of just rule. Governing under the rubric of justice and moderation would be synonymous with a balanced, prudent, and wise interpretation of the law. The individual and his property would be protected against arbitrary appropriation by the ruler, who must see to it that security and prosperity are provided. Understood in this way, freedom requires that the leader should refrain from oppressing his subjects.[49] Freedom involves applying good laws in a just manner, not the fundamental right of the population to participate in making the laws. Thus justice presupposes a just and good ruler, not laws resulting from the free will of a sovereign people.[50]

The argument from cultural anthropology that the difficulty encountered in translating concepts reflects more than mere differences in linguistic usage has to be taken seriously.[51] The power of language can bring out differences in the way values are ranked. It is an open question whether in the Arab and Muslim value scale "justice" stands higher than what is associated with "freedom." In any case, the AHDR cites surveys showing that modern ideas of freedom and democracy meet with high rates of approval in the Arab world. Only in attitudes toward the equality of women and equal treatment in professional life is there a massive deviation from the global trend.[52] Tahtawi would probably have agreed with the authors of the report. After all, the privileges of freedom in whatever culturally specific form should also benefit those who did not participate in the historical emergence of either idea or institution. The fact that the idea of freedom is a specific outcome of the Western experience does not make its validity less universal.

If freedom has proved to be a productive force in the knowledge-based societies of the present, what, then, is the state of productivity in the Arab world? Here as well the AHDR tells a tale of woe. The dry statistics will keep us from viewing the future too hopefully. Despite the widespread and false impression that Arabs are immensely rich, Arab states must be considered poor. A glance at the gross national product reveals the true situation. The figure of $604 billion per annum, which is all the entire Arab world has to show, is only slightly more than that of a European country the size of Spain ($559 billion), but falls far short of what, say, Italy produced in the same period ($1,074 billion).

As far as productivity is concerned, when compared with other national economies in the process of catching up, Arab countries are falling far behind. Whereas, according to World Bank data, in 1998–1999 China posted a growth rate of 15 percent, Korea 8 percent, and India 6 percent, in those Arab states with the best rates growth was much less.[53] Current data estimating future growth are no better. In World Bank forecasts for industrial goods and high tech—both areas where capital is reflected in the form of knowledge—Arab states once again bring up the rear.[54] The consumer goods industry, which makes up the lion's share of production in Arab countries, relies on foreign licenses and thus on foreign know-how. Knowledge-based production is not to be expected from that quarter.

In the AHDR's view, the deficit in growth as well as the drastic under-supply of knowledge potential have their origin in oil production. On closer inspection, the blessing of oil turns out to be a curse—in that the wealth spurting from the ground brings in mountains of cash, but does nothing to stimulate productivity. Quite the contrary: wealth drawn from oil strangles productivity and the urgently needed culture of knowledge.

What are we to make of this paradox? In describing a form of wealth that hinders development, the authors are describing a phenomenon that bears all the hallmarks of inevitability. It begins with the fact that access to such abundant financial means has led to a massive shift in the social values of oil-producing Arab countries. Learning, knowledge, and creative abilities and skills have been depreciated by oil wealth. Wealth flowing from the ground has devalued income earned by conventional activity. For those with academic training and those who earn their living by working, this change has meant a serious loss of authority. Having money has become more important than how it was acquired in the first place. The result is that gainful activity as such has decreased in value, especially since every kind of good and every kind of expertise can be bought. And since buying goods and expertise from abroad is easier and quicker than laboring to develop the skills needed to produce them at home, people take to consuming the vast array of goods on the world market. This becomes a habit, and a chronic one at that: habit hardens into structure.

This phenomenon of hampered development resulting from the sheer limitlessness of available wealth has nothing to do with either Arab culture or Islam. It rests on a form of income known as a ground rent.[55] In principle, there is nothing wrong with rent; in the form of ground rent, it may also be justified in various domains connected with creating value from the earth and from nature—but only as long as it remains in proportion with other ways of creating value in a national economy, above all through labor. In countries whose wealth derives chiefly from the extraction of raw materials, however, a social situation can arise in which all development grinds to a halt. This happens when a country enjoys such a high income from ground rents that the value realized by all other forms of work seems pointless.[56] Moreover, access to so much money encourages an intoxicating consumption that can be satisfied only by buying goods and services produced abroad. Because there is no incentive to forgo desired goods, consumption, which is limited only by the price of oil on the world market, triggers within the country a process of spending resources to achieve status. The principle is: If you spend, you're somebody. Nations that live exclusively, or chiefly, by selling their natural resources are called "rentier states."[57] Most Arab countries fall into this category. Libya, Iraq, and Algeria are all dependent on ground rents, nor can Egypt, Syria, Sudan, and Yemen get by without oil-derived revenues. The Gulf states and Saudi Arabia need not be mentioned in this connection. Iran, as a non-Arab but Muslim oil producer, is not treated in the AHDR.[58]

The wealth accruing from ground rents is a new phenomenon for these countries. From the beginning of the twentieth century until well past its midpoint, it was other firms and agencies that knew about the value of oil. Since the so-called D'Arcy oil-field concession of 1901 and the British navy's subsequent switch to oil-fired boilers, the traditional rulers in the region were content with royalties.[59] Only toward the end of the 1950s or in the early 1960s did this tribute-for-concessions relationship begin to break down. During the years of decolonization and the Cold War, Western concessionaires and the political and military powers behind them saw their hold on the Middle East wane. That was the great age of nationalism, primarily Arab, in the region. National independence meant control over territory. But it also meant control over underground resources and transportation facilities, such as oil pipelines or the Suez Canal, traversing a state's territory. The canal's nationalization in 1956 marked a high point of national self-determination and the beginning of withdrawal by the traditional colonial powers, Britain and France.

Newly won sovereignty over the region and the founding of OPEC, the Organization of the Petroleum Exporting Countries, in 1960 enlightened member states as to how the market value of oil was determined. OPEC—originally an agency providing oil-producing countries with information about the stages and mechanisms shaping prices—bore the trappings of a monopoly. In the first five years after the wake-up call of the nationalization of the Suez Canal, revenues to the oil-producing states rose sevenfold.[60] After the 1973 oil crisis, energy sources were finally sold at market prices. From then on, the wealth stored in resources could be trapped at will by the country or its ruler. This does not mean, however, that development was initiated. Nothing more clearly shows the difference between true and false wealth than the income from ground rents. The extent to which ground rents foster stagnation can be seen outside the Arab world, too. Take the frequently overlooked example of the former Soviet Union, one of the leading oil-producing and energy-exporting countries of the postwar era. The steeply rising price of oil in the early 1970s resulted in the Soviet Union, along with the other oil-producing countries, receiving large amounts of foreign exchange—so large, in fact, that they could conceal the consequences of the notorious stagnation during the Brezhnev era. Thus the Soviet Union self-destructed as a result of declining productivity and innovation, though it took the United States to reveal this by intensifying the arms race.

The fact that the Arab and other Muslim states have become rentier states has grave consequences, especially where the institutional spillover is misjudged or ignored and certainly where a striking lack of freedom is evident. I am referring to the area of political power and rule.

The power to control the wealth bubbling from the ground is a source of patronage for the autocratic state. Such is the arbitrariness of unlimited, or nearly unlimited, power that only one man—or at best a clique—controls the purse strings. The ruler can deny citizens, or rather his subjects, any rights of participation, while showering them with favors from his personal, or the state's, virtually inexhaustible coffers—or, indeed, do anything he pleases. The ruler has given—and taken—at whim.[61]

Control over and distribution of wealth by and through the state lends support to the traditional Muslim notion of "just rule." A ruler is just when he underwrites the fair distribution of goods. And fair distribution of goods is legitimated by the canons of Islamic law. Hence the ground rents realized on the global market in the form of oil revenues allow Middle Eastern states to preserve an early, premodern practice of traditional rule that is rooted in historically diverse manifestations of the centralized state. Here the primacy of rule over the social fabric seems to prevail in cultural anthropological terms.

Whether a regime legitimizes itself in a socialist or a Muslim order, control of the wealth realized through ground rents generates a bureaucracy to regulate its distribution. Since power and wealth are controlled by the same person or group, no separation pertains between politics and economy, between state and society, such as is indispensable for a bourgeois or middle-class society, not to say a rational economy. Rule is absolute—no matter how enlightened it might be.

Tahtawi's diary is eloquent on the subject of traditional rule in the Middle East and how "modern" it is—as when he quotes directly from Mehmed Ali's letters urging the scholars living in Paris at state expense to study constantly and without rest.[62] The menacing tone and threats of punishment to which his admonitions frequently give way depict Mehmed Ali as a despot who controls everything: power, wealth, the land, and, not least, the minds of his subjects.

The impression given by Tahtawi's diary does not err. Mehmed Ali ruled over almost everything in Egypt. His absolute power began with his monopoly over the land. In order to see his modernization project through, he made himself the sole beneficiary of ground rents. Between 1805 and 1814, Mehmed Ali personally appropriated every single acre of land in Egypt. Control over the land established by Oriental despots had, and has, a twofold purpose: first, to gain control of agricultural production, and second, to underwrite political power, that is, the exercise of power over subjects. The integration of the means of rule and wealth, indeed, their complete fusion, is characteristic of stable political autocracy based on a monopoly on wealth coming from ground rents rather than from productive work and the taxation of the population, which then would be able to claim its rights.[63]

The intermeshing that undercuts the distinction between state and society in the Middle East extends to obscure linkages between political elites and the economic world. It is not an orderly, transparent procedure in line with the norms of economic viability that brings success, but rather proximity to the ruler. The result is corruption, to put it bluntly. Thus the intermeshing of politics and economy, not untypical of Arab countries, results in a client system that undercuts the rational administration of the state in line with bureaucratic guidelines, at the same time making it harder to achieve a rational economy.

Corruption pervades state and society alike, undermining the very basis for achieving a constitutionally regulated polity. The conclusion is clear enough: it is impossible, without constitutionality and good governance, to produce the conditions under which mere wealth turns into productivity, much less to evolve structures that the AHDR insists the Arab elites will need if they are to grow a knowledge-based society in line with global standards. That the first step toward this goal is precisely the opposite of the steps taken in past decades by nationalistic regimes—namely nationalization, in particular nationalization of the oil industry—will not be pursued here.

Instead, we will turn to the particular nature of the state in Arab-Muslim countries. All the parameters in the AHDR suggest that the state and the domain of power in the Middle East must be considered problematic. Thus, the omnipresence of state power—or conversely, the lack of freedom—in the Arab-Muslim world can hardly be ignored. That the idiosyncrasies of power cannot be traced back solely to the peculiarities of oil production—although the ruling power's monopolistic control over oil certainly does its bit to reinforce these idiosyncrasies—should be apparent.

The insufficiencies in the Middle East raised by the AHDR are not new, even if they present themselves with greater urgency today because, in contrast to earlier stages of historical development, despite all the differences among cultures and civilizations, the world is tending to become one. And in this one world people communicate more directly and compare themselves with one another—which is the fly in the ointment. When all the comparisons have been made and the verdict is in, people are no longer willing to accept their lot. They call for action. The frenetic effort to understand the undeniable gap between the West and the Arab domain is a source of vexation in the Middle East. But there *is* an opportunity: that the West, as a burning preoccupation, might be able to enlighten Middle Easterners about themselves.[64]

Enlightening oneself about the reality of one's own life does not yield a sense of humiliation. Rather, it is an expression of self-determined freedom and thus of dignity. In any case, it certainly does not spring from "Orientalism." Thus, Middle Easterners can subscribe without further ado to Tahtawi's judgment from the early 1830s: in his admiration for the achievements of the French—and, by extension, of the West generally—he felt obliged to emphasize that, of the multitude of things he found to praise there, it was the care lavished on knowledge that was the best.[65]

2 GEOPOLITICS AND RELIGIOUS ZEAL
Radicalization in the Muslim East

Between Palestine and Kashmir—Cold War and Decolonization—
England and Russia—Gladstone and Disraeli—Caliphate and
Pan-Islam—Kemal Pasha and Enver Pasha—Hindus and Muslims—
Colonialism and Alienation—Arabism and Islamism—Mawdudi and
Sayyid Qutb—Political Theology and Civil War

WHEN THE *ARAB HUMAN DEVELOPMENT REPORT* first appeared
in 2002, it aroused interest throughout the world, and not without reason. After the events of September 11, 2001, this document seemed as
though it might provide an answer to the biggest question of all: what
had induced the perpetrators to act as they did. Yet the UN report on the
condition of the Arab world cannot be considered a reaction to the attacks on New York and Washington, any more than the phenomenon of
stalled modernization that the report describes can be considered a compelling reason for carrying out such attacks. True, the symbolism of the
twin towers at the financial heart of New York and the Pentagon in Washington may fuel speculation—but no causal connection is discernible.
But even though it stops short of causality, a certain convergence can be
discerned: between the hampered development in the Arab world as diagnosed by the AHDR, and violent political eruptions, of which the Middle East had seen many portents.

Indeed, there does seem to be a link between the endemic standstill in
the Middle East and the events of September 11.[1] But what is it? To those
who led the terrorist attacks on the twin towers and the Pentagon, targets
that were symbols and incarnations of Western superiority, there *was* a

link, and an obvious one at that. No need for post hoc explanations or for laboriously assembled hypotheses. The act, for them, was self-explanatory: the West—in this case America—must be punished *because* it is the West.

The AHDR published in 2002 was not intended as an answer to the events of 2001. A blunt situation report long in the making, its theme was the crisis in the Arab-Muslim world, which by the 1990s had become glaringly obvious and was diagnosed as structural. If the crisis has reached notorious proportions, it was due to two only seemingly interconnected factors: a massive spurt in global productivity driven by new technologies, and the decline of Communism with the collapse of the Soviet Union. Between these two factors there is again more convergence than causal connection. The end of more than forty years of Cold War made it possible to develop commercial applications of the multiplicity of high-tech innovations that had formerly been reserved for the military. Furthermore, the opening of a broader global market in the name of freedom unchained an extraordinary economic dynamic. Technological innovation, growth, and democratization meshed in previously unknown ways. This unusual economic activity also affected regions and communities in which growth had previously been weak. The trend was ubiquitous—except in the Arab-Muslim world.

The decline of Communism and the collapse of the Soviet Union exposed the fact that the Arab world suffered from significant, qualitative deficiencies in development. Not that this poor showing, which took the form of chronic stasis, had not been previously identified. The figures were available, and experts had been concerned for years about the strange absence of scientific, technological, and social progress in the region. What was new was that the hampered development had passed the point of deniability. The lamentable state of Arab countries became obvious and impossible to ignore with the demise of the Soviet Union, for now the West was seen as undeniably superior. Nor could the Muslims' own miserable situation be denied when compared with the West. Up to that point the Soviet Union had, by its very existence, distorted Middle Easterners' perspective because, despite its familiar material shortages, the Soviet Union seemed to offer—in contrast to the overheated modernity of the West—a moderate and thus palatable variant of the same process.

The Soviet Union was not only a world power, it was a superpower with atomic weapons, and because of its strategic nuclear arsenal it could claim equality with the West. True, this was equality in the capacity for destruction, but it was also more than that: for decades—especially in the era of decolonization, which was contemporaneous with the Cold War—it freed peoples in Asia and Africa, and particularly in the Middle East, from immediate dependency by offering a model of modernity that could be seen as an alternative to the Western one. In this model, priority would be given not to the demands of Western individuality, which Middle Eastern culture deemed excessive, but rather to the collectivity that provided protection and security. Trust would be placed not in the abstract, virtually invisible mechanisms of the market with its inherent mood swings, but rather in the steady hands of state planners. The countries opting for this model did not seek to become players in the alliances dividing the world into Eastern and Western blocs, but rather to remain unaligned—even if their sympathies tended to be with the Soviet Union.

This ploy of tacking between the blocs found expression in the efforts Third World countries made in the areas of agriculture and industry, in voting behavior in the United Nations and other international organizations, and above all in the weapons technology that the Soviet Union, with seeming selflessness, made available to them. If countries in the Third World supplied themselves primarily with Soviet weaponry, it was not only because when they approached the West they were turned down because of their declared political nonalignment, or because the purchase of weapons would have to be paid in hard currency and not in kind, but above all because Soviet weapons technology of acceptable quality was less complex and easier to handle. Thus, not by accident a whole era found its icon in the Soviet AK-47, the Kalashnikov automatic rifle.

But that was then. With the passing of the Soviet Union, it is not only that the wellsprings of a technology thought appropriate to the Third World's stage of development have run dry. What has gone is more than the materiel from the arsenals—meager, in any case—of the former socialist countries. An alternative has been lost, but it is not that of directly imitating Soviet Communism—the "developing countries," as they were then called, were either unwilling or unable to follow this path. No, what the demise of the Soviet Union finished off was the idea that there was an alternative path to modernity. The collapse of this never very convincing model affected the nations of the Third World in its entirety. The perspective of a softer, more acceptable modernity was gone for good. What remained was the Western yardstick of a ruthless modernity, based on the uncomfortable demands of freedom, individuality, and the habitual modes of accelerated time.

The end of the Cold War put an end not only to the hope of a transitional modernity of sorts but also to a well-established system of regulating international order. For more than forty years, this system, although accompanied by warfare among proxies, had had a relatively stabilizing effect on a conflict-ridden region such as the Middle East.[2] Here I am referring to the regulating effect of the opposition between the superpowers—an opposition that was able to adapt to its internal logic the conflicts associated with the process of decolonization and its aftermath in the area from the Eastern Mediterranean to the Hindu Kush. Thus the principal conflicts in the region were subordinated to the East-West opposition. This holds for the Arab-Israeli conflict and for the rash of wars that accompanied it, as well as for tensions between India and Pakistan and the recurrent armed confrontations between the two countries. Both conflicts—between Arabs and Israelis, and between India and Pakistan—went back to 1947, the year Britain withdrew from South Asia and soon afterward from Palestine.[3] These withdrawals were related in time and space to other events. Shortly after the announcement that the British would pull out of their colonial possessions in the Eastern Mediterranean and in Asia, the Truman Doctrine, which guaranteed to Greece and Turkey American support in the event of a threat—real or imagined—from the Soviet Union, was proclaimed. This proclamation marked the early beginning of the Cold War.[4]

The Cold War rewrote in terms of its own logic the conflicts situated between Palestine and Kashmir.[5] In 1989, however, the decades-long system of control by the informal hegemons, America and the Soviet Union, ceased. The shifting sands of the Middle East would from now on be deeper than ever.

The Cold War had hardly been interred when Saddam Hussein invaded Kuwait in 1990, resulting in a war with an Arab coalition led by the United States. It seems unlikely that Saddam would have risked attacking

Kuwait had the Soviet Union still claimed its old superpower status, with commensurate influence in the region. The Soviet ambassador in Baghdad, acting in accord with customary Cold War protocols and bent on avoiding a quarrel with America, would have seen to that. But at the time the Soviet Union was already imploding and only a shadow of its former self.[6]

In the 1980s, two conflicts in the Middle East evaded the usual Cold War scenario of regulation by the opposing superpowers. One was the violence in the Hindu Kush, that is, in Afghanistan; the other—very different in kind—was the Iran-Iraq war that Saddam Hussein triggered without pretext in the wake of the Islamic revolution in Teheran. In Afghanistan, however, the superpowers used the country as a venue for settling their own accounts. As had happened earlier in Vietnam, Afghanistan became a sparring ground for a Cold War that was heating up militarily.

In contrast, the Islamic revolution in Iran stepped beyond the familiar Cold War battle order. Armed with this special status, it initiated in February 1979 a process leading into previously uncharted waters, not to say an imponderable future. It struck out at an oblique angle to the bloc formations reflecting the opposition between the superpowers. With its theologically impregnated politics, the new regime cut the country off from the rest of the world, making it an island unto itself. No one grasped quicker than Saddam Hussein that Iran, following the Ayatollah Khomeini's revolution, no longer had the backing of either superpower, so he took advantage of this scenario by launching a frontal attack on his Persian archenemy. He hoped to realize long-standing territorial claims in the Shatt al-'Arab and Khuzestan, and also to deal a knockout blow, in the name of Arab nationalism, to the Islamic revolution.[7]

This project failed because of the religious zeal of the holy warriors mobilized by the revolution. In this sense, Iraq's sudden attack on Iran in 1980 anticipated a situation that would come about only ten years later—after the Cold War—and then on a global scale. For without the deterrent of mutually assured destruction, without the damping effect of the opposition between the nuclear-armed superpowers, regional conflicts could spiral endlessly.[8]

Almost concurrently with the upheaval in Iran, the Soviet Union gave in to the temptation to intervene in Afghanistan. Based on their proximity in space and time—both occurred in 1979—these events could be seen as related. Yet because of the different circumstances surrounding them, they are, in fact, very different. Whereas the revolution in Iran did away with the pro-Western regime of the shah, which was supported by the United States but deeply hated by large segments of the population, the Soviets hastened to rescue the Communist regime in Afghanistan, which was also little favored by its people—as if the land in the Hindu Kush, located in a gray zone of the world power game, were covered by the Brezhnev Doctrine. It may have been that conflicts among Communist factions in Kabul made the leadership in Moscow speculate that it could act there as it did in "friendly foreign countries" in Eastern Europe; it may also be that Afghanistan's proximity across the border proved seductive.[9]

The Soviet invasion of Afghanistan ended that country's traditional role as a buffer between great geopolitical rivals. This role was residual—a leftover from an earlier age when Russia and Britain competed for influence on the fringes between the Ottoman Empire and British India. When the Cold War changed the colors on the world map, including the map of the Middle East, Afghanistan remained as gray as ever—a hitherto undisturbed area that belonged to an older, late nineteenth-century configuration. It may have been this impression of tranquility that led the Kremlin to imagine, in late 1979, that it could ignore Afghanistan's long-standing neutrality and, because it had a Communist regime, view it as an appendage to the Soviet Union's legitimate sphere of interest. In any case, Afghanistan was not deemed to be on the Western side in the Cold War.

The miscalculation in Afghanistan—that gray zone in time and space— did not, as many have concluded, immediately cost the Soviet Union its very existence; but the operations there, which dragged on interminably, did indeed lead to massive bloodletting. In any event, the Americans decided to let the Soviets bleed to death in Afghanistan, so creating their own future enemy. The Mujahedin unleashed there against the Soviet infidels were supplied by Saudi Arabia and supported by Pakistan. They were also boosted by the followers of a radical brand of Islam, who streamed into Afghanistan from Arab countries, mostly governed along secular and nationalist lines. In the Afghan no-man's-land of the old certainties of the Cold War, the seeds of future conflagrations were sown. A hot war whose outcome is still uncertain was about to begin.

In the midst of the dramatic events in Iran and Afghanistan, another important event occurred. In November 1979, a few hundred armed Sunni fanatics besieged the Great Mosque in Mecca. This was a challenge to the Saudi dynasty to assume its role as the "guardian of the two holy places" (*khadem al-haramayn*) of Islam. After bloody fighting in which the palace summoned to the holy site French counterinsurgency experts—specially converted to Islam for the purpose—the rebellion was put down. Its leader, Juhaiman al-Utaybaī, who belonged to an extreme Wahhabi faction, came from a leading family in the Najd region of Saudi Arabia. His grandfather had risen to prominence as a follower of Abd al-Aziz ibn Sa'ud at the beginning of the twentieth century. Members of his clan were prominent representatives of the Ikhwan, a brotherhood espousing the puritanical teachings of Muhammad ibn Abd al-Wahhab. Steeped in this tradition, Juhaiman al-Utaybaī accused the House of Sa'ud of corruption, of living in luxury, and of imitating the West. These were the very accusations used by the Ayatollah Khomeini to dethrone the shah. The Saudi royal family was deeply alarmed.[10] From then on it strove more assiduously to prove its Islamic legitimacy, principally by supporting Wahhabism everywhere. In what was essentially a holding action to maintain its rule in Saudi Arabia, it contributed to the spread of Wahhabism, particularly to Afghanistan.[11]

The kind of Islamism that established itself in Afghanistan in those years had an even longer history. The fact that it took root there, following the Soviet intervention, was chiefly a matter of chance. But the significance of this country, in terms of past and present upheavals in the realm of Islam, is deep. Geographically as well as historically, Afghanistan is located at the crossroad of historical trends that created what would become radical Islam. These trends involved, on the one hand, the transition from the Ottoman Empire to the Turkish Republic, and on the other, the transfer of radical interpretations of Islam from the Indian border region to the Arab heartland. Central to these developments, however, is the year 1924.

The year 1924 holds the key to understanding the crisis in the Muslim world.[12] It was then that Mustafa Kemal Pasha (1881–1938), the founder of the Turkish Republic, inaugurated the decisive reforms connected with his project of modernization. Atatürk, as he would soon be called, abolished the central Islamic institutions: the caliphate as well as the office of the supreme Islamic arbiter, the *sheikh-ul-islam*, of crucial importance to Sunni Muslims throughout the world. Thus the symbolic link between divine rule and this world was severed.[13]

The liquidation of the caliphate and the *sheikh-ul-islam* was to have consequences reaching far beyond Turkey.[14] Muslims felt orphaned and abandoned—especially Muslims in British India, who then constituted the largest Muslim community in the world. When in 1928 the Turkish Republic did away with the Arabic alphabet and replaced it with the Latin one, the secular attack on religion seemed to have reached its zenith. In his speeches and legal advisories, Osama bin Laden was to allude to these events as a catastrophe that had befallen Muslims some eighty years earlier.

If the Kremlin was ready to launch a military invasion of Afghanistan in 1979 and to get involved in the quarrels among Afghan Communist factions, in doing so it was following Bolshevist and even older traditions from the czarist era.[15] This continuity may have gone unrecognized by the actors themselves, but this armed intervention in intra-Afghan troubles, which quickly floundered, was always linked to the battles that had followed the revolutionary period and ended only with the relatively late establishment of Soviet rule in Central Asia at the beginning of the 1930s. Up to that point, resistance, including armed resistance, was the order of the day. In the early 1920s, in an extension of the Russian civil war, the Red Army moved into Turkistan to put down the Basmachi revolt. Some twenty thousand fighters, reviled by the Soviets as bandits and brigands, operated in an area of deep Muslim awareness.[16] The fighting reached its climax in 1921. One year later the leader of the Basmachi—Enver Pasha—was killed as he rode, saber drawn, to attack a Soviet machine gun emplacement.[17]

The historically informed reader will know Enver Pasha from other contexts. As first among equals, he represented the Young Turk government in the First World War. Moreover, he had married into the family of the sultan-caliph in Istanbul—which endowed him with a prestige he was able to exploit in the Islamic mobilization of the Basmachi. In 1919, following German advice, he seems to have made contact with the Soviets.

The following year Enver even participated in the Comintern congress in Baku. In organizing this meeting, the Bolsheviks intended, according to their own declarations, to incite the people and workers of the East to anti-imperialist resistance against the British presence in the North-West Frontier, especially in Afghanistan, and in India. The head of the Comintern, Grigory Zinovyev, even called for a holy war.[18]

No less anti-British and directed against the Allies were undertakings launched by former Ottoman officials who had fled to Central Asia when Ottoman rule in Turkey collapsed. Djemal Pasha, also prominent in the earlier Young Turk government, set himself the goal in Afghanistan of turning that country's army against Britain. Mustafa Kemal Pasha, on the contrary, ignored these rather esoteric undertakings, preferring to fight in Anatolia against the Allied troops and their Armenian and Greek allies. Djemal Pasha's various undertakings were, unlike those of Kemal Pasha, quite adventurous. He dreamed of bringing down British rule in India and establishing a Muslim body politic alone the lines of the long-defunct Mughal Empire.

The conflicts in the early 1920s can be seen as distant reverberations of what Rudyard Kipling called "the Great Game," played out in the nineteenth century between Russia and Britain as strategic rivals in the Middle East and Central Asia. Britain regarded this area as a buffer zone around its possessions in India, the imperial core. Russia—so the British assumed—was trying to break through this belt stretching from the Mediterranean to Central Asia, and even the Far East. Under the terms of the Turkmanchay peace treaty, signed in 1828 after a second war between Russia and Persia, the Caspian Sea was open only to Russian vessels. London feared that in the future the czar's troops might land on the southern shores of the Caspian and quickly advance on the Afghan city of Herat, thus opening a gateway to India. In the following year, after yet another war between Russia and the Ottomans, the treaty of Adrianopolis made continued Russian expansion into the South Caucasus possible. The czar seemed within a stone's throw of the British Raj.[19]

The opposition between Britain and Russia lasted throughout the nineteenth century,[20] in fact until the 1907 concord between the two powers to divide up Persia into respective spheres of influence. While the "Great

Game" played out in Central Asia, the "Eastern Question" engulfed the Ottoman Empire.[21] The "Eastern question" refers to the process of disintegration of the Ottoman Empire in the nineteenth century, affecting the European balance of power—the informal system regulating the policies of the Great Powers among themselves—and the emergence of ethnically impregnated nation-states, especially in the Balkans.[22] In the framework of the "Eastern question," British policy in the nineteenth century, favoring the Ottomans and opposing the Russians, was based on the touchstone of Britain's imperial policy: protection of its possessions in India.

This historical constellation came to a head in the autumn of 1914 when the Young Turk government entered the First World War on the side of the Central Powers, Germany and Austria-Hungary, breaking with the Ottoman tradition of the nineteenth century. In doing so, the Ottomans were opposing not only their historical arch-enemy, Russia, but also their traditional patron, Britain. It was a gamble that did not pay off. After its defeat in 1918, the Ottoman Empire met the fate from which British policy within the European balance of power had long shielded it: dismemberment.[23]

The last third of the nineteenth century was a time of estrangement between Great Britain and the Ottomans. Three consecutive events had strained relations: the Russo-Turkish war of 1877–1878, which led to the peace of San Stefano and severe humiliation for the Ottomans; the Anglo-Afghan war of 1878–1880; and the British military occupation of Egypt in 1882. All three events increased tensions between Britain and Muslims, whose consequences for English colonial rule in India could not be foreseen—especially when it became evident that the sultan-caliph in Istanbul was conducting a pan-Islamic policy and considering whether to extend his quarrel with Britain, his historical protector, to the Raj itself.

British thoughts about the possibility of replacing its unreliable ally on the Bosporus with the Arabs, who were not on very friendly terms with the Turks, go back to this period, though they were not acted on until the First World War.[24] Constantly mindful of its Indian Muslim population and obsessed with its communication routes to India and the Far East, which passed through the Middle East, Britain put in place a policy of making tactical use of the Arabs—chiefly the sharifs of Mecca, who, as the protectors of the holy places of Islam, commanded great prestige among Muslims. It is said that there was even talk of establishing an Arab caliphate to compete with the Ottoman caliphate.[25]

The cooling of relations between Britain and the Ottomans began with the Serbo-Turkish war of 1876. This conflict broadened into a major clash between Ottomans and Russians, a disastrous defeat for the Turks, incurred the draconian peace settlement of San Stefano. Anti-Ottoman uprisings in the Balkans and the fighting that followed in their wake led to internal political debates in England. Prime Minister Benjamin Disraeli, who had declared that Britain was, from an Indian point of view, a "Muslim power,"[26] was more inclined to favor Turkey; in any case, his romantic admiration for the Orient was notorious.[27] The British Liberal opposition under the leadership of William Gladstone was never tired of waging, against the Conservative Disraeli, a campaign to publicize Ottoman brutalities in the Balkans.[28] Gladstone's pamphlet on the "Bulgarian atrocities" rallied public anger in England.[29]

It was more Liberal public opinion than actual British policy with regard to the Ottomans that upset Indian Muslims. Their expectation, like that of Turkish Muslims, was that Britain would—as it did during the Crimean War of 1853–1856—side with the Ottomans and defy Russia. The Crimean War was a conflict of global dimensions. Disraeli called it, with an eye to British interests in Southern Asia, an "Indian war," and considered the 1878 Anglo-Ottoman pact regarding the protection and maintenance of the Ottoman Empire, which included Turkey's cession of Cyprus to England, as mattering less for Britain's Mediterranean policy than for its Indian policy. The point was to offset the territorial gains made by the czar in the Russo-Turkish war (i.e., in the South Caucasus, especially the city of Kars). In the opinion of the British government in India, this expansion could lead to a Russian move into Mesopotamia and then into the area of the Indian Ocean.[30]

The fear of Russian machinations in Asia that gripped the government of British India in Delhi, which was showing a conspicuous independence from the government in London, bordered on obsession.[31] In order to counter Russia's presumed designs, the government of British India attempted to forge a pan-Islamic, Central Asian alliance with the Muslim khans—and especially the emir of Bukhara—who were coming under pressure from St. Petersburg. Of course, this was years before the

Ottoman-Russian war of 1877–1878, which brought about a change of sentiment in British-Muslim relations. In 1870 the British still labored under the illusion that by exploiting pan-Islamic agitation they could transform the region—as a secret dispatch to London put it—into a hot plate on which they could make the Russian bear dance.[32] The Russians had warned the British about the dangers of pan-Islamic agitation. It was a two-edged sword that would cause the British trouble in India. Not that it took British propaganda to sow pan-Islamic feeling among Muslims. As it was, that policy had been prescribed by Sultan-Caliph Abd ul-Hamid II (ruled 1876–1909). Moreover, British colonial policy played its own part in arousing Muslim anger.

The Indian Mutiny, as it came to be called, provided a foretaste of what was to come. It shook British rule on the subcontinent; from then on, England was careful not to put too much pressure on Muslims, entirely for the sake of its imperial policy. In the spring of 1857, Indian soldiers, or sepoys, in the service of the British East India Company mutinied. A revolt broke out when sepoy troops refused orders from their British officers to bite off the ends of the cartridges used for the new Enfield rifles. A rumor had spread that the grease used to lubricate the cartridges was a mixture of pig and cow fat—a serious affront to the religious beliefs of Hindus and Muslims alike.[33]

The mutiny was a symptom of discontent brewing in the native population, which spelled serious trouble for the colonial power. Through the East India Company, the British had made deep inroads into the country's traditional structures and had wrought changes that stirred up Hindus and Muslims against them.[34] The activities of Christian missionaries, the introduction of a Western-style system of education, the legalization of remarriage for widows (which ran counter to tradition), to name some of the chief grievances, fueled the unrest. After the mutiny had been brutally put down, the East India Company was dissolved. The new colonial administration would henceforth strive, by establishing suitable institutions, to give Indians a role in governmental activities.

Pan-Islamic feeling among Indian Muslims was therefore first awakened after the Russo-Turkish war of 1877–1878, as was a sense of political and religious closeness to the sultan-caliph in Istanbul. From then on, the sultan-caliph's name was mentioned in the reading of the *khutba* during

Friday prayers in the country's most important mosques—thus did the faithful express their recognition of him as their sovereign.[35] Indian Muslims had entered the orbit of the Ottoman Empire's institutions.

The 'Urabi rebellion in Egypt—which paradoxically prompted Gladstone, who had positioned himself as an anti-imperialist in opposition to Disraeli, to occupy the Nile valley—also contributed to a feeling of commonality among Muslims as far away as India. Ahmad 'Urabi Pasha, a high-ranking Egyptian military officer and politician who was close to the people, had opposed the khedives' indulgent policies toward foreigners and set up an early nationalist regime.[36] After the British had defeated 'Urabi's army at Tall al-Kabir and banished him to Ceylon, his prestige spread from the site of his internment to India. The British governor had 'Urabi removed from Jaffna, which was only thirty-five miles from the Indian mainland, and confined him away from the coast.[37]

When after the First World War the victorious Allies' intention to divide up the Ottoman Empire became evident, this caused great difficulties for British rule in India, where Muslim politicians and writers founded the caliphate movement.[38] The goal of the latter's protests in the British Crown Colony was to pressure Britain to preserve the last Muslim universal empire and its Islamic institutions in Istanbul. The accompanying demonstrations combined the solidarity with the Ottomans awakened by the caliphate movement with an ever growing desire to secure independence for their own country. Thus the defense of Islamic institutions in Istanbul linked up with the anticolonial battle for Indian independence, which, for the time being, could still unite Muslims and Hindus. But when Turkish nationalists dissolved these Islamic institutions in 1924, the Indian caliphate movement petered out. The battle for independence, however, continued unabated.

The new leadership of Turkey, secular and nationalist by persuasion, expelled the caliph and abolished his office as well as the office of the *sheikh-ul-islam*—an event that Muslims everywhere saw as a decisive break with Islamic tradition, indeed an abomination.[39] This was to have unfortunate consequences. For all the Ottoman Empire's territorial losses over previous decades, one thing had always remained inviolate for Muslims living outside its borders: the *sheikh-ul-islam* in Istanbul had had the legal authority to appoint the supreme judge in all Muslim countries. This was the case in Bosnia-Herzegovina, annexed by Austria-Hungary in 1908, as well as in the Italian protectorate established in Libya in 1911; and in the case of Bulgaria, it was written into the 1913 Constantinople agreement.

After the Turkish Republic abolished the caliphate, attempts were made in the Arab-Muslim world to resurrect the office of caliph, which had so dramatically become vacant. These attempts, however, were either put down by force (as in the case of the sharif of Mecca, Husain ibn Ali, who claimed the office of caliph for himself and was put down by the Wahhabist al-Ikhwan in alliance with the house of Ibn Saud in 1924) or were strenuously ignored by other Muslims and thwarted by the British (as in the case of the Egyptian king Fuad I, who ruled 1922–1936).[40] Discussions at Islamic congresses during the 1920s and 1930s regarding the reestablishment of the caliphate also came to nothing.[41]

This lent all the more impetus to movements demanding a return to true Islam. These movements enunciated the counterprogram, as it were, to the nationalization and secularization of the Muslim community being pursued by Turks and Arabs. Thus, in the Orient of the 1920s there were movements in both directions. Kemal Pasha's dissolution of Islamic institutions in Istanbul, seen by devout Muslims as a brazen affront, and the antireligious secularism of Turkey, which had succumbed to nationalistic pride, both served the adherents of a radical Islam as warnings of the destructive potential of Western ideas. These ideas had to be opposed.

Turkey committed further sacrileges. In order to eradicate Muslim traditions more completely, the Arabic alphabet was abolished in 1928. It was said that it was not suited to the Turkish language, especially to Turkish phonetics. This claim may have reflected pragmatic intentions, but its symbolic result was to set the final seal on a secularization imposed from above. With the abolition of the Arabic alphabet and its replacement by romanized script a blow was struck at the sacred. This reform was justified by the apparently innocent, and also accurate, remark that 80 to 90 percent of the Turkish population was illiterate and needed to be taught to read and write as quickly as possible—a project that could not be carried out using the complicated Arabic script, at least not in the foreseeable future. But eliminating the Arabic script not only made it easier for people to learn to read and write, it also did away with the aura of the sacred surrounding the Arabic characters. Concurrent efforts to use Turkish rather than Arabic as the liturgical language were less successful. On the other hand, abolition of Arabic and also Persian in the schools was achieved.[42]

During the Ottoman era, especially at the time of the great reform projects in the mid-nineteenth century, attempts were already made to simplify the complicated Arabic script and to devise a solution to the problem of representing Turkish vowels. The sense that the Arabic script hampers learning to read and write, and thus delays the acquisition of knowledge, is strengthened by comparisons between religious groups. Whereas Christian and Jewish children in foreign schools in the Ottoman Empire quickly learned the Greek or Hebrew alphabets, because of their greater simplicity, as well as the Latin alphabet, and so were soon able to use them to gain knowledge, Muslim children had to struggle much longer with the complex Arabic alphabet. Thus they were slower to absorb the contents of what they read. The result was a significant gap between the educational level of Jews and Greeks on the one hand, and Muslim children on the other.[43] And it was hard to counter the pragmatic argument advanced by the nineteenth-century reformers that use of the romanized script made it easier to learn a great many European languages quickly.[44]

Although many efforts to simplify the Arabic alphabet (or to replace it entirely with the Latin alphabet) had been made in Turkey's Ottoman past, they were initially stymied by the sacredness inscribed within the Arabic letters. This explains why romanization of the writing system does not date from the time of the basic reform of Islamic institutions—that is, their abolition in 1923 and 1924. At the time, romanization seemed a bridge too far. The secular coup was extended to the Arabic alphabet only four years later, in 1928. What had happened in the meantime?

The abolition of the Arabic script had indeed been urged by Turkish nationalists; their urgings were given further impetus by the Soviets' anti-Islamic reform projects across the Turkish border.[45] Attempts to use the Latin alphabet to represent Turkish began in Soviet-controlled Azerbaijan and the North Caucasus in 1922.[46] In 1925, the Supreme Soviet of the Republic of Azerbaijan introduced the use of the Latin alphabet for Azeri, a Turkish dialect. At a conference held in Baku a year later, Soviet experts on Turkish-speaking people urged the romanization of all Turkic languages in Soviet Central Asia.[47]

These events beyond their borders could not fail to impress Turkish nationalists, even if only those committed to a Turkish territorial state in Anatolia. If contacts with other Turkish peoples were to be preserved, a common script on both sides of the border would have to be maintained. So pan-Turkish tendencies in Turkey were what made the difference— overcoming previously entrenched opposition to replacement of the Arabic by the Latin alphabet. This was indeed a step that increased the distance from the Ottoman, and even more from the Islamic, past.

Atatürk was anathema to devout Muslims everywhere, as was the secularization in Turkey associated with his name. This was especially true of those tendencies within Islam that were trying to fend off Western colonialism, and the West in general, by radicalizing their own belief. That such tendencies toward radicalization reached a high point in the 1920s was not due solely to the political iconoclasm of the Kemalists in Turkey. True, radical groups found in these events a consistent narrative that would accompany them from then on; but their cause lay in a prehistory and in experiences that were peculiar to the region. Two mutually reinforcing tendencies can be discerned, one located in British India, the other in Egypt.

At the beginning is a paradox. Although India had the largest Muslim population in the world, they lived in a condition of diaspora.[48] This sense of living in a diaspora was based on the fact that, apart from the Mughal dynasty of the sixteenth to eighteenth centuries, no truly Islamic rule had ever been established there. Moreover, many Muslims worried that independence would result in Hindu domination. A significant number of Muslims could not be content with such a prospect.[49] Although Muslims as well as Hindus opposed British colonial rule, Muslims wondered what would happen once independence was achieved.

Anticipating such a scenario, some Indian Muslims conceived the idea of creating a state of their own on Indian soil. The state would be Muslim but not Islamic, inasmuch as it would provide a secure home for the Muslim nation in India. Its foundation was to be political, not religious. Those who wanted to establish a Muslim state in India embarked on a collision course with those who envisioned an Indian union composed of all its inhabitants and with those who envisioned a Muslim state of a strict Islamic order, in which Muslims would be conceived as part of the *umma*, the universal community of believers. When in 1947, a fateful year for decolonization, the subcontinent was partitioned and two geographically noncontiguous Muslim areas emerged following "ethnic cleansing" on religious grounds, involving the flight of millions of refugees to the northwest and northeast, the state of Pakistan was born.

Pakistan was a paradox because it was established as a secular state on a purely religious basis. Its founder, Mohammed Ali Jinnah (1867–1948) maintained that state and religion should be separated, that belief was a private matter. For him, Indian Muslims constituted a peculiar political community based on Islamic culture, a specifically Indian Muslim nation—a conception not accepted by devout Muslims.[50] For them, the universal community of believers was the only valid yardstick. Islam is either universal or it is nothing. So from the outset, Pakistan was involved in a Kulturkampf between those who maintained that its character was Muslim and those who maintained that it was Islamic.[51] This polarity sparked violent conflict when shortly after independence Mohammed Jinnah died. It was never to go away.[52]

Among those who sought an Islamic but not Muslim state was Abu'l-'Ala' Mawdudi (1903–1979). Soon after Pakistan was established, he was thrown in jail for his ideas; he was even condemned to death in 1953, only to be freed shortly thereafter. Mawdudi was the most important scholar associated with an increasingly radicalized Islam in India. His influence went far beyond the question—which he considered too narrowly posed—of the Islamic or Muslim character of Pakistan.[53] Thus he represented a brand of Islam the more radical for being on the periphery of the Muslim world, an Islamic creed to be construed as political theology. It would be of great significance in the confrontation between Islam and Western modernity.[54]

The ideological radicalization brought to Islam by Mawdudi grew from a threefold challenge: first, the confrontation with the West per se, with secularism and individualism, and with the Western separation between belief and knowledge, between religion and state, and between this world and the next; second, the experience of Indian Muslims who, despite making up the world's largest Muslim population, lived among people of another religion, Hindus; and third, the struggle with the consequences of the colonial experience and the associated loss of authenticity. What Mawdudi says in his correspondence with an American Jew, Margret Marcus, who converted to Islam and took the name Maryam Jameelah, regarding the then prime minister of India, the secular Hindu Pandit Nehru, reminds us of what the anticolonial theoretician and psychiatrist Frantz Fanon himself concluded: Nehru's Indian body housed an English soul.[55]

Such were the unusual parameters behind the Indian Muslims' experience of straddling cultural and religious boundaries.[56] In contrast to other Muslims—especially those whose self-esteem stemmed from the cultural and political experience of being a majority predestined to rule, as was the case in the core lands of Islam—Indian Muslims, despite their belief in their religion's superiority, were reacting to their experiences as a minority. Their behavior was to that extent defensive—to the point of founding their own state, Pakistan.[57]

It was from this defensive posture that Mawdudi wrote his first apology for Islam, treating the doctrine of jihad. The occasion was the murder of the leader of the Arya Samaj (Society of Aryans), Swami Shraddhanand, in 1926. Arya Samaj sought to bring Hindu converts to Islam back to the true religion, and its activities aroused indignation among Muslims in North India. Debates over the murder of Shraddhanand led to Hindus accusing Muslims of having spread Islam not by persuasion but by the sword alone. This accusation had to be answered.[58]

It was also necessary to respond to Muslims' sense of being overwhelmed by the West—by its institutions, its rational and scientific culture, its military power. Many Indians, both Muslims and Hindus, were impressed by the civilizing institutions of the British. The superiority constantly paraded before their eyes gnawed at their self-esteem. For Muslims, whose monotheistic religion was measured by the yardstick of secularized Western Christianity, the West posed a constant challenge to the foundations of their belief.

Mawdudi's teaching freed Muslims from this Western yardstick in an apodictic way, by excluding from the outset all possibility of comparison. It eliminated any conceptual nexus, any shared point of cognitive reference, that might connect the Islamic framework with that of the West. And without this conceptual common ground—assumed to be universally valid, but reserving a priori a history of development for the West—Islam was set free, free from humiliating comparisons, free to adopt a point of reference mirroring itself only. Thus an insurmountable religious obstacle was placed in the way of the "idolatry" proceeding from Western secularism and materialism. Muslims had had enough of the sacrilege of Westerners' control over time, enough of the splitting of the person into different, conflicting parts, enough of the division between worldly and religious, enough of institutional barriers between public and private, enough of religion and state as discrete entities. Islam, Mawdudi maintained, should rely on its own set of rules in the areas of culture, the legal system, politics, and economics. Islam should grant transcendence in God to those whom modernity had caused to be lost in inner conflict and doubt.

Mawdudi's teaching made Islam impervious to the consequences of Western modernity by rejecting lock, stock and barrel the Enlightenment that had preceded it. The key element in Mawdudi's worldview is as simple as it is radical: man must no longer have control over his fate. Man is neither autonomous nor free. Not man, but only God has the power to make decisions. God has sovereign control over humans, and this control is exercised through Islamic law.

With this clear and uncompromising distinction between the Western Enlightenment and modernity on the one hand, and Islam on the other, Mawdudi sharpened Muslims' awareness of their own cosmos. Islam is seen as a perfected constellation that constrains belief and life. This Islamic cosmos rests on the unshakable conviction that God alone rules. In striving for the loftiest goal, that of being one with God, humans have a duty to submit to Sharia, the infallible Law of God. And because Sharia is of divine origin, it is perfect and complete; everything is included. It is a perfect, internally coherent system of regulations, standards, and duties. There is nothing to quibble about, nothing to change. Nothing is superfluous; nothing may be added. In the contemporary world of conflict and doubt, what matters is to stand by an uncorrupted, pure Islam and its sources or else to return to them. The path is shown in the Koran and the Sunna. God is to be taken at His word.

At first glance, Mawdudi's teaching looks like a doctrine of subjugation and blind obedience. It is, however, a doctrine of rebellion and revolt.

A revolt in the name of God and His Law, to be sure, but a revolt none-theless. At first, it was directed against British colonial rule, against insti-tutions that were thought superior and secretly admired. It focused its hostility on the whole of Western civilization and its achievements. But it did not stop there. Later, and in a radicalized form, it was directed above all against Muslim rulers and their regimes that were accused of being unfaithful to Islam. This extension of Mawdudi's teaching was under-taken in the 1950s and 1960s by the Egyptian Sayyid Qutb, turning it into an Islamic political theology of civil war.[59]

Mawdudi sought to spread his comprehensive, integrated interpreta-tion stressing doctrinal purity. He was constantly writing articles, books, and commentaries. Along with Qutb, Mawdudi was the most productive and important Islamic political theoretician of the twentieth century. His masterpiece is a commentary on the Koran, on which he worked for more than thirty years. But he also turned his pen to current issues. In ar-ticles written for periodicals, he partook in the political debates over the Muslim or Islamic character of Pakistan. In addition, he helped organize a renewal of Islam, in the sense of a return to its roots. And he established contact in the Arabian peninsula with representatives of Wahhabism, the orthodox, purist brand of Islam promoted by the Saudis. He was in-volved in establishing an Islamic university in Saudi Arabia and in the activities of the Muslim World League.[60] His influence was greatest, how-ever, in Egypt, where his works were widely read from the early 1950s on.

In Egypt an independent movement of Islamic renewal and self-discovery had arisen, a popular movement that also made social demands—the Muslim Brotherhood (*al-Ikhwan al-Muslimun*), founded in 1928 by Hasan al-Banna (1906–1949) in Ismailia.[61] Transformed and much degenerated by the 1970s, it spawned terrorist organizations prepared to use violence. Persecuted by the Egyptian government, these organizations found refuge in Afghanistan among like-minded Islamists who had gone there from Arab and other Muslim countries.

The Egyptian Muslim Brotherhood did not mark the beginning of a development; rather it was the outcome of a paradoxical, earlier trend to-ward Islamic renewal: the *salafiyah*. The *salafiyah* is paradoxical because, as a modern religious movement, it seeks to accommodate modernity by returning to Islam's origins.[62] It draws its self-understanding from the tradition of the *salaf* (or pious ancestors) of Islam. The way out of the decadence of Arab and Muslim societies, out of their weakness and decline, passes through awareness of original, pure, uncorrupted Islam, an Islam freed from the burden of the interpretations piled up by theologians across the centuries, an Islam that rejects all writings that have appeared in the interim, basing itself solely on the Koran, the Sunna, and their classical interpreters. Among the latter are members of the ninth-century purist legal school of Ibn Hanbal; Ibn Taymiyah, whose judgments were delivered in Damascus in the thirteenth and fourteenth centuries; and Abd al-Wahhab, who was active in the Arabian peninsula in the eighteenth century.

It is in the context of renewal that we should also see the great figures in the Islamic reform movement, such as Jamal al-Din al-Afghani (1838/39–1897), his student Mohammed Abduh (1849–1905), and his successor Rashid Rida (1865–1935), who reacted to the challenge of the West by trying to elaborate an Islamic way of coming to terms with modernity.[63] In the nineteenth century, Muslims' self-perception was shaken by the innovations, discoveries, and inventions of the West. How were Muslims to react to technological innovations such as railroads, telegraphs, and steamboats? These novelties not only changed everyday life and made it easier, but they also aroused doubts about God's sovereignty and the eternal character of the Koran as the book of revelation. Islamic purists saw these modern machines as works of the devil challenging God's control over time. They challenged both belief and believers. Such speeding up of the world's pace could only end badly. Muslims making use of such machines risked being seen as deviants by interpreters who followed the pure doctrine of the Koran and Sunna.[64]

This kind of purism was not the program of the *salafiyah*, at least not of that stream of the *salafiyah* associated with Afghani, Abduh, and Rida. In trying to mediate between Islam and modernity, these figures went quite far—so far, in fact, that they even considered a linguistic reform to ensure the use of Arabic as a language of education as well. In addition, they strove to secure antidespotic political reforms. The *salafiyah* connected with the name of Mohammed Abduh spread through the whole Arab and Muslim world, from Morocco to India. On the Indian subcontinent, its chief exponent was Muhammad Iqbal (1873–1938), a scholar, poet, and Muslim popular leader who did not conceal his admiration for Western achievements. Thus the *salafiyah* was anything but monolithic. The return to the original and the pure that the movement demanded paradoxically opened up a broad field of interpretation. *Salafiyah* was chiefly, therefore, a matter of interpretation.

When Hasan al-Banna founded the Muslim Brotherhood in 1928, he brought organizational talent into a political vacuum lacking in overall vision. The ideas of the *salafiyah* were omnipresent, but the renewal movement had not been communicated to all levels of the population. It had no social dimension. Up to that point, it had been confined to the elite—to the intellectual rather than the religious elite. In founding the Muslim Brotherhood, Banna created a mass movement. Turning idea into political action was inevitably accompanied by some radicalization. And it was this radicalization, manifested in the form of a mass movement, that made it possible to discern in the Muslim Brotherhood a modern phenomenon. Its ideological—not to say theological—underpinnings were open to further interpretation along radical lines and may also have been influenced by Wahhabism.

In the 1920s, things were still in flux. The urgent priority was to put an end to the vacuum left by Atatürk's abolition of the caliphate. In that respect, the founding of the Muslim Brotherhood can also be considered a reaction to the events of the period 1924–1928. Moreover, the consequences of the collapse of the Ottoman Empire for Arabs and Muslims were not limited to the sphere of religion and religious institutions, but involved the political sphere as well. Colonial power was extended to those parts of the Middle East that had earlier been under the control of the sultan-caliph in Istanbul but were not part of Turkey. England and France divided this area up between them, concealing their colonial presence behind an (on paper) less offensive mandate system. On the other hand, Arab plans to establish an empire failed and were thwarted by the colonial powers. Also, the issue of Palestine cast a spell over Arabs and Muslims.

It was the Muslim Brothers who made this conflict their own. Palestine was not only dear to their hearts but also an effective way of rallying support. Eventually, they would achieve a synthesis between Islam and

Arab nationalism, which was no easy thing to do. Nationalism linked to Islam differed from Arab nationalism, which was based on secular foundations. Whereas Islamic nationalism saw itself as merely a first step, a transitional stage on the way to a universal Muslim community, the *umma*, Arab nationalism was rejected by the radical Islam that later emerged from within the Muslim Brotherhood, which saw it as an expression of heathenism and racism, and repudiated it as the nadir of unbelief. The Egyptian territorialism beyond Islam propagated in Egypt by Taha Husain and Salama Musa was also rejected as heathenism and loathed by pious Muslims. The same goes for Ali Abdel Razik's theses proposing a complete separation of Islam from politics. All this characterized the political cacophony of the 1920s and 1930s.[65]

The year of the founding of the Muslim Brotherhood in Egypt, 1928, therefore marks the point when Islam became a political movement. Not only the year, but also the place of founding is instructive concerning the motives behind the Brotherhood's establishment. The young Hasan al-Banna, born 1906, chose as its seat the city of Ismailia. It was an obvious choice, since Banna taught Arabic at a school there. But Ismailia was more than just the place where the founder of the Muslim Brotherhood happened to work.

Ismailia was a newly established city closely connected with the British Empire's central artery, the Suez Canal. Named after a descendent of Mehmed Ali, the khedive Ismail Pasha, the city was not only the seat of the canal's administration, but also a manifestation of an importunate European presence. It was a bastion of European colonialism in the form of the British presence in the country, which even after Egypt gained formal independence in 1922 continued to operate in a covert albeit constantly perceptible way. The social contrasts were more evident there than elsewhere in Egypt. As a teacher in Ismailia, Banna was confronted every day with this humiliating backdrop of colonialism, poverty, and cultural devaluation. And so in the Muslim Brotherhood's program the question of social justice fused with ideas about a renewal of Islam and the battle against the colonial presence.

The Muslim Brotherhood developed into the most important Islamic organization to have emerged from the crisis of the 1920s. It was rooted primarily in Egypt, where it reached not only the urban and rural masses, but also educated people and bureaucrats, as well as important figures at the royal court. The Muslim Brothers engaged in philanthropy and were active in social welfare. They built schools, set up factories, and also maintained paramilitary forces—something unheard of in Egypt or elsewhere in the Arab world in the 1930s. In everything they did, they strove to create a kind of countersociety. By the late 1940s, it was said that they constituted a state within the state. Their military attacks on British installations, especially in the Suez Canal Zone, increased tensions between them and the government. In 1948, this led to a fatal attack on the Egyptian premier, Nuqrashi Pasha. The government reacted by having Hasan al-Banna murdered in February 1949.

That the Muslim Brothers had good contacts with Gamal Abdel Nasser's Free Officers, who were to overthrow the monarchy in 1952, is no surprise given their wide-ranging network.[66] The liaison between the colonels and the Brotherhood is said to have originally been Anwar el-Sadat, one of the more traditional among the military conspirators. Differences of opinion soon appeared between the Brotherhood and the new regime, however, and grew into overt hostility. This hostility led to an attempt on Nasser's life on October 26, 1954. As he was making a speech in Alexandria before hundreds of thousands of people, an assassin fired eight shots but missed his target. The government struck against the Brotherhood, arresting thousands of its members and throwing them in jail or incarcerating them in prison camps. Torture and other forms of abuse were the order of the day. One of those tortured by the security forces was a man who, basing himself on Mawdudi's teachings, quickly became the ideological beacon of radical Islam: Sayyid Qutb.[67]

Sayyid Qutb is considered one of the leading Islamic intellectuals. He was born in Upper Egypt in 1906, and thus belongs to the same generation as Mawdudi and Banna. From childhood on, he received an Islamic education. By the age of ten, he is said to have been able to recite the Koran by heart. He fell in with the Muslim Brotherhood in the late 1930s, when he was an official in the Education Ministry. Shortly after the Free Officers' putsch, he is even said to have sat at the table of the revolutionary command as the Brotherhood's liaison. But soon estrangement set in, leading to an open rift. The Free Officers had no intention of acting in accord with the Brotherhood's values, whereas for Qutb, the regime had thrown in its lot with those exponents of modernity that the Brotherhood so much detested. The rift widened further when the government moved toward increasingly close relations with the godless Soviet Union.

Sayyid Qutb came into contact with Mawdudi's works, which had been available in Arabic since 1951. He put a sharper edge on Mawdudi's ideas, one that emerged from his experience of oppression under Nasser. Qutb despised Nasser's regime and other nationalist regimes in the Arab and Muslim world, which he regarded as blasphemous. Their ultimate foundation was not universal Islam, but rather an Arab nationalism based on ancestry and ethnic affiliation. According to the theory that Qutb gradually developed and wrote down mainly while he was in prison, nationalism is an expression of apostasy—a heathenism analogous to the barbarous ignorance of the pre-Islamic Arabs, the time of *Jahiliya*. But this heathenism is more reprehensible than the pre-Islamic *Jahiliya* because its exponents have already been enlightened by Islam. Since they have turned away from true belief, they are apostates, and their apostasy is a continuation of Islam's greatest fall from grace, represented by what happened in Atatürk's Turkey. Radical Islam and Arab nationalism are mortal enemies.

Sayyid Qutb was hanged by Nasser's government in 1966, by which time this unusually productive thinker and writer had churned out a sizable body of work. At the core was a Koranic exegesis in thirty volumes. Like his other writings, this interpretation sought to renew Islam along the lines Mawdudi had proposed: Islam depicts a self-contained, divine truth that cannot, and need not, be compared with the knowledge-fixated culture of the West and the modernity it had spawned. Muslims live in a timeless temporal order imbued with the sacred, for which any historical conception of time is anathema. Everything is laid down in the Koran and the Sunna. Any alteration is tantamount to heresy. Compromises or adaptations to other worldviews are to be resisted by all means.

In a radical Salafist way Qutb consistently rejected intellectual assimilation to Greek ideas and especially to Neoplatonic philosophy, which had flowered in the Islamic Middle Ages in tandem with Islamic scholarship. His criticism of the West—its materialism, its lack of moral and economic restraint, its neglect of God—was unrelenting. He thought he knew the West at first hand; after all, he had spent two years in the United States studying English as well as educational theory. The disgust he felt for the American way of life, which he found to be completely unrestrained, is thought to have led him to the views today associated with his name. But Qutb's criticism goes further and deeper. It advances into areas of fundamental importance for the development of Western modernity.[68]

In the Islamic assumption of the unity of God and man, Qutb saw the basis of all order and orientation. Only in this unity can man find himself, find reconciliation with himself and the world. In Qutb's view, this monotheistic unity had been sundered by Christianity at the outset, ever since the separation of religion and political power proclaimed by Christ. This separation, which is characteristic of Western modernity, is already implicit in the injunction to render unto Caesar the things that are Caesar's, and unto God the things that are God's. The conflict implicit in this early separation was later secularized in the cultural context of the West.

Sayyid Qutb is not wrong here: a fundamental institutional tension does in fact run through Western culture, whether in the various interpretations of the "two swords" theory in the high Middle Ages or in the earlier distinction between *imperium* and *sacerdotium* inherent in the fabric of the Holy Roman Empire. The individuality and freedom so important to the West can be traced back to a basic question in medieval Christianity: who should be obeyed—the emperor or the pope? These two authorities struggle for supremacy in the heart of the perplexed, who can choose only one of them. Thus the birth of freedom is the expression of a deep internal rift. It stems from the individual's doubt and despair. Freedom springs from conflict and the discord associated with it. And in this conflict the individual is left all alone. Only conscience born of this discord can provide a sense of direction—but conscience is not infallible.

Islam, on the contrary, speaks of unity—the unity of religion and rule, transcended in God and represented on earth by the caliph as God's shadow. True, the Byzantine emperor, the *basileus*, was both spiritual and earthly ruler—a unity disparagingly referred to, albeit from a Western perspective, as "Caesaropapism." But the Eastern Orthodox Church had its own religious hierarchy, in which tensions and disputes found regulated expression. The office of emperor and patriarch were separate. And

Byzantium did make a distinction between *imperium* and *sacerdotium*.[69] In contrast, Islam has no clergy. Everything is subsumed into one—into God and His Law.

In Western Christianity, the individual is exposed to constant conflict. This conflict reaches from the cosmos of belief into the world of the profane. Partitioning and internalization of the spheres of the intimate, the private, and the public underpin the regulation of different areas of lived experience.[70] It was precisely in this sundering of the unity of man and God that Sayyid Qutb saw civilization's fall from grace. The duality that is constitutive of Western man reminded him of the psychiatric condition of schizophrenia—as symptomatic of a festering spiritual ailment. But when there is no partitioning of functional spheres and no internalization thereof, the external institutions regulating society and politics are in a bad way. That this leads to the phenomenon of alienation—blamed on the West—is widely believed, if accepted with resignation, but that alienation contributes to cultural deepening, and thus to what we recognize as development and civilization, is not adequately recognized.

Qutb challenges the West's secularized but no less religious existence. This makes him a political theologian. And his challenge is anything but reassuring. For he questions the legitimacy with which the secularized Christian West presumes to impose on other cultures an alien canon.[71] And he questions the psychological dispositions that go with this canon. After all, isn't it imperialism, in the sense of a secularized Christian colonization of other cultures, when institutions based on Western notions of the state and Western political theory are transferred to other societies— in this case, to Muslim society? Wasn't it argued somewhere that all the key concepts in the modern theory of the state are secularized theological concepts—in this case, concepts of Christian origin?[72] Isn't it the case that the *umma*, the community of believers, is led into apostasy when alien concepts with a disguised Christian bias are imposed on it?

Further questions arise: In his *Leviathan*, the basic text of the Western theory of the state, didn't Thomas Hobbes constantly intone that *Jesus is the Christ*, a religious proposition conducing to the internalization of state rule?[73] Wasn't it Jean Bodin who brought a sovereign God down from heaven to earth, making men the source of all legal authority? And wasn't the division of the sovereign's authority into three powers, each holding the others in check, preceded by an idolatrous sundering of the divine unity? Couldn't this have originally been a secularizing shadow of the Christian Trinity? And wasn't this sundering of the unity of God into mediating instances, tantamount to transforming the divine into the worldly, the original sin, the step into depravity, that has given rise to Western modernity? If people strive for democratic control over everything, no limits are set to their greed and corruptibility. For that reason, God is the ultimate and sole authority over them and their desires. According to Mawdudi and Qutb, this authority is guaranteed only by the Koran and Sunna. Nothing may be subtracted from the literally transmitted word of God. Nothing is superfluous, nothing may be added.

This bulwark against modernity is religiously sealed off. To seek to break through it and carry out reforms, to adapt to Western regulation of the Muslim lifeworld and the values that go with it, is to show that one is the enemy of Islam, or at least of Islam thus interpreted. Such enemies of Islam are legion. In the form of imperialism and colonialism, they strive to destroy Muslim culture from the outside by proffering and even imposing their institutions. And from the inside, so-called modernists turn their energies on Islam by comparing the condition of Muslims, which they regard as lamentable, with the achievements of the West, which they portray as superior. It is hardly surprising that in a comparison undertaken using Western yardsticks Muslims come off worse. But such comparisons must be rejected as sacrilege. Those who make them are destroyers of Islam. Their prototype was Rifa'ah at-Tahtawi, whose Paris diary extolled to Muslims the advantages of the West and urged their emulation. Despite the fact that Tahtawi taught at al-Azhar in Cairo, or precisely because of this fact, for radical Islamists he is anathema. The most dangerous foe is the foe within. In the early 1960s, Nasser in Egypt and Habib Bourguiba in Tunisia were considered destroyers of Islam. Mawdudi and others saw them as belonging to the tradition of the apostate Atatürk.[74]

To oppose the ideas of these Westernized Muslims who were reviled as apostates was one thing; to come up with an Islamic alternative was quite another. Things were in fact not going so well for Muslims. The not particularly edifying condition of Islamic civilization required both diagnosis and therapy. How, after all, had Muslims got themselves into such a lamentable impasse? The answer the radicals reached is as astonishing as it is simple: They had strayed from the path of true belief. And if that was so, then a return to the origins held out the best promise of improvement. Thus retrospective nostalgia is trained on a past utopia and its restoration. That ideal is early Islam, the age of the Prophet and the righteous caliphs—the holy age of Islam.

To be sure, external influences had also played a role in the decline. These, however, had to be explained historically—without reference to God. Among these influences, the prime candidate was the crusaders.[75] But the Christian interlopers had been repulsed by the Muslims. The Mongols seemed, on reflection, a better candidate. After all, they had destroyed Baghdad in the middle of the thirteenth century. But then the Mongols had soon converted to Islam and become an integral part of the *umma*. It is true that Ibn Taymiyah, highly esteemed by Sayyid Qutb, tried in his legal interpretations based on Ibn Hanbal to deny the Mongols membership in the community of believers, on the ground that they were not true Muslims; however, this was hardly enough to put them definitively beyond the law.[76]

Qutb offered another explanation of the decline that was at once historical and theological. It focused on the Renaissance, the era in which the civilizations of Islam and Christianity began to move apart. Europe was at the beginning of its rise to unprecedented power and wealth. Through its conquests—which it called "discoveries"—the West subjugated the world. In Qutb's view, the reason for this superiority was obvious: Christianity had usurped medieval Arab learning in order to make use of it instrumentally, based on a separation of knowledge and religious belief. By cutting knowledge loose from its moorings in belief, the West had given itself a ready means to ruthlessly conquer the world. Yet for Qutb the West's superiority was temporary: Islam's spirituality would ultimately win out over crass Western materialism.

Qutb's diagnosis is not so false as it seems at first glance. Applying usual standards of historical explanation, we can, in fact, discern at the time of the Renaissance, the Reformation, and the "discoveries" an emergence of complex conditions that would, from then on, shape the divergent developments of Western Christendom and the Muslim world. Qutb, however—and here he is acting in accord with a self-conception dominant in the Orient—does not trace these changes back to causes explicable in purely secular terms; instead, he translates them into the language of conspiracies, cabals, and other machinations directed against Islam. Attempts such as Qutb's to explain complex relationships in such terms are an expression of a fundamental illusion that arises whenever premodern cultures collide traumatically with modern civilization. The idea of a conspiracy turns on linking a misunderstood notion of Western modernity to experiences drawn from Muslims' own lived experience. On the model of courtly or patrimonial contexts, in which personal favor is the true source of power, the abstractions of modernity are construed in personalized terms. A willingness to move from everyday experience to the greater whole—from the micro to the macro level, so to speak—is what is behind this conspiracy fantasy. Not that this phenomenon is unique to the Muslim cultural context, or even its Arab subcontext. It occurs everywhere, not least in cultures generally considered to be admirably enlightened in the social sciences.[77]

Belief in transcendence is, of course, far distant from the Western disenchanting of social life. In essence, this disenchantment involves putting in place an interpretation of the world generated by historical thought in which God is completely absent. On the other hand, the natural sciences, and especially their technological applications, were of interest to fundamentalist reformers. Thus, unlike the Islamic traditionalists and purists of the nineteenth and early twentieth centuries, Sayyid Qutb was not at all opposed to Western achievements in these areas. Here we are not dealing with a general technophobia. On the contrary, many Islamist activists are trained in technical disciplines, notably engineering. But this only sharpens their sense of the distance separating Islamic culture from the West. Nothing more than the poor state of basic research in Muslim countries reveals to technicians and engineers the widening gap between the two civilizations. Qutb was convinced that Islam did not impede research into the foundations of knowledge. But science was expected to adhere strictly to Islamic standards; research had to be pursued without individual autonomy and in sole obedience to the word of God.

In 1967, soon after Sayyid Qutb's execution, Arab armies suffered a severe military defeat at the hands of Israel, which was reviled as a "crusader state." Islamists took the defeat as confirmation of their doctrine of *Jahiliya*. For them, this catastrophe refuted the modernizing claims made by the despised regime of the apostate Nasser and by Arab nationalism in general.[78] And so the turn to a new, purist interpretation of Islam took its course.[79] The "proximate" enemies to be fought were the radical's own governments, denounced as apostate. Nor did these governments remain inactive. They persecuted radical Islamists with the relentless severity characteristic of civil war. Sadat acted against them before he was assassinated in 1981.[80] In 1982, the Baathist regime in Damascus, which considered itself secular, landed a telling blow. The artillery shells of Hafis al-Asad, himself deemed an apostate, rained down on Muslim rebels, mostly belonging to the Muslim Brotherhood, in the city of Hama. Thousands are thought to have been killed.

Another high point in the conflict between nationalist Arab regimes and radical Muslims was reached in Algeria in 1991 when the Front Islamique du Salut (FIS), the Islamic Salvation Front, emerged victorious from the National Assembly elections. The election results were immediately nullified by the army. This was undemocratic and proved everything the Islamists had been saying about the government. The FLN (National Liberation Front) government saw no obligation to honor the results of the ballots, "one man, one vote"—and probably "one time" only. Indeed, the military and bureaucrats of the old FLN cadres had no intention of forgoing the sinecures provided for them and their clients by oil revenues.[81]

Besieged by regimes they deemed infidel and corrupt, and driven out of their countries of origin, Islamists during the 1980s assembled in Afghanistan. In an area where the state's power barely reached, they formed Islamic international brigades to battle that paragon of irreligion, the Soviet Union. Their religious fervor was stored by the Wahhabi interpretation of Islam, supported by Pakistan and fueled by Saudi Arabia. A circle seemed to be closing—a circle whose starting point was the end of the Ottoman Empire, the dissolution of Islamic institutions, and the abolition of Arabic script in Turkey; a circle that began in the fateful year 1924 and appeared to end in 1979. The end of the Cold War, along with the eclipse of the Soviet Union and the slow-paced version of modernity it had represented for decades, accelerated the crisis in the Arab-Muslim world. The origins of the stasis in that world, its thwarted development, lie far deeper, however.

3 TEXT AND SPEECH

The Rejection of the Printing Press

One God, One Book—Mechanical Reproduction and Profanation—
Consonants and Vowels—Arabic and Hebrew—Baruch Spinoza and
Walter Benjamin—Romanization and Secularization—Recitation and
Reading—Literacy and Diglossia—*Fusha* and *Ammiya*

FOR THE AUTHORS OF THE *Arab Human Development Report,* one
of the factors hindering development of an indigenous modernity is the
fact that Arabic comes in two discrete variants: high Arabic, used chiefly
in writing, and colloquial Arabic, used in everyday social intercourse. This
division has led to two mutually exclusive spheres of communication—
writing and speech—that get in each other's way.

Classical Arabic, the language of the Koran, has, so it seems, a sacred
character even when used to convey secular content. The linguistic dilemma that results is obvious: knowledge crucial to development is communicated in written Arabic, but the written language, because of its
complexity, is far from easy to use. Conversely, everyday life and the
changes taking place in it, which are experienced and expressed in colloquial Arabic, can enter the storehouse of the written language only with
great difficulty, if at all.

In order to be rendered into writing, any new expression must clear a
very high hurdle—not in the first place because of a rigorous policy set
by diverse academies or other bodies keeping watch over the language, but
because everyday experience, which is spontaneous and largely unregulated, finds it hard to gain entry into the regulated canon of such a refined

written language as high Arabic. The difficulty of rendering social events, subjects, and artifacts into Arabic is as old as the confrontation between the Middle East and modernity. Rifa'ah at-Tahtawi struggled with it. He was the first to have attempted to formulate, in a necessarily free way combining high and colloquial Arabic, what he had seen in the West and found novel and different. We should not take such an achievement for granted. The combination of different variants existing within a single linguistic community, which differ significantly in their use and are traditionally associated with specific domains and situations, can certainly be seen as breaking a taboo.

High Arabic hampers appropriate elaboration and dissemination of knowledge; it decelerates social time. The sacred dwells within high Arabic.

The special religious status of Arabic becomes evident when we compare it with other languages used by Muslims—Persian, for instance. Although Arabic characters are also used in Farsi, for Iranian Muslims it is Arabic that is sacred, not Farsi. Thus, Iranian Muslims have two different languages at their disposal, meaning that the sacred and the profane can easily be distinguished, despite the use of Arabic characters in Farsi. The same goes for Urdu, which is used in Pakistan. On the other hand, Muslim Arabs have available to them only one language, Arabic, to express profane as well as sacred meanings. The sacred holds the profane in check. This does not, of course, suffice to explain why it is so difficult to achieve secularization, but it does point to some of the dilemmas that confront Muslim Arabs as opposed to Muslim Turks, Muslim Iranians, and Muslim Pakistanis.

The notion that the sacred works to decelerate social time is best demonstrated by the example of printing. Astonishingly to an outside observer, the printing press was first introduced into the Middle East some three centuries after its invention in Europe. Kemal Atatürk himself hammered home the dramatic importance of this fact. In November 1925, when dedicating the school of law in Ankara, he referred to a paradox from the time of the Ottoman conquest of Constantinople in 1453. Just as the Ottomans had reached the zenith of their power, the ulema (official scholars of Sharia), in his view, prevented the introduction of the printing press, which had been invented in Europe at that very historical moment.[1] From the middle of the fifteenth century on, Atatürk implied, the Western path to modernity had increasingly diverged from that in the East.

Johannes Gutenberg's invention of the printing press, the *ars impressioria*, was a major revolution in the culture of knowledge.[2] Realization of its potential in Europe made this evident everywhere. The extent to which development was accelerated by printing is easily demonstrated. In the fifty years following the fall of Constantinople in that very year of 1453, some eight million books were printed. That was far more than all the copyists in Europe had managed to produce in the more than one thousand years from the founding of Constantinople in A.D. 330 to the historical turning point represented by the invention of printing.[3]

Moreover, the invention of printing with movable type involved more than introducing a new technology; mechanical reproduction of texts and the almost unbounded spread of knowledge it made possible led to enormous upheavals in the most diverse areas. First and foremost was the Reformation. It is inconceivable that Luther's rebellion against papal authority could have succeeded without the dissemination of printed literature. That it was possible to circumvent the authorities by creating public opinion that was hard to control, is due entirely to printing. If a manuscript could not be published in one territory, the author simply had it published in another. Since a printed book could be reproduced in an endless number of copies, printing was like air and water, forcing its way into every nook and cranny. And if the printing of one book was forbidden, another would spring forth from the indefatigable presses.

But the causality also flowed the other way: Luther and his Reformation triggered an unprecedented boom in printing. During this time the flood of printed matter, and especially polemics and propaganda from both sides of the confessional divide, created for the first time public opinion worthy of the name.[4] Participants in the heated debates provoked by the Reformation were obsessed with disseminating their own points of view; what resulted was a proto-Enlightenment, a dialectic of argument and counterargument constantly fueled by the printing press.[5]

During the first three decades of the sixteenth century, ten thousand pamphlets were published, and the total number of copies printed was around ten million. Thus printing became the chief medium of communication for the culture as a whole. This trend was stimulated by both the zeal of the religious reformers and the interest in antiquity aroused by the humanists during the fifteenth century, the latter resulting in the systematic construction of libraries and ever-increasing translation of Greek texts—the first fruits of the Renaissance. The alliance between printing, on the one hand, and intellectual curiosity and erudition, on the other, meant that the literature of the classical tradition, which in an earlier age had had to be copied by hand, not only was systematically stored in the new medium, but also was distributed on a grand scale. Like the Reformation, the Renaissance was closely connected with printing. The resulting acceleration of cultural development was unprecedented. The project of transposing the knowledge of the ancients into printed form began in the year of Gutenberg's death, 1469. By 1530 or so it could be considered completed.[6] This early industrial instance of mass production resulted in that most ubiquitous of goods, knowledge.

The very nature of knowledge was altered by printing: it became public property because now nothing could prevent its spreading. The sheer volume of printed matter made knowledge, in theory, accessible to all. Previously it had been treated as a secret treasure to be guarded and kept under wraps. Handwritten books and manuscripts were usually stored away from prying eyes, in chests and secluded chambers. The new "knowledge" made public by dissemination in print differed from traditional "wisdom," insofar as knowledge treated as secret differs from knowledge that can be examined and verified in public. Thus printing and publication not only rescued the accumulated store of knowledge from oblivion, but also contributed to formation of reflective knowledge based on the autonomy of available, visually retrievable information. This went hand in hand with reorganization of the extant hierarchy of sensory input—thus, in the transmission of knowledge, individual reading replaced collective listening.[7] Now there were no limits to the acquisition of knowledge. Writing expanded into the realm formerly dominated by the spoken word.[8]

The situation was quite different in Muslim civilization, which managed for centuries to evade the revolutionary inroads of print culture. Texts were transmitted essentially by the spoken and recited word, that is, through listening. In contrast to a European civilization increasingly characterized by printing and the acquisition of knowledge through individual reading, Islamic civilization remained committed to an orally transmitted culture based on scripture. Thus the language of the Koran is construed as speech recorded in writing.[9] Muslim culture is essentially an oral culture supported by the written word. Traditional communication of knowledge from teacher to pupil was via the spoken word, often recited the better to memorize it—a phenomenon not without relevance for further development of Arabic under modern conditions.[10]

Relying on listening and memory limits the quantity of knowledge that can be acquired and transmitted; indeed, this limitation comes to be seen as a virtue. We know that during the Muslim Middle Ages, or the classical era, when knowledge and erudition had attained great heights among Muslims, resistance to "excessive" writing set in. Warnings were issued about having too may books, new writings were greeted with public displays of skepticism, and the written word came to be generally distrusted. There were complaints about the long-windedness of thick tomes. There were grumblings that though life was short, books were many. The legal school founded by Ibn Hanbal (780–855) maintained that only the Koran and the Hadith (the corpus of Muslim oral tradition) were worth putting in writing. Everything else simply confused believers. Thus while the written expression of knowledge and experience was not prevented, its dissemination in the form of handwritten copies was limited. Limited too for another reason: despite the plethora of scribes, scholars often had to copy out works themselves if they wanted to possess knowledge they considered important. All of this led to modesty and humility becoming much esteemed virtues.[11]

On what is the primacy of the spoken word in Islam based? How are we to understand the fact that the act of writing was barely tolerated and even the possession of books was suspect? Did these mores and customs, deeply ingrained in the culture as they were, engender a mindset that would later, in the early modern period, retard the introduction of the printing press?

In Muslim tradition can be discerned a striking hesitancy, if not an open aversion, to putting things in writing (*qahr al-kitab*). The founder of modern Islamic studies, Ignaz Goldziher, spoke of a genuine "antipathy"

(*Widerwillen*) toward writing.[12] The roots of this astonishing phenomenon reach far back into the time of early Islam, when Islam was trying to differentiate itself from the other monotheistic religions, especially from Judaism, to which it is related. This differentiation was paradoxical in that it contained two contrary tendencies: one mimetic or imitative of Judaism, the other distancing from it.[13]

The mimetic tendency is illustrated by the fact that early Muslims were guided by the Jewish tradition when they refused to recognize—in analogy to the Torah, the five books of Moses—any written text other than the Koran as the authentic word of God. The commentaries on the Hebrew Bible—and especially the traditions of religious law of rabbinical Judaism, which were written down in the third century in a collection known as the Mishnah—are held, in contrast to the holy book of the Bible, to constitute an oral tradition, an oral Torah (*thora she b'al peh*).[14] This distinction was later codified when it was necessary to preserve, following the guidelines of the Babylonian and Palestinian Talmuds, a distinction between the written word, on the one hand, and oral speech that had been written down, on the other.[15] It was accepted that everything handed down orally must also be handed on orally, and everything handed down in writing must also be handed on in writing.[16] Thus an "oral book" is not an oxymoron.[17]

It was through Jewish converts to Islam, presumably, that the oral tradition of interpretation entered the Muslim canon. Like the Jews' "oral Torah" before it, the Hadith is bound to the principle of orality. As in Judaism, the "heard" tradition (*sama*) took precedence over what was merely written (*kitab*).[18] Thus the Hadith stands in relation to the Koran as oral teaching does to written teaching in Judaism.[19]

That is the first, mimetic line of tradition, which links Judaism and Islam. The second line of Islamic tradition leads away from Judaism. Islam was at pains to distinguish itself from Christian traditions, but even more so from Judaism, to which it bore greater affinity, because Islam understood itself as the religion based on the final and conclusive word of God. Islam was revealed because the other religions had distorted and misrepresented the doctrine originally communicated to them. This misrepresentation occurred when the Jews, by editing the Mishnah, attempted to make authoritative a second book alongside the Torah.[20] Thus

Muslims adopted the rabbinical scholars' principle of orality while condemning their written practices. It is one of Islam's founding dogmas that no book can enter into rivalry with the Koran; beyond God's word, no other scripture can be admitted.[21] Just as there can be no God but God, so there can be no book but the Koran. Accordingly, the suspicion with which the scriptural is constantly regarded is rooted in Islam's absolute monotheism.[22]

This mistrust of the scriptural fed a general suspicion of the activity of writing per se, which might produce a second book, and gave rise to a great tradition of orality, recitation, and memorization. Early Islam has left many documents about people suspected of having circumvented the taboo on writing. While this taboo proceeds from the Hadith, which is identified as oral doctrine, it refers not only to the writing down of tradition, but also to literature in general, and in particular to books. All written texts other than the Koran are the object of intense suspicion.[23]

It was part of the culture of early Islam that before dying, one destroyed everything one had written during one's lifetime. Thus people were admonished on their death beds or before riding into battle to dispose of all written documents—preferably to burn them or in some other way to make them illegible and thus unusable. This practice had nothing to do, as one might expect from a modern point of view, with ensuring that a person's intimate secrets died with him. Instead, what mattered to those departing this life was that they should leave behind no written documents that might later give rise to distortions or misrepresentations contrary to true belief. Furthermore, scholars did not care to have it said after their deaths that they had possessed books, perhaps many books. The taboo against permanent written records is even said to have gone so far that it was thought unseemly to keep a book in one's house overnight.[24]

Not that this strict taboo applied to all forms of writing. A distinction was drawn between the possession of books, which was deemed improper, and the possession of other written documents such as letters. Possession of a book was considered a public matter and thus was subject to (imaginary) public scrutiny. Letters, on the other hand, were assigned to the private, and for that reason little attention was paid to their contents.[25]

How then was knowledge—especially the Hadith, so central to handing on the tradition—transmitted, if writing came under such suspicion?

The answer is: by great feats of memory. Those able to demonstrate great mnemonic skills were respected. But those who had trouble remembering had to resort to mnemonic aids, which could only be in the form of writing. It was important that these aids be provisional, however; they were to be destroyed as soon as the text had been memorized. This suggests that blackboards or even walls found favor—the temporary nature of anything written on them made them fitting media. Writing was eventually washed off a wall by rain or other weather conditions, and a blackboard could be wiped clean. Moreover, because of the provisional nature of these mnemonic aids, whole sentences were not written down.

In some places, the taboo on writing was so strictly enforced that it was expressly forbidden to try to remember something by writing it on the palm of one's hand or on one's sandals—though evidently this was a common practice. If a teacher became aware that a pupil had made written notes of the lessons he had given orally, or if the pupil reminded the teacher of an earlier statement that he had written down, the pupil was required to destroy his notes immediately. If something learned was in fact written down, this was done in a quiet room at home, away from public scrutiny. Anything else was considered a gross violation of the rules and punished accordingly. Even the best memory cannot get by entirely without writing, however, and therefore written documents and even books were inevitably used as aids to memory. Ultimately this kind of orality is based on writing, even if the latter is read aloud. This was especially true in the scholarly domain. Pupils were not allowed to read books without supervision, however. In order to confirm that the pupil had not read the text unsupervised, the teacher marked his presence on the text. It was, after all, easy to misread an Arabic text. Imagine a pupil acquiring his knowledge from books or manuals whose text he has only read, not heard. If the written text is not provided with the correct diacritical marks, specifying the vowels, this can have significant consequences. It is said that the incorrect use of diacritical marks in the names of certain drugs sometimes resulted in patients' deaths.[26]

Good reasons can be given for this tendency to orality in Arab-Muslim civilization. For instance, the spoken word is probably closer to what is meant than the written word.[27] In addition to the written word's notorious unreliability, its lack of spontaneity, vividness, and immediacy can be noted.[28] Using the oral language also makes it easier to keep open the possibility of interpretation; and in any case, a "shackling of knowledge" (*taqyid al-'ilm*) is avoided. Furthermore, the flexibility of interpretation that goes hand in hand with orality makes it less likely that dangerous schisms will occur. And not least, the oral language serves to confine knowledge to a small circle of professionals.

In addition to the control factor, accompanied reading has the practical advantage of ensuring correct understanding of the text. Moreover, in acquiring knowledge two sense organs are equally implicated: sight and hearing, the latter especially. In an oral tradition, it is receiver's ability to hear, not his ability to speak, that is important. Sight in any case is subject to cultural suspicion. One need only think of the figure of the sightless seer, who hears everything with utmost precision and is granted the dubious privilege of not being blinded by appearances when making judgments.

Noting the significance of hearing raises the question of the extent to which orality in the Islamic tradition is solely the consequence of religious reservations concerning writing. What, in fact, is the basis for the primacy accorded to orality? Might not other peculiarities of Arabic render it necessary to put hearing before reading? And might it be that the prohibition of writing on religious grounds is based on something that, although rationalized in terms of religion, is actually founded in cultural anthropology? Or, as so often happens, it might turn out that both have equal weight: a circumstance that turns on both cultural anthropology and its religious rationalization—the latter intensifying the former.

At stake, once again, is the issue of authenticity, truth, and the pure, undistorted tradition that must be discursively certified over the temporal distance separating the *fons et origo* of the text (in the revelation to Mohammed) from the present. Here too the meaning of the text is imbued at every turn with religion and the sacred—even if in this context it is the cultural conditions determining the technology used to communicate it that count.[29]

Isnads—the unbroken lines of authoritative transmission of the Hadith from generation to generation—are of central importance to oral tradition because they alone guarantee its authenticity and its sacred status.

Only the genealogy of traditional transmission of the text, the validation of the transmitting scholar, confers genuineness and the sacred status that emanates from it.[30]

The text is handed down by means of oral recitation; this eases the task of memorizing, especially since it is only through the immediacy of orality that a direct link can be forged between teacher and pupil. Thus it is by the teacher's authority, as communicated by his personal recitation of the text, that truth itself is assured.[31] Independent reading would not yield this kind of immediacy—especially because in the antagonistic discourse of religious interpretation, texts can easily be suspected of being forgeries.[32] Only in the physical presence of the teacher and in the recitation of the versified text, only in the trust-inspiring tonality of chanting, do the original character of the knowledge communicated (and thus also its authoritative truthfulness) find expression.[33] Many of the fundamental texts in law, as well as in other areas, were originally composed in verse and were traditionally studied in that form.

There are good reasons for this need to transmit knowledge orally and to listen to texts being read aloud, which lie in the complex phonology of Arabic and the structure of its script. Only in the act of speaking are consonants and vowels conjoined, because in Arabic written characters represent only consonantal phonemes and long vowels. Short vowels, the absence of vowels, and double consonants are not represented. Although it is possible to guess the correct reading with correctly accented vowels, more often than not, from individual words consisting only of consonants, sometimes it is necessary for the meaning of the whole sentence to be understood first. And since a word's semiotic meaning may differ from its phonetic meaning, a statement's meaning depends on its being given the "correct" intonation.[34]

Correct intonation alone conveys the authenticity, the divinely guaranteed accuracy, of the written text. Only the spoken or recited text is the authentic word. Intoning the text is what gives it its eternal, immutable meaning, which can be grasped only by hearing, not by seeing. For the same reason, the meaning of a validated sequence of oral transmission is crucial. Only when the transmission of a text from one generation of scholars to another in an unbroken chain can be established does its correctness and truth seem original. Only then is the text deemed to have been fully preserved in all its loftiness and sacredness. Conversely, the dilemma involved in putting texts into writing is palpable: although the word is saved from oblivion by being written down, it loses its original meaning.[35]

In his *Theologico-Political Treatise*, Baruch Spinoza refers to the problem of obscurity or "ambiguity" in writing with reference to Hebrew. He notes that in Hebrew there are no vowels and there is no punctuation to elucidate meaning or separate clauses. Although the lack of vowels and punctuation has generally been supplied by points and accents, he argues that such substitutes are unacceptable, inasmuch as they were invented by men of a later age whose authority should carry no weight.[36] Vowels are therefore an expression of human interpretive freedom—at best the consonants can be attributed to God, Spinoza adds ironically. A kabbalistic interpretation would attempt to go back even behind the vowelless text to an ur-Torah, the *thora kelula*. In this interpretation, the word of God is not revealed—not even in the numbering of the consonants. Writing retreats behind orality, that is, behind an unending exegetic quest to decipher the word of God.[37]

This favoring of orality over writing, coupled with the presence of the sacred, may have contributed more than anything else to the delayed acceptance of printing in the Muslim world. Anthropologically informed linguistics makes it clear that this is not a problem of Islam as a religion; a culture of orality has simply been preserved more fully in Muslim culture than it has been in other civilizations, especially in the secularized Christian West. Thus toward the end of the nineteenth century, the linguist Ferdinand de Saussure, following Jean-Jacques Rousseau, regarded the primacy of writing over speech in the West as a usurpation, because through the spread of printing, the written sign had won out over its auditory counterpart even though the natural relationship is the reverse.

The sequence is enlightening: first comes sound, then writing. The fourteenth-century Arab historiographer Abd ar-Rahman ibn Khaldun (1332–1406) was already aware of this order of precedence and sequence.[38] Ultimately, speech and writing are two different systems of signs, and writing is simply an aid for representing speech. Rousseau thought it odd to pay more attention to the image composed of signs than to the object conveyed by the sign, namely the spoken word.[39] Saussure went beyond Rousseau by noting that writing obscures the expressiveness of speech. In his view, writing does not so much clothe speech, if you will, as disguise it.[40] From this he concluded that writing claims an authority it does not deserve—above all, because the development of the child shows that we first hear and then we see.[41] The retroactive effect of writing on the spoken word can be detrimental, and it is widespread. According to Saussure, the culturally established primacy of the written over the spoken is a "pathological emergence,"[42] a process from which all life has been drained. Jacques Derrida has spoken in this connection of the "testamentary" character of the graphic.[43]

In a Muslim civilization based on the sacred, orality aided by writing reflects in its specific way a universal constant: the aura of the sacred is lost when texts are mechanically reproduced and made available to everyone as individual readers. The original text, imbued with the sacred by being recited orally, loses its pristine religiosity as soon as it is written down. This is the loss that Walter Benjamin recognized and described in his celebrated essay "The Work of Art in the Age of Mechanical Reproduction." Benjamin explains that mechanical reproduction violates the living core of the artwork, the authority contained in its originality, its unimpaired authenticity. For Benjamin, authenticity is the essence of all things handed down *ab origine*—ranging from their material duration to their historical testimony.[44] In contrast, reproduction destabilizes all historical authenticity and thus the authority of the thing itself. The technology of reproduction, by detaching the object reproduced from the domain of tradition shakes the object's very foundation. This process is symptomatic; and its meaning, Benjamin notes, extends well beyond the realm of art.[45]

From the perspective of a culture of orality, wary of all forms of reproduction in writing, the scale of the upheaval caused by Europe's printing revolution (and the mentalities it subsequently spawned) is understandable. The technology permitting reproduction of a written spiritual or intellectual good has far-reaching consequences that are subjective as well as objective. The author does not submit reverently to a tradition that preceded him; rather he demonstrates his individuality—whose value is specified by dissemination of the written work associated with his name. Only printing makes knowledge eternal and the author immortal.

In addition to provoking excessive bouts of writing, printing provides a yardstick to measure the author's fame and wealth by the number of copies of his work in circulation. Thus the boom in printing initiated by the Reformation found in Luther a best-selling author as subversive as he was celebrated. The extent of his success, kindled and at the same time consolidated by development of a public readership, is evident in the fact that as early as 1519—that is, only two years after he nailed his theses to the church door in Wittenberg—his printed works no longer bore his full name; his initials sufficed. More than a million copies of his translation of the Bible were sold during his lifetime.

Luther's Bible was not the first non-Latin Bible: translations of the holy scriptures into vernacular languages had already appeared. Since the beginning of the fourteenth century it had been common to promulgate the Christian message in French, Italian, and German—but never, before Luther, to print it, to mechanically reproduce it, in the vernacular. The significance of Latin as the universal language of Europe had been on the wane since the eleventh century, as the vernaculars emerged and began to be written down.[46] The rise of written vernaculars led to a distinction being made between the universal language as a medium of the sacred, on the one hand, and the vernaculars as profane idioms diluting the sacred, on the other. A parallel development can be seen at the same time in South Asia, with Sanskrit in the role of universal language. There too, written vernaculars were emerging. Only Arabic, another important universal language, remained unaffected by this development.[47]

Not that the sacred disappeared with the rise of European vernaculars in tandem with print culture. Luther virtually consecrated printing to religious ends by praising it as the "last and at the same time the greatest of God's gifts." No other gift like it would be forthcoming from heaven before Judgment Day.[48] Thus printing was elevated to part of the divine message. It was there at God's command. Revelation had culminated for Christendom in the reception of printing.

So it was that independent, individual reading of the Bible, first made possible by Luther's printed German translation, came to possess ritual significance. It was a call to faith. In the sixteenth century, holy scripture became identical with the printed word of God. For Luther, the divine word had to be revealed in printed form, if it was to be perceived as such. This transformation of the religious, by construing scripture as something now to be read by the individual believer, amounted to a conversion of the sacred. All-inclusive religion was denominationalized by individualization of the relationship with God, and thus partly secularized. The idea that each person stands in direct relation to God—and therefore there is no need for a mediating clergy—became possible only in the age of printing.

The conception of eternity also changed in the wake of the printing press. The new technology allowed the Bible to be distributed on a massive scale, its very ubiquity and universal accessibility helping to make the Christian message eternal. This was accompanied by a new relationship to time. Whereas formerly the sacred had been bound to eternity and thus to emblems of immutability, the Church now accepted the idea of accelerated time, for only by this technology could the blessings of Christianity be spread to the ends of the earth. Hence despite (or perhaps even because of) its obligatory religious character, the printed Bible, translated into the vernacular, turned out to be a Trojan horse for modernity.

Thus the new age was adumbrated in the relationship between the vernacular and the printing press. The Church of Rome opposed this alliance because it saw the use of the vernacular as destroying the old Latin concepts, distorting their traditional meaning, and destabilizing the hierarchy of belief—that is, it saw this alliance as endangering orthodox religiosity and annihilating spiritual and worldly bonds alike.[49] The Catholic Church sought to stem the flow of information unleashed by printing to counter the great confusion it saw as having resulted.[50] No less than in the world of Islam, in the Middle Ages Christianity deemed the accumulation of knowledge both menacing and dangerous. It seemed better to restrict knowledge to its professional custodians, the clergy and university professors.

The new art of printing was also opposed by scribes, who saw it as a threat to their livelihoods. In this they were backed by the Church hierarchy, which was only too willing to sing their praises. An ancient and venerable calling had to be preserved. Moreover, copying was considered a sacred act of inner reflection and peace, a form of worship. To no avail: in the Christian world the contemplative slowness of laboriously copying out texts by hand was now, due to human invention, replaced by hasty, greedy printing—the *multiplicatio librorum*, the multiplication of books.[51] To religious conservatives, the craving for fame and wealth that printing created seemed a sacrilege. The printed book, which could be reproduced in an endless number of copies, pointed the way to a world of commodities; it was a prototype of early industrialization. As a "free art," the printing industry still, for the time being, stood outside brotherhoods and guilds, severely challenging the old craft traditions. Everything to do with the later emergence of the mechanized world is prefigured here. The complex, long-term, and expensive process of producing and marketing books presupposes the investment of large amounts of capital. As the provider of significant sums over time, an investor in the book industry was taking on significant risk—a risk later undertaken by people we now know as publishers. Thus all the hallmarks of an incipient modernity were implicit in the printed book.[52]

Three hundred years had to pass before printing was introduced into Muslim lands. How could it have been fended off for so long? What prevented this revolutionary industrial craft from gaining entry into the domain of Islam? In Islam, despite the oral tradition, a highly developed culture of writing prevailed. Printing could only have helped to disseminate Islam's holy scripture, that is, the Koran. But the density of the sacred resisted the introduction of movable metal type. It was sufficiently strong to prevent mechanical reproduction.

In Christian Europe, with its multiplicity of territories, religious and secular authorities were unable to stop the spread of printing, whereas their counterparts in the Muslim world were quite differently placed. There may be two reasons for this: first, a practical one, that respected religious figures wielded greater power over local communities in the Muslim world than was the case in Europe; and second, in the East the taboo of the sacred was far more impenetrable, the unity of the believer with God more complete, and the influence of the holy more absolute than in the West.

The impact of the impenetrability of the sacred can be perceived by its effects. One of these was the firmness with which the innovation of

printing was rejected. At the outset came an authoritative ban on printing, issued in 1485 by the Ottoman sultan Bayesid II.[53] But would such a
formal ban be sufficient to fend off the printing press? Had the public
been truly impressed by the mechanical reproduction of texts, such a ban
would have been no more effective in stopping it than the resistance of
scribes and copyists trying to protect their trade (which, as we observed,
was fruitless in Europe). In fact, historians have been tempted to put the
successful banning of the printing press in the Muslim world down to the
influence of scribes.[54] But this does not go far enough—and even if true,
it applies less to the professional aspect of their activities than to the ritual,
liturgical aspect. For not only is the handwritten copying of sacred texts a
personal blessing for the scribe, it also places him in the line of transmission of these texts—concerned in direct spiritual connection, therefore,
with the early age of Islam and its promise of salvation.[55] Thus the resistance to printing reflected an attitude prevalent among Muslims that set
them apart from Jews and Christians living among them in the Ottoman
Empire, who unhesitatingly accepted the mechanical reproduction of
their texts.[56]

The comparison with that other religion of the law, Judaism, is instructive. Whereas Muslims living under Muslim rule were generally unable to circumvent the sacred taboo against mechanical reproduction,
Jews made active use of printing. Here it was helpful that, as a diasporic
population, Jews lived in (and between) two worlds—the world of their
Law and the law of the land. Printing had hardly been invented before
the rabbis made it clear that they perceived its utility. They distinguished
between texts serving liturgical ends and those that might have religious
content, but served chiefly for study or for mnemonic purposes. The
former—among which were (and still are) the Sefer Torah, the parchment scrolls in phylacteries or tefillin, and the mezuzah (parchment scrips
affixed to the doorposts of houses)—were to be copied only by hand.
Everything else could be mechanically reproduced without religious scru-
ples. Since that includes the lion's share of all Jewish texts, we can assume
that Jews living in Christian as well as in Muslim lands were able to enjoy
the advantages of printing in full measure.[57]

Things were otherwise for Muslims living under Muslim rule. Their
resistance to printing testifies to a deep-seated rejection stemming from a

highly tenacious taboo. This taboo finds expression in intuitive adherence to the authority of scripture transmitting the sacred. Such authority is not revealed directly, but rather is grounded in a variety of rationalizations, which in Islamic culture can assume a technical, legal, esthetic, or theological (or other religious) character. Common to all these rationalizations is an enigmatic rejection of the printed book.

Just how profound the Muslim rejection of texts printed in Arabic was is shown by an event from the year 1588, when Venetian merchants offered for sale in the Ottoman Empire books by Arab philosophers of the Middle Ages that had been printed in Italy. Although Sultan Murad III expressly upheld the merchants' right to put these books on sale, there were no buyers. No one was willing to purchase books printed in Arabic script. People objected to the printed characters, which they considered esthetically corrupt. Furthermore, the books were full of typographic errors. The idea that mechanical reproduction spread errors and irregularities endlessly was anathema to Muslims. But even apart from typographic errors, the esthetic quality of printed books from Europe could not bear comparison with handwritten Arabic texts.[58]

When technical advances eventually improved the quality of books printed in Arabic in the West, resistance coming from the ulema became evident. Indeed, the ulema—and the *qadis* (judges) as well—exercised absolute control over the written and disseminated word. Their position of power was an expression of their monopoly over Muslim cultural production. The ulema and scribes controlled the whole process, both the texts and the network relating to the production of texts. This monopoly included not only writing, copying, and distributing texts, but also reading them aloud to public audiences. Moreover, the ulema and scribes controlled not only the distribution of manuscripts but their preservation as well. In short, they held the keys to the written word. Thus, for example, in Istanbul booksellers were strictly supervised by the ulema and *qadis*, and by the judiciary through which they operated. This absolute control over the Muslim textual canon continued even when printing was allowed (within limits). Members of the censorship council set up by Sultan Abdulhamid I in 1784 to exercise spiritual supervision, the ulema, and the *kuttab* (the state bureaucracy) continued to play a leading role in monitoring all texts intended for wide distribution, whether handwritten or printed. In institutions such as these, Islam's authority found clear expression.[59]

The ulema's and *qadis'* control over the text was in no way lessened when in 1727 Sultan Ahmed III first allowed the printing of books in the Ottoman Empire. This tardy introduction of printing to the Islamic world was not to have any social consequences. There was no upheaval like that in Christian countries in the early modern period. In contradistinction to Europe, where printing began with none other than the reproduction of a holy book, the Bible, in the Ottoman Empire the printing of religious books was explicitly banned. The ban was not just for the Koran; it extended to all texts treating Islamic subjects. Given that nearly all Muslim discourse is imbued with elements of the sacred, this was a wide-ranging restriction that, in practice, allowed the printing only of grammars, language textbooks, and technical manuals. Among the external manifestations of the religious was the commonly heard suggestion that the movable metal type associated with mechanical printing was a Christian invention, and therefore should be kept as far away as possible from the language of revelation.[60] Thus it is not surprising that in 1747 the printing house that had been opened in Istanbul twenty years earlier was closed down. During the time it was in operation, it produced only seventeen titles in twenty-one volumes—showing that the mechanical reproduction of texts was given no particular priority in the Muslim world.

Outside the domain of Islam, in countries under Christian rule, works having an Islamic content were continually printed. Even the Koran was typographically reproduced in Christendom—as early as 1537, in Venice, intended for scholarly use.[61] Later there was an upswing in the printing of the Koran when, in 1774, the Treaty of Küçük Kaynarca brought areas inhabited by Muslims, primarily around Kazan and in the Crimea, under Russian control. Catherine the Great in St. Petersburg, committed as ever to the Enlightenment, took pleasure in printing Islam's holy book for her new Muslim subjects, now under Christian rule.

In the first third of the nineteenth century, the English Church Missionary Society's press in Malta served a variety of ends. It produced printed materials for the religious edification of Christians in the Orient. As did the American missionaries, whose press was also first located in Malta before moving to Beirut, the English missionaries promoted, through the rationalization and standardization of printing, a trend toward the modernization of Arabic. Thus were put in place some of the foundations for the *nahda*, or Arab Renaissance, which began in the early nineteenth century. Another landmark was the production in 1836, also on Malta, of an Arabic grammar printed in a modern typeface and proudly styled *editio princeps* (first edition). Among those participating in this project was the Oriental Christian Faris al-Shidyaq, who later converted to Islam and in 1860 entered the service of the Ottoman sultan. Now called Ahmed Faris, he drew on what he had seen of the Christian printing of Arabic in Malta and Beirut, this time in the context of an Islam that was slowly opening up to modernity. Immediately after the Ottomans' law changed to permit printing, he was appointed chief corrector to the imperial printing house.[62]

In Egypt in 1822, under Mehmed Ali's watchful eye, a state printing house—then the most important in the Orient—was set up in Bulak, a suburb of Cairo. By 1843 it had published some 250 titles, not counting teaching materials for use in schools. Most of these were connected with Mehmed Ali's modernization drive—chiefly books on military and naval matters, but also books of an intellectual or instructive nature as well as others treating the natural sciences and technology. Rifa'ah at-Tahtawi alone wrote or translated thirty-eight books on very diverse subjects, and these were printed, along with his famous diary, in Ottoman-Turkish, Arabic, and Persian.[63]

The first printing house in Egypt had been set up by the French in 1798, during their occupation. It produced pamphlets and other materials intended to familiarize the local population with the ideas of the Enlightenment and with human rights. It met an abrupt end when an excited mob broke into the premises and destroyed its type plates and other equipment.[64] We do not know whether this was motivated by religious zeal. What we do know is that in the early nineteenth century a small number of books with religious and sacred content were being printed in Cairo or Istanbul. These books alone, and not profane publications, allow us to discern a slow movement toward cautious secularization. If books of a religious nature could be entrusted to mechanical reproduction, indeed we can speak of a lifting of the religious taboo against printing. Whereas in Istanbul between 1803 and 1817 only eight books of a religious nature were printed, from 1818 onward there was an upturn in publishing activity.

The Koran itself was first mechanically reproduced by Muslims for Muslims in 1828 in Teheran. The technique of hot-metal composition with movable type was still banned, so the text had to be printed lithographically.[65] This method preserved the impression of the handwritten original, leaving the aura of the sacred attaching to it undisturbed. To this day the Koran is not printed with moveable type, but either lithographically or using photo offset technology. This also holds for the Azhar Koran, which was—after long preparation—printed in 1924, a critical year for the Muslim world. For Muslims, the Azhar Koran is the authoritative text. It meets the demands of traditional Muslim scholarship with regard to the original consonantal text introduced under Caliph Othman (ruled 644–656). It also includes the aids to reading necessary for professional recitation.[66]

The text of the Koran is read aloud. It is recited. This recitation has liturgical significance. Thus it is on the basis of intoned scripture that we must understand the fault lines of linguistic communication in Arabic. We can see what a powerful sacred taboo weighs down Arabic and any attempt to adapt it to modernity. Any change in the language is tantamount to an attack on the sacred. Conversely, any attempt to take control over language and writing, to subject it to the project of modernity—in short, to reform it—carries the stigma of profanation.

Arabs distinguish two languages within the one family: classical Arabic, considered to be the "high" language, the *al-lugha al-arabiyya al-fusha* (the language of sublimity); and colloquial Arabic, which varies from place to place. If the Egyptian variant, so-called *ammiya* or colloquial Egyptian, is more important than other regional "dialects" of Arabic, it is because it has spread far beyond that country's borders as a result of the leading role played in the Arab world by Egyptian cultural productions, especially in film and music.[67]

The juxtaposition of two variants of the same language is called diglossia, a phenomenon by no means limited to the Arabic-speaking world.[68] It is found in the most diverse linguistic cultures—for example, in those parts of Switzerland where both High German and Swiss German are spoken. In the case of Arabic, a child learns the dialect as his true native language, and this will remain his natural idiom of spoken communication throughout his life. In this supposedly unregulated language a sure feeling for language develops that enables another speaker's phonological, syntactical, or lexical deviations to be identified as such. In contrast, high Arabic in its various levels—which because of its complex system of rules is acquired later and is, in any event, used chiefly in writing—is learned as a foreign language, much as Latin used to be in Europe. So hardly any feeling for the high language develops.

Nor can these two coexisting languages be used interchangeably; each is bound to certain situations. True, for some decades now they have begun to blend as a result of the mass media. Thus a simplified, modernizing "third" language has sprung up in the role of go-between. But in principle, high and colloquial Arabic still inhabit separate worlds of communication. Moreover, the separation is problematic in that while the contexts of high Arabic are written, those of colloquial Arabic are not. And since the written language, imbued as it is with the sacred, by and large rejects the profane aspects of life, secular linguistic footprints are rare. The richness of daily experience is lost. Thus the lifeworlds associated with different languages in the same family get in each other's way.

The authors of the AHDR, referring to the resulting social deceleration, noted the inescapable need to develop a mode of written Arabic to meet the demands of modern communication. In the ensuing debate over the authors' explanation of the Arab world's hampered development, it was suggested that the twofold form characteristic of the Arabic language—which otherwise would pose no problem—reflects a fundamental difficulty, namely a delayed secularization of society. The form of diglossia specific to Arabic mirrors not only a functional separation of social spheres expressed in linguistic usage, but also, far more dramatic, a basic distinction between sacred and profane.

Why is it so hard to overcome this separation? How is it that a sense of the sacred, lodged in the very pores of written classical Arabic, has persisted so tenaciously? What saps all political will to change the language? What is it about this taboo that prevents any fundamental change to high Arabic, or any serious upgrading of colloquial Arabic by conceding to it a written form?

Saturation with the sacred and, with it, reverence for high Arabic begins in early childhood. It occurs in parallel with the learning of colloquial Arabic. Reverence for high Arabic is mediated by the ubiquitous audibility of the impressive tones of the *adhan* (the call to prayer) and the familiar sound of the Koran being recited—whether on the radio, on tape, or in the familiar milieu of one's neighborhood. Children imbibe these sounds from earliest childhood. These sounds are the seed from which the sacred grows into all other spheres of life, and above all into reverence for high Arabic. The impact of the sacred, which is imparted to the child through recitation, in later life will be expressed through the medium of high Arabic in its written character. Colloquial Arabic, in contrast, is absorbed through the sounds of daily life, and therefore remains free of the sacred.

Thus, the sacred is first absorbed by listening to texts identified as holy, that is, by means of liturgy and ritual, and then it makes its way into written Arabic. For language to retain its sacredness, it must conform to the highest grammatical and syntactic canons. Only correct Arabic can convey truth. Any attempt to alter high Arabic, any linguistic reform based on functional parameters, would injure the sacred reposing within. For that reason, it is highly resistant to change.[69]

When proposals for changing the written language to suit the changing times are rejected, two lines of argument are cited. The first is Islamic in character, the second based on Arab nationalism. The Islamic—in no sense Islamicist—position stresses that Egyptians do not truly own the language; at best, they have custody of it. Although the holy idiom was entrusted to their care, only its original speakers, the Arabs of the Arabian peninsula, have full rights over the language. The Arabian peninsula, after all, is where Islam originated; and the Bedouins who live there are seen as the true Arabs—at any rate, as those speaking the purest and least corrupted Arabic. It is from them that the holy language derives. This attitude, repudiating any alteration of the language, is based on the notion that it was created by God. Because of its holiness, it is eternal. Humans may not lay hands on it.[70]

The argument that high Arabic is the language of all Arabs also has a religious component—even if disguised. In its ideal form, Arab nationalism relates to the Islamic corpus more as history than as religion, and to the exceptional status of the Arabic language in that corpus. It is not just that Arabic, as a lingua franca, is seen as indispensable for understanding the indivisibility of the Arab nation.[71] Arabic also is constitutive of Arab national consciousness. Arabic is an abiding expression of an age regarded as "epic," because belief in the language's sublimity as emblematic of a glorious past still has the power to shape the present.[72] Any injury to, let alone loss of, this pure and perfect language would also destroy the collective memory of the epic age that is bound up with it.

Thus Arabic guards the heritage of the Arab nation in a magical way that far transcends the functional.[73] Precisely because the glorious Arab Empire does not exist in reality, it is preserved in high Arabic. Any written form of colloquial Arabic would bear the stamp of the region where it is spoken, and therefore would undermine the linguistic unity of Arabs elsewhere. Arab self-perception is based on this fiction of a shared language, compensating for an Arab unity otherwise lacking.[74] So any substantial adaptation of high Arabic to meet the demands of modernity would probably desecrate the canons of religion and nation alike. On either plane—religious or national—the present eludes high Arabic. High Arabic (*fusha*) functions as *catechon*: it actually arrests time.[75]

Arabic is not unique in being seen as a sacred language exposed to the demands of modernity. Hebrew too is essentially a sacred language.[76] In Yiddish it is called the "holy tongue," *loyshen koidesh*. When in the course of the nineteenth century Hebrew was revived as a literary language, especially by Jews no longer observing religious law, it was not at all obvious that Hebrew would be applied everywhere. When it was applied at all, it was with reservations. For the truly profane, for the mundane as well as for the coarse, Yiddish or other Jewish colloquial languages were used. In addition, there was the matter of Hebrew letters and the problem of the holiness residing in them—just as we have seen with Arabic letters.

When the most important Jewish figure in the German Enlightenment, Moses Mendelssohn (1729–1786), translated the Hebrew Bible into German at the end of the eighteenth century, he used Hebrew characters.[77] There may have been practical reasons for this—despite the Jewish population having scant knowledge of the Hebrew language, the use of Hebrew letters was ubiquitous. Yet this explanation of why Mendelssohn used Hebrew characters focuses only on the practical. But there are other, deeper reasons. To have used the Latin alphabet would have been a step too far, a step Mendelssohn drew back from taking, instead using Hebrew letters to lessen the profanation of the sacred.[78] A translation of the five books of Moses into German using Latin letters would have made excessive demands on the same Jewish reading public Mendelssohn hoped to win over.[79] The mere fact that in everyday Jewish usage Latin letters were pejoratively called *galkhes*—a word derived from Hebrew that referred to the clean-shaven heads and, in contrast to the Jews, clean-shaven faces, of Christian priests and monks (*galakh/galokhim*)—points to the religiosity vested in the respective alphabets. For people poised on the brink of modernity, the Latin, Hebrew, and Arabic alphabets were imbued with religion to different degrees.

Despite his use of Hebrew letters, Mendelssohn's translation was accorded less than an enthusiastic reception by the rabbinate, though it stopped short of excommunication (*herem*). Mendelssohn must have suspected that his project involved crossing the threshold between the sacred and the profane. In any case, he made no attempt to obtain a rabbinical *haskama* or approval for his translation of the Bible. Claiming that since the text was written in German rather than Hebrew he did not need the rabbis' approval, he made the extent of his transgression clear.[80] In 1813–1815, two incomplete versions of Mendelssohn's translation were published using a Latin alphabet; but the text as a whole was not published using Latin letters until it appeared in the 1845 edition of his complete works. For Jews, switching to the Latin alphabet was no minor matter.[81]

During the transition from the early modern to the modern period, Central European Jews moved in a broad field of German-Jewish linguistic variety. Different mixtures of German and Hebrew were used—from Yiddish to Jewish German to the increasingly used High German. This hybrid diglossia, even polyglossia—not to mention the continuing use of Hebrew and Aramaic for religious purposes—allowed Jews to linguistically differentiate the various realms of life in terms of the tension between the sacred and the profane.

Another case of diglossia, similar to that of Muslim Arabs, was found among Orthodox Greeks well into the twentieth century, who also had two variants of the same language at their disposal: Katharevousa, the purist, archaizing written language used in public documents, the courts, and so on; and Demotic, the popular language used by the great majority of Greeks. In Greek, too, the linguistic forms are differentiated in terms of their proximity to the sacred. Thus the Greek Bible is written in the "pure" language, Katharevousa, while everyday life is transacted in Demotic. When in 1903 the New Testament was first published in Demotic, there was unrest among the people. The act of translating from one linguistic form into the other was perceived as a sacrilege.[82] Only after the fall of the military dictatorship in 1974 and the later socialist takeover was the popular language given the status of an official national language. Only then was the Greek language fully secularized.

In Egypt, the most populous as well as the most culturally and politically important country in the Arab world, article 2 of the constitution establishes Islam as the official religion and Arabic—that is, high Arabic—as the official national language. Thus the link between religion and language is accorded constitutional status. The sacred penetrates society through language. No explicit introduction—or reintroduction—of Sharia, the Islamic religious law, is even required. The elevated language by itself establishes direct proximity to the sacred. As the only permitted written language, high Arabic is not truly mastered, however, by large parts of the population. The great majority continue to communicate in the vernacular, *ammiya*. Television programs use *ammiya*, as do theater and film. The news is read in high Arabic, even if ratings are lower than for programs broadcast in the vernacular. Yet no written form of *ammiya* is being planned. What's more, all past attempts to provide a written form came to naught. They failed, not only because authorities resisted such efforts, but also because—as in the case of printing—people resisted what they saw as a transgression. Just as printing once seemed to detract from the sacredness of writing, so systematically planning for a written form of *ammiya* would seem to be breaking a taboo.

Classical Arabic is already imbued with the sacred by the mere fact that human beings use it to talk to God. In contrast, they converse with each other in colloquial Arabic. For colloquial Arabic to be put in writing would be for human beings to usurp the place of the divine Sovereign. And indeed, this would be a sign of profanation—which makes all the more evident classical Arabic's significance as a hindrance to secularization.

However much classical Arabic is revered for its sacred character, so far as its use in everyday contexts and the acquisition of knowledge is concerned, it is the source of much grumbling in the general population. Egyptians freely admit the difficulty they have in using high Arabic. Whenever possible, schoolchildren and university students, instead of plowing through long tomes in classical Arabic, resort to books written in European languages—or more precisely, books of various kinds printed using the Latin alphabet. Authors are obliged to "translate" their works out of the colloquial Arabic of everyday discourse into high Arabic, the only language deemed fit to print. The Egyptian president, Hosni Mubarak, may give a speech in *ammiya*, but in tomorrow's newspaper he will read it in *fusha*. When Gamal Abdel Nasser in July 1956 delivered his famous speech on nationalization of the Suez Canal, there was a roar of applause from the crowd every time he shifted from the classical tongue to the vernacular. Though it may be an exaggeration to say so, it is not inconceivable that the crowd's excitement on hearing the announcement about the canal was less a response to its nationalization than to Nasser's switching from *fusha* to *ammiya*.

The lines of defense surrounding the sacred are numerous and impregnable. If iconoclastic reformers succeed in breaching one, another is there to repel them. The barriers erected to keep the vernacular at bay are virtually impenetrable. It all begins at school, where colloquial Arabic is dismissed as mere slang—a language for the dumb and ignorant, a language without grammar or fixed rules. The teacher's chief task is to extirpate the use of the vernacular, on the grounds that it is vulgar. If a pupil is so imprudent as to slip words from *ammiya* into a composition in high language, he is punished by the mockery of his classmates. Fear that the syntax of the vernacular might contaminate the classical language is everywhere discernible. It is a fear that the classical idiom will be corrupted. Even Naguib Mahfouz (1911–2006), a Nobel Prize–winning author known to be close to the people, spoke of colloquial Arabic as a detestable expression of cultural poverty and depravity.[83] In his view, the world of shamelessness, coarseness, and filth is the world of *ammiya*. Assailed from all sides, the vernacular's back is broken. Out of it no language can develop around which cultural self-awareness might coalesce. Self-awareness must be achieved only through the high language—which has the sacred at its core.

Attempts were made in the 1930s to raise *ammiya* to the level of an official language, but they came to nothing.[84] These efforts came from the political left, which saw them as a way to promote secularization. In the 1950s, however, during the high tide of Arab nationalism with its anti-imperialist and socialist rhetoric, the Egyptian left saw an attractive strategic option in their country's reliance on the Soviet Union and therefore supported the idea of pan-Arabism, including the linguistic unity of all Arabs in the high language.[85] Thus they sacrificed on the altar of Arab nationalism their efforts on behalf of the vernacular as the people's language.

4 RISE AND DECLINE

Ottoman Perplexities in the Early Modern Period

Europe and Asia—Ottomans and the New World—Gold and Silver—Piri
Reis and Selim I—Mamluks and Venetians—The Price Revolution and
Mercantilism—Janissaries and Bureaucrats—Merchants and Craftsmen—
Inflation and Rebellion—Stasis or Crisis—Mustafa Ali and Katip Çelebi

IN EUROPE, THE RENAISSANCE AND REFORMATION mark the
transition from the Middle Ages to the early modern period. The rebirth
of classical knowledge (which began with the fifteenth-century humanists) and the incipient confessionalization of religious belief were signs of
an earlier phase of secularization—a secularization prior to secularization,
so to speak. The impact of the transformation of Christendom into the
modern West grew apace and was accompanied by spatial expansion.
With the physical appropriation and ensuing intellectual assimilation of
the New World, the emergence of a new era was sealed.

But in the Ottoman Empire, the discovery of America attracted little
attention. Whereas Westerners eagerly devoured all reports from the other
side of the ocean, news of the New World barely engaged the Ottomans.
Here and there we find signs of desultory interest, but nothing of the first
order. The fact that the Ottomans possessed a copy of Columbus's navigational chart—indeed, the oldest one extant—is no proof of the contrary. The Ottoman admiral Piri Reis (died 1553) included it in a lavishly
decorated map he put together in 1513 and presented to Sultan Selim I in
1517—a key year for Ottoman territorial expansion, then still ongoing.[1]
Piri Reis, who also composed the famed work *Bahriye* (*On Navigation*)

and who, being the nephew of the great admiral Kemal Reis, had grown up from childhood with seafaring, had the navigational chart copied for purposes of study and edification. It was never intended to show Ottoman ships the way to America. It is true that Piri Reis had marked out a part of America on the map and labeled it a *vilayet antilia*, or area of Ottoman administration. But this territorial claim can hardly have been meant literally. From it can be deduced neither concrete intentions nor an intimate knowledge of conditions in the New World.

Neither is the anonymously authored book *Tarih-i Hind-i garbi* (*History of West India*), completed around 1580, proof of any especial Ottoman interest in the New World. This work, compiled from Spanish and Italian sources, is unique; repeatedly copied in the seventeenth and eighteenth centuries, it remained for more than three hundred years the only Ottoman source dealing with the events surrounding the discovery of the new continent. Nor is there any evidence that a broader audience may have taken a greater interest in these events, let alone developed a wider-ranging curiosity.[2] Yet it is true that broad swathes of the Turkish population became very fond of smoking tobacco, which was introduced into Turkey in 1601 by English merchants.[3]

The fact that the Ottomans ignored the discovery of the New World does not mean that they remained undisturbed by the changes it wrought, especially when these affected the traditional structure of the Ottoman Empire as a centrally organized military and fiscal state. Here two different but linked phenomena were involved: on the one hand, the price revolution triggered by the influx of precious metals from America into Europe, and on the other, the rise of mercantilism in Europe itself. American gold and silver were among the factors propelling the latter development too.

The massive inflation witnessed by Europe in the sixteenth century must be attributed to the price revolution.[4] Over a period of about a hundred years, prices generally rose by 100 to 200 percent, depending on the region, while in some pockets the price of food rose by 600 percent or more.[5] The reasons for the rise in food prices vary. For instance, after the demographic collapse caused by the Black Death in the late Middle Ages, population numbers began to rise again; as a result, the demand for agricultural products increased.[6] Growing trade between city and countryside and over longer distances required an increase in the money supply. There was talk of a downright "hunger" for precious metals. Demand for silver rose; and the precious metals flowing in from America drove prices still higher. First there were steep price hikes in Spain. These then spread across the rest of Europe and from there into the Middle East and Asia.

The economic significance of this massive inflation in the mid-sixteenth century did not escape the attention of thoughtful contemporaries. Jean Bodin, a philosopher and theoretician of the state, wrote in 1568 of the phenomena associated with these price increases.[7] Much later, in the first third of the twentieth century, historians were able to demonstrate Bodin's knowledge of the effects of the influx of precious metals from America. The quantity theory inspired, in part, by his work would become an important school of monetary thought.[8]

The massive inflow of precious metals damaged the complex institutions regulating the highly centralized Ottoman state; what is more, it damaged them in a way that the premodern Muslim community had never before witnessed. This is shown by the inflationary indicators of the time. Thus, under Suleyman the Lawgiver (ruled 1520–1566) state revenues amounted to some ten million pieces of gold. By 1653, although nominal revenues had not decreased, their value was only slightly more than four million pieces of gold.[9] For a social formation like the Ottoman Empire, whose bureaucracy used the mechanisms of monetary stability to regulate what was, in effect, a highly complex community, these were not insignificant losses. It also became clear that the institutions of the Muslim centralized state could not match the dynamic developments in the emerging capitalist world market that was just then being launched by the West.[10] Its institutions were not compatible with the demands of an accelerated social time, but a return to the traditional, self-contained economic and governmental system was not possible.[11] This gap between "no longer" and "not yet" was to dog the Ottoman Empire for generations.

The integrating power of the delicately poised Ottoman system of regulation was shattered by the steady inroads of inflation. Because there was no separation of the spheres of politics and economics, damage to the economy spilled over into government and vice versa. A weak state, further weakened by the military defeats and territorial losses that began to pile up in the seventeenth century, could not but affect internal stability and therefore prosperity as well.

This factor—the fusion of political power and economic utility—goes far toward explaining the decline of the Ottoman Empire, a decline that set in with the chronic economic stagnation apparent from the late sixteenth century on. Whereas with the rise of mercantilism in Europe, the spheres of politics and economics began to separate, the Ottoman Empire notoriously remained committed to its traditional fusion of these spheres. And in this seamless fusion of political power and economic utility the sacred was inscribed.

The influence of the sacred on economic activity consists in religious regulation of what is and is not allowed in getting and spending. These regulations enjoined the renunciation of desire while reining in the all too human drive to enrich oneself. In contrast, and even in opposition, to this religiously decreed ban on greed, the mercantilist system developing at the time in the West abetted the search for profits. Furthermore, mercantilist encouragement of desire for material gain increased secularization. Mercantilism and secularization went hand in hand, not least because, in parallel with the growing separation between government and economic life, the socially accepted modes of acquiring wealth were freed from the restrictive bounds of religion and ethics.[12] Thus the spirit of mercantilism drove a morally agnostic mentality committed to the ceaseless expansion of profits. That economic theories considered the phenomenon of the legitimate acquisition of wealth was itself a consequence of the price revolution—as was already apparent to Jean Bodin. The flow of precious metals from America was bound up, as we have seen, with huge fluctuations in prices, which, along with a new order of commerce focused on economic success alone, led to acquisitive behavior coming to the fore—a reorientation now fundamental to political economy.[13]

Thus the burden put on the delicate fabric of the Ottoman Empire by galloping inflation from the end of the sixteenth century on came just as mercantilism, a robust new form of state-directed economic activity, was gaining a foothold in Europe.[14] Mercantilism was robust because it allowed people to operate with scant regard for traditional structures—even at the price of the destruction of the guilds and other cooperative institutions. In contrast, Ottoman regulations were based on reverence, steeped in religion, for the traditional ways of engaging in trade and earning a living.

European mercantilism, whose hallmarks were the dirigiste production of commodities and aggressive foreign trade, can be thought of as a system of production for production's sake. The contrast with the Ottoman system of balancing production and needs could not have been greater. In accord with traditional theories of the state, the Ottomans adhered to the conception of an ideal closed, self-sufficient, balanced, and religiously impregnated order. Both systems—the Occidental and the Oriental—sought to accumulate, with thoroughly bullionist intentions, a store of precious metals, the better to increase the state's reserves; where they differed is that the mercantilist system saw itself as an enterprise geared to constantly increasing economic returns, and it acted accordingly, with all that this implied for the social disciplining of the population. And so a ruthless mode of production entered the world.[15]

The Ottoman order pursued different goals, in ways that had profound consequences. True, the Ottomans also sought to increase the state's reserves by importing precious metals—gold, and especially silver—and they took every administrative measure possible to prevent currency from leaving the country. But being committed to the idea of a good society, the Ottoman Empire was, at the same time, obliged to facilitate imports of benefit to its people. Protecting manufacturing centers against cheaper and ruinous foreign competition never occurred to the Ottomans—in contrast to European mercantilism, which staked all on protecting its own manufacturing centers by means of high tariff barriers.[16]

The effects of these different kinds of economies and the political orders associated with them were not felt for a long time, because there was little demand in the Ottoman Empire for most products offered by Europeans. Before the industrial revolution, trade between Europe and the Ottoman-dominated East was limited to a handful of goods such as woolen fabrics and metal products.[17]

But that was hardly the issue. It was not the influx of European products—which began, in any case, only in the first third of the nineteenth century—but rather the different and opposing economic mentalities and attendant institutions established in the seventeenth century that caused East and West to drift apart. This would become dramatically evident in the age of industrialization.[18]

The system of traditional equilibrium was shattered not by Western imports but by Ottoman exports. This questionable opening up was caused by the efforts of Ottoman merchants to realize higher prices abroad—especially for agricultural products. These exports flouted Ottoman standards of economic behavior. That is to say, they were illegal exports, a kind of large-scale smuggling that caused an uncontrolled outflow of goods at a time when the Ottoman Empire was being flooded with foreign currency. Hence the bouts of inflation that persistently shook the traditional Ottoman institutions. The extent of illegal foreign trade and its concomitant currency fluctuations is said to have been so great that, in the first third of the seventeenth century, the sultan at times even lost his grip on the privilege of minting money that symbolized his sovereign power. The Ottomans' defensive bullionism was caught in the slipstream of a rampant European mercantilism. From the mid-eighteenth century on, the differences between West and East became ever more striking. The widening gap with Europe was now evident and can, from our perspective, be diagnosed as unequal development.[19]

No matter how we rate the thesis of a structural monetary crisis triggered alike by the gold and silver flowing from America to Europe and by the inflation transmitted to the Ottoman Empire in the second half of the sixteenth century, there was an interrelationship, even if a looser one, between the dramatic course of Ottoman history and the gold and silver closely associated with the discovery of America.[20] In addition to the sharp increase in European demand for precious metals recorded in the annals of the monetary history in the late Middle Ages—a hunger for silver—the search for exchange equivalencies that would be acceptable everywhere was driven by a constant problem: the recurrent deficits run by European trade in commodities with Asia. These deficits were notorious, and the reason for them was obvious: there were no European goods that could be exchanged for the commodities—chiefly spices—coming in from South Asia. There was no demand there for what Europe had to offer.

The first Europeans to come in contact with the much sought-after spices of the Orient were the crusaders who invaded the Holy Land in the twelfth century. From that time on, these spices enjoyed great popularity in the West as goods for elite consumption and also as medicinal ingredients. But this consumption came at a price: since exchangeable goods were lacking, spices had to be paid for in cash, primarily silver. The flow of silver from Europe to South Asia, and even to China, was chronic—as Marco Polo's exotically colorful narrative shows.[21] The complex commercial geography of these exchanges shows that the control exercised by Muslims over the trade routes linking Europe with Asia necessarily involved transfer taxes and increased overhead.[22]

Starting in 1517, a key year in history, the Ottomans extended their rule to the whole of the Middle East. Thus they now controlled all the relevant trade routes through the region. Even earlier, transit trade moving through the region was under Muslim control—that is, it was run by the Mamluks in alliance with Venice, whose influence extended from Egypt as far as the Indian Ocean.[23] When in the sixteenth century the Ottomans, as a result of their conquest of the Islamic heartland, replaced the Mamluks, the rivalry between Istanbul and Venice increased. The latter's traditional dominance of the eastern Mediterranean was tantamount to a logistical monopoly over trade between Asia and Europe.

Despite the vicissitudes of the struggle between the Venetians and the Ottomans for control of the eastern Mediterranean, in their unending opposition they would paradoxically share the same fate. After all, prosperity for both the Christian and the Muslim power was bound up with the geography of commercial exchange between Asia and Europe. The decline of the traditional caravan routes as a result of the new sea link to India around Africa, combined with the growing importance of transatlantic trade, spelled a loss of influence for Ottomans and Venetians alike.[24] From the middle to the end of the seventeenth century, both played ancien régime to the new sort of commerce represented by the English, French, and Dutch.[25]

It is probably impossible to determine just how much the hunger for precious metals, whetted by the trade deficit with Asia, was magnified by the fact that the Muslims controlled the transit routes; or whether this hunger contributed to the discovery of America, which later turned out to be so fateful for the Ottomans. A certain paradox is instructive: at the very moment when Admiral Piri Reis presented to Sultan Selim I the map (including Columbus's chart) on which he had marked off a *vilayet antilia*, the Ottomans saw the most imposing expansion of their empire in the heart of the Old World. From 1517 on, they controlled the intersection of three continents and the crossroads of the most important global trade routes. Piri Reis's symbolic act in a Cairo just conquered from the Mamluks is of epistemic significance for the question of why the Ottomans turned a blind eye to the upheavals caused by discovery of the New World: they simply had more important things on their minds.

A glance at the geography and chronology of these events is instructive. Within a short time, the area of Ottoman rule expanded in an unprecedented manner. The sultan's armies drove farther west than ever before. In 1521 they conquered Belgrade and were knocking at the door to the plain of the Danube. Buda fell in 1526, Vienna was first besieged in 1529, and Transylvania was occupied in 1541. In the east, Syria and Palestine were incorporated in 1516; in 1517 the Ottomans took Cairo, at that time the largest city in the Muslim world after Istanbul. And they overran the Hejaz, with its holy cities of Mecca and Medina. From then on, the Ottoman sultan could view himself as the protector and standard-bearer of Islam. In 1534, Baghdad, and a few years later Basra, were incorporated into the Empire—thus allowing the Indian Ocean to be reached not only via the Red Sea but also via the Persian Gulf. With the occupation of Aden in 1538 and that of southern Yemen soon after, this campaign of expansion was complete.[26]

The sultan's navy as well as his army had a hand in this expansion that made him the leading power in the Middle East. With the conquest of Rhodes in 1522, the way to the Aegean and the Mediterranean was open. In 1487, Sultan Bayesid II had already been tempted to support Muslims under pressure from the Spanish *reconquista* in Andalusia. To that end a fleet led by Admiral Kemal Reis was sent to the far reaches of the western Mediterranean. A half century later, the Venetians lost their dominant position in the region when Andrea Dorea was defeated by Cheireddin Barbarossa in the naval battle at Prevesa. When it proved necessary to protect Muslims from attack by the Portuguese, who had circumnavigated Africa and were operating in the Indian Ocean, Ottoman galleys were dispatched as far as Morocco in the west and Aceh in the east.

Given such imposing feats on land and sea, it is not surprising that the Ottomans barely registered the discovery of America, which was so crucial to the West, and that they did nothing about the newly discovered lands on the margins of the world. That the discovery of America was indeed a major event, heralding a new age, initially escaped European attention, too. It mattered more to the Ottomans that they had reached the zenith of their power in the old heartlands of civilization, and that they had now achieved a monopoly over the transit trade between Asia and Europe. They controlled the intersection of all the routes—east-west as well as north-south. The enormous wealth they derived from this locational advantage flowed into the coffers of the Ottoman financial and military state, based as it was on taxes and other revenues. Thus it is no surprise that only those excluded from the benefits of control of the transcontinental trade routes, namely Western Christians, should try to circumvent the Muslim world in search of gold and silver.

The discovery of America by Christian navigators was the result of an attempt to sail westward around the world to India avoiding the Muslim-controlled areas in the Orient. This discovery was at first nothing more than compensation—a mere substitute—for the Muslim monopoly over the trade routes between Asia and Europe. That this enterprise would open up far more was neither foreseeable nor indeed intended.

When the Christian navigators—first the Portuguese, then the Spanish—began to quest for a sea route to India, they did so with a sense of religious mission. In order to secure financing and papal certification of the sought trade monopolies, such enterprises were carried out under the banner of the Cross. And since these might result in delivering Jerusalem from the hands of unbelievers, they acquired the character of crusades—crusades between the eras: between the old, medieval understanding of the world that was still imbued with the sacred, and a new, more profane, secularizing world with incipient nonreligious contours.[27] God and gold, salvation and trade had still not parted company; that would occur in more profane times to come. First the Protestant powers, England and Holland—which were, as it happened, on friendly terms with the Ottomans—and France, which was constantly quarreling with the pope and the Hapsburgs, would engage in overseas commerce or, more precisely, in overseas robbery. In his 1605 book on the law of plunder, *De Jure Praedae*, Hugo Grotius sought to legitimate this practice by giving it a secular foundation in jus gentium.[28] But all this was still to come.

In the foundational act of the new age, the discovery of America, things were still as one might expect for a transitional event: old and new had still not parted ways, sacred and profane had not yet diverged. Thus from Columbus's logbook we can infer that his *empresa de las Indias* was an enterprise that included elements of both crusade and political cunning. A Genoese navigator in the service of the Spanish Crown, Columbus wanted to reach out to the Mongols in order to forge an alliance between Christendom and a receptive Great Khan. His goal was to sail around the Muslim lands. Above all, he sought to circumvent the Middle East and the Mamluks controlling the trade routes to India, to find the fabled land of gold, Eldorado, and to conquer Jerusalem for Christianity.[29] In his religious beliefs, Columbus was steeped in medieval ideas. Doubtless he never suspected that his voyage would open the door to a new age little disposed to a naive trust in God.[30]

As always, everything had begun much earlier—in 1291, to be exact, when the Genoese Vivaldi brothers, trying to find a way to India by circumnavigating Africa, had been shipwrecked on the North African coast. Their story would not be worth mentioning here were it not that the year of their misfortune indicates an instructive fusion of the religious and the profane that led them to take such risks. For it was in 1291 that the fortress of St. Jean d'Acre fell—the last bastion of the crusaders in the Holy Land. This accords with the notion that the search for a passage to India that circumvented Muslim lands was conducted, among other things, under the sign of the Cross. Christianity and commerce were bedfellows, the common goal being to break the Muslim monopoly on transit trade. Thus in 1317 the Portuguese king Dinis made the Genoese merchant Pessagno an admiral, so the latter could lead a fleet built with funds provided by the pope and embark, with the papal blessing, on a campaign against the Muslims. The first visible results of such campaigns came in 1415, when Henry the Navigator took Ceuta with the aim of using this North African bridgehead to wrest control of the caravan routes to Morocco from the Ottomans and then move farther toward West Africa. The prizes he sought were gold, ivory, and slaves.

The Ottoman conquest of Constantinople in 1453—an event seen in the annals of Christianity as a great misfortune—strengthened the resolve of crusading sailors questing for riches and religious rewards alike. When

in 1497 Vasco da Gama succeeded in circumnavigating the Cape of Good
Hope, there was little to prevent the Portuguese from taking control of
the sea routes to the Indian Ocean and South Asia. The galleys of the
Mamluks, who had traditionally been active in the lucrative spice trade,
were no match for the Portuguese sailors' tall, three-masted caravels,
which were highly maneuverable and heavily armed with cannons.[31]

The monopoly of the Asian spice trade sought by the Portuguese was
finally achieved when they gained control of the key strategic points at the
entrance to the Persian Gulf and the Red Sea. This monopoly, supported
by military force and certified by the sale of *cartazas*, or transit passes,
struck a blow not only against the Mamluk sultan in Cairo but also against
the Mamluks' Venetian middlemen.[32] By controlling the sea routes to Asia
and Africa, the Portuguese sought to bring the Venetian merchants to heel:
they were to purchase spices only in Portuguese markets.[33] Buyers of these
precious commodities immediately adapted to the new situation. In 1501,
only a few years after Vasco da Gama had rounded the Cape, Antwerp
received its first shipment of spices directly from Portuguese sources.[34]

Predatory commerce coincided with a divine mission. Alfonso de Al-
buquerque, the conqueror of Hormuz on the Persian Gulf and Malacca
in Malaya, placed himself at the disposal of Pope Leo X, noting that control over the Straits of Hormuz opened the way to Jerusalem. But Albu-
querque was not able to carry out his other plan: to take Mecca hostage
by landing in Jeddah, and then exchanging Islam's holy city for the city
of Jerusalem so dear to Christians. Moreover, Portugal was about to pass
the zenith of its power in the Orient. One after the other, the rising Protestant powers of England and Holland broke Portugal's lucrative monopoly with Asia. Meanwhile, the Ottomans had defeated the Mamluks and
incorporated the heartlands of Islam into their mighty empire. Had the
Ottomans determined to cut a canal across the Isthmus of Suez so that
they could move their Mediterranean fleet quickly and without hindrance
into the Red Sea, and so into the Indian Ocean, this might have coun-
tered the Europeans' transatlantic claims on the riches of America, which
they pursued alongside their trade with Asia.[35]

The shift of trade in spices and other prized Asian goods from land to
sea foreshadowed a development in which scholars of economic history
only a few decades ago discerned the origin of a worldwide revolution in

trade.[36] This revolution seemed to them to have two causes: first, the displacement of the traditional caravan trade from Asia to Europe to the sea route around the Cape of Good Hope, and second, the increasing volume of transatlantic trade.

The dangers and manifold tolls, taxes, and duties connected with transportation by overland routes made commodities much more expensive. Transportation by sea routes could reduce costs significantly—in some places, it is said to have been by a factor of twenty.[37] Furthermore, maritime logistics were securer and transportation quicker—particularly important for perishables. Yet it is not necessarily the case that increased trade by sea or the growing transatlantic trade negatively affected the Ottoman Empire, which from the beginning of the sixteenth century exercised control over all routes. Trade revenues rose, and the increased recourse to shipping did not necessarily mean a decrease in trade by caravan. At times the English and Dutch considered trade with the Levant, which passed through Ottoman ports, more profitable than trade with India conducted exclusively by sea.[38]

From the influx of commodities via the traditional caravan routes, the Ottomans drew significant profits over the long term. The duties on trade passing through its territories were not the sole or even the principal source of revenue for the Ottoman fiscal state, the income from agriculture being greater. Nevertheless, they were a source of revenues whose loss would have been painful indeed—revenues the Ottomans were willing to fight for. Thus in planning the occupation of Aden and Yemen, we know an annual income to the state treasury of several hundred thousand gold pieces and jewels was expected. As it turned out, between fifty and sixty ships passed through the port of Aden every year, yielding a revenue of some two hundred thousand gold pieces. Despite all the fees traders had to pay the central government in the form of taxes, this modus operandi was more advantageous than paying protection money to various groups in the absence of a central government. So, it actually conduced to foreign trade that both Hormuz and Aden were under Ottoman control.[39]

The extent to which costs were increased by the high duties imposed on goods passing through Ottoman territory—duties flowing ineluctably into the coffers of the state—can be gauged from the tax payable on one camel load of spices, weighing about 250 kilograms, for a single leg of the long and arduous land route. For example, if a ship coming from South Asia put in to Jeddah on the Red Sea, the Ottoman treasury and the traditional local authority—the sharif of Mecca—split the transit tax paid. The ship's cargo still had a long way to go, however. That way passed through Damascus and Aleppo before reaching a temporary warehouse in Bursa, a trading hub. But before arriving there, the cargo had been taxed again. In Damascus, the duties for a single camel load were set at seven gold pieces. If the commodities were purchased by a "Frankish," that is to say, a European trade partner, a princely nineteen gold pieces had to be paid—nine of them by the Europeans themselves.[40]

In addition to the Indian spices that reached Europe by various routes across the Middle East, silk was another traditional commodity traded. Silk was produced in Persia and reached Bursa, and later Aleppo as well, via east-west trade routes controlled by the Ottoman Empire. Control of the silk trade and its tax revenues had amounted to no less of a monopoly than the spice trade. Indeed, the lure of monopoly led to fierce competition among the powers involved in trade. In the Indian Ocean, European national companies vied with each other for monopoly status. On land, Muslim rulers contended for control of the caravan routes. In 1514, the Ottoman sultan Selim I tried to strangle the Iranian economy with a rigorous embargo against silk. The Persian shah Abbas I reciprocated when, at the beginning of the seventeenth century, in the course of a decades-long standoff with the Ottomans, he exploited a weakness deriving from the latter's war with the Hapsburgs to divert the hotly contested Silk Road away from Ottoman territory and in the direction of the Indian Ocean with its sea routes. The Safavid Persians benefited when the English and Dutch, who had replaced the Portuguese as the chief powers in the Indian Ocean, refused to pay the high duties demanded in Ottoman ports. Thus it is unremarkable that in 1603 the trade war between the Ottomans and the Iranians, waged by means of all-out reciprocal blockades, again spilled over into armed conflict. Reflecting the international situation, the standoff between Ottomans and Persians became part of the front line in the incessant wrangling between the dominant powers of the day—the Ottomans and the Hapsburgs.

The Ottomans were an integral part of the prevailing European balance of power. As continual opponents of the Hapsburgs, they were directly or indirectly allied with all those opposed to the emperor and the pope or their Venetian allies. In the sixteenth century, the chief beneficiary of Ottoman support was France. That France could develop into a territorial state with national contours would scarcely have been possible without Ottoman backing in its war against the Hapsburgs. Similarly, without Ottoman support, the Protestant side in the confessional wars, not least the Calvinists of Hungary and Transylvania, would hardly have been able to withstand pressure from the Catholics. The bonds of mutual sympathy seem to have been so enduring that in Europe talk of "Calvino-Turkism" made the rounds.[41]

The Ottomans also used trade policy to intervene in internal European conflicts such as that between the Ottomans' archenemy, the Hapsburgs, and the Low Countries, which were detaching themselves from the Holy Roman Empire. Thus the sultan granted European merchants from friendly countries—especially the French, but later the English and Dutch as well—trade privileges in the form of so-called capitulations. These trade privileges were intended not only to help supply the city of Istanbul with European goods, but also to channel trade between Asia and Europe through the trade routes and ports controlled by the Ottomans. Thus capitulations were granted to the English just as they were on the point of switching to a trade route leading through Russia, the Caucasus, and Iran to Hormuz.[42]

The capitulations were also an instrument of high policy, however, because they let Western powers active in the Levant trade, but with no love for the Hapsburgs or their imperial authority, further consolidate their independence. In connection with their transatlantic activities and the precious metals reaching them through Spain for their final products, Western European coastal states developed the economic system of mercantilism, soon fundamental to the European way. From the mid-eighteenth century on, the capitulations granted by the sultan were transformed into unequal contractual relationships that allowed Europeans to penetrate the Middle East.[43]

The reasons for the decline—more exactly, for what comes across as Ottoman stasis by the yardstick of European development—are as many and varied as they are controversial. But however we assess the principal events, we can discern in the Ottoman Empire by the end of the sixteenth century an accumulation of changes that caused traditional institutions to drift into decline. And then there is the fact of territorial contraction. Not that territorial expansion is a sufficient indicator of a polity's power and prosperity. But in the premodern period—in which agriculture was still the dominant factor, and especially in a Middle Eastern fiscal and military state like that of the Ottomans, in which service in the cavalry was rewarded with a fief that involved collecting taxes for the treasury— the loss of territory, combined with the loss of control over communication routes for the transit trade, could have far-reaching implications.

The Battle of Lepanto in 1571, in which the Ottomans lost almost their entire fleet, was a bad omen. But it was the Hapsburg-Ottoman war, which lasted from 1593 to 1606, the outcome of which was not very advantageous to the Ottomans, that first indicated that Ottoman expansion was coming to an end. In addition, Persian power was growing in the east, leading to territorial losses for the Ottomans in the Caucasus. Decades of warfare with Persia ended in 1638 with a final demarcation of borders, yet the ultimate result was financial deprivations for the Ottomans. In the 1660s, a large-scale Ottoman offensive against Austria came to a standstill; and the war between the Hapsburgs and the Ottomans at the end of the century, which included the inconclusive second siege of Vienna, ended in 1699 with the Treaty of Carlowitz, which obliged the Ottomans to make the biggest territorial concessions yet. Hungary, Transylvania, Slavonia, and Croatia fell to Austria; Kamieniec, Podolia, and the Ukraine to Poland; the Peloponnesus and a large part of Dalmatia to Venice. These dramatic territorial losses continued with the Treaty of Passarowitz, which ended the war between the Ottomans and the Hapsburgs in 1718—a date that lies, however, outside the critical period from the late sixteenth through the seventeenth century that concerns us here.

Ottoman territorial losses relating to Russia's rise and its southward expansion likewise fall outside this period. With the 1774 Treaty of Küçük Kaynarca, so momentous and humiliating for the Ottomans, Russia signaled its future role as nemesis of the last Muslim universal empire. From that point on, it was the European balance of power that saved Turkey from Poland's fate—Poland was first partitioned in 1772—or at least it did so until the Young Turk government's ill-considered decision to enter the First World War on the side of the Central Powers brought defeat in 1918.[44]

The territorial contraction of the Ottoman Empire that began in the seventeenth century may have been cause as well as symptom of what was even then perceived as a decline. What caused this decline and, indeed, whether the events are correctly characterized as such is still a matter of debate.[45] What is not open to debate is that something led to a change in the military and the revenues derived from military service, both of which were vital to the social fabric of the Ottoman Empire. This something was a shift away from military service based on direct allegiance to the sultan, and to a standing army of infantry, the janissaries.

Many causes lay behind this transition, chief among them being Western innovations in weapons technology.[46] The Austro-Turkish war had shown the sultan that his heavily armored cavalry, equipped with sabers and lances, was no match for the emperor's foot soldiers, who were armed with muskets. In order to accommodate the new situation on the battlefield, the sultan had to establish a standing army of foot soldiers (the janissaries), equipped with firearms, and artillerymen, with heavy equipment in tow.[47] In addition, depots for gunpowder and shot had to be set up throughout the empire. The sultan's coffers had to finance these installations and compensate the new standing army in cash.

This change affected more than just the military: it had far-reaching consequences for the social order as well. This is due to the dual nature of the traditional cavalry (the *sepahi*), which lost its function. As timariots, or fiefholders, traditionally they had been obliged to perform military service for the sultan in exchange for agricultural revenues from the fiefs they had been granted. Because firearms replaced sabers and a standing army equipped with muskets became indispensible, the fief system lost its relevance. From now on, a mode of agrarian taxation based on leasehold, payable in cash, had to be introduced. The sultan, as owner of the land, would henceforth auction off leases to the highest bidder. The consequences for the tenants were severe; their exploitation increased.

Thus, a further monetizing wave swept through the complex social fabric of the Ottoman Empire. The janissaries were already remunerated in cash for their services. Expanding this part of the armed forces necessarily placed additional financial burdens on the state treasury. State regulation of currency values now became increasingly important. The stability and welfare of the Ottoman state depended on money—both the financial means available in the form of coins made of precious metals and the actual quality of the coins, which determined their value.

What was it about the Ottoman Empire's social fabric that caused it to react so sensitively to the monetary upheavals coming in from outside the empire? And how did its monetary regulations differ from the forms of institutionalized commerce then emerging in the West—that is to say, mercantilism?

The Ottoman social environment was characterized by an interweaving of economics and politics, whose growing separation in the West would be so important in the later development of modernity. Moreover, in the Ottoman context, the interpenetration of the functions of politics and economics was reinforced by another factor—the sacred.

The presence of the sacred, even where it is least expected, is not peculiar to Islam. Such interconnections were standard in the premodern period as a whole—but especially in the Orient, where a dominant power regulated everything. This was no less true of Byzantium, whose institutions the Ottomans had adopted in many respects and, following Persian-Iranian tradition, further centralized. The effect of the sacred can be seen in the specific liturgical semantics and in the regulations that accompany it, which are part and parcel of the centralized state's constant interventions in the social and economic lifeworlds.

The structure of status and rank in the Ottoman Empire was twofold. On the one hand, there were merchants, craftsmen, and farmers; on the other, the bureaucracy and the military. The first group, that of the producers, was expected to support the second, that of the officials representing the highly centralized state, by the taxes and fees it paid. True to Oriental tradition, the Ottomans' centralized fiscal and military state constrained the social fabric into a web of regulations and controls. The social fabric, in turn, was configured by institutions facing inward toward the central power. Absolute priority was given to supplying Istanbul, the empire's control center and hub, with food and other goods for daily consumption. This privileging had a functional significance, since it served to stabilize the bureaucracy and military as basic pillars of the Ottoman state.

At the heart of government was the state treasury, the bulwark of stability and prosperity. The extent of its assets reflected the condition of the empire. Thus, for its own preservation, the government sought to maintain or increase the value of the treasury by importing precious metals. It had to protect the currency and show itself benevolent and well disposed toward the people. Good governance was symbolically expressed, as when the sultan used the occasion of religious holidays to publicly hand out goods, thus demonstrating that he possessed the virtues of munificence and magnanimity. These displays—reminiscent of ritual acts—included mass slaughtering of sheep to feed the poor and the distribution of highly prized woolen clothing to the janissaries.[48]

Among the taxable groups of merchants, craftsmen, and farmers, the merchants had the greatest prestige. This may have been connected with the fact that trade was essentially responsible for bringing in riches and ensuring their geographic movement. In addition, officials skimmed off revenues in the form of money, and this is most easily done when money is circulating. But it is precisely when money is circulating that, owing to its abstract character, it is most likely to evaporate and thus evade the clutches of the state treasury. For a state based on tax revenues, merchants constitute an indispensable but problematic clientele. The relationship between the two was marked by constant mutual mistrust.

In Muslim tradition, merchants were highly praised. Beyond this praise, however, merchants' prestige derived from their vital role in supplying the cities, those havens of imperial life, power, and bureaucracy. In addition, the organs of government saw to it that the trade routes passed within striking distance of the capital and other centers of regional trade such as Bursa, Edirne, and later Aleppo. Likewise, the Ottoman policy of territorial expansion, whose great phase peaked in the year 1517, was resolved on, in part, in order to profit from the caravan trade. This was evident in the major thrust toward the Indian Ocean as well as in the wars against the Safavid Persians.

The sultan's control over Ottoman social life was absolute. This could be observed when urban centers were established and populated by decree following territorial acquisition by war or other means. For this purpose, populations could be transplanted and resettled (the praxis of *sürgün*), as in the case of the Sephardic Jews, expelled from the Iberian peninsula and Italy, and resettled by Sultan Bayesid II (ruled 1481–1512) in the domain of the Ottoman Empire. Through the skills they brought with them from an early mercantilist setting, they enabled the Ottoman Empire to reap the benefits of superior European knowledge and manufacturing in the fields of weaponry and medicine. Furthermore, in the port cities of Salonika, Izmir, and Istanbul, the Iberian Jews represented a highly specialized population oriented toward foreign trade and exchange. In Salonika, they established a center for Ottoman production of woolens and established a close relationship with the janissaries, who were institutionally on the rise and in need of this material. Resettlement in accord with Ottoman policy proved less advantageous for some 1,500 merchants and craftsmen from Cairo and Tabriz. After Sultan Selim I's armies conquered their cities, they were sent bag and baggage to Istanbul.[49]

Central to the state's control over economic life was the Ottoman institution of *narh*, which allowed government officials to set prices for goods sold on the market. Maximum prices for foodstuffs and other items of daily consumption were fixed by the state, albeit in consultation with representatives of guildlike vocational associations. *Narh* was an Ottoman rather than a genuinely Islamic institution, and it indicates the centralist and regulatory nature of the state. The various schools of Islamic law recognize a contractual partner's freedom to negotiate the price of a commodity. Only in exceptional cases, for example, in famines or other shortages, is it permissible in Islamic law to impose prices.

In the Ottoman system, fixed maximum prices served to supply the population in accord with the yardsticks of cheapness, fairness, and predictability. It expressed the state's concern for the welfare of its people, but even more, it preserved the public peace and so shored up state control. This was particularly true of bread prices. If these were raised, this could spark unrest in Istanbul, the center of power, which might then threaten the state—something the sultan tried to avoid at all costs. Bread prices and the public peace were very closely related. The question of bread prices was so delicate that the sultan even had trusted allies spy on the grand vizier, who personally controlled bread prices—just to be sure that the information collected by his chief minister regarding current bread prices was accurate.

Hence, in the Ottoman Empire, the process of determining prices was anything but free. There was no such thing as a market price, regulated by supply and demand. In setting prices, merchants and craftsmen were more constrained agents of the state than freely contracting agents of a particular interest. Moreover, becoming unduly rich was not well regarded, and required approval as "fair profit." Permissible profit was seen as a bonus for services rendered; and service was seen as a duty owed to the sultan. While free trade was in any case out of sync with the spirit and values of the age, these regulations make it clear what hurdles, both mental and habitual, would have to be cleared when the times made fundamental change necessary.

The restrictions placed on the effort—so central to a market economy—to earn the highest profits possible are evident also in the forms of distribution practiced. Thus commodities were never freely available, but always subject to conditions and constraints. Further, they could not be put on sale just anywhere, but only in certain parts of the city and only in certain streets designated for this purpose. Then there were the modalities of price controls. For many goods, prices were set on a daily basis, while for others—chiefly meat and dairy products—the price fluctuated with the season and the holiday. That prices were administered was evidenced in the fact that they were decreed on a daily basis. No one could ignore these public prices without offending customers or, for that matter, attracting attention from the supervisory agencies monitoring merchant behavior in the marketplace.[50]

The institution of *narh* was therefore a means of political regulation and equitable social distribution. It was based on the assumption, promoted by the ruling military caste, that the merchants' drive to enrich themselves was fundamentally untrustworthy. After all, the intrinsic goal of profit-seeking was to serve the individual's own interests. Thus reservations about profit-seeking, which was deemed to proceed from disreputable motives, could be grounded both ethically and functionally. Anyone seeking profits was suspected of evading his duty to the community. Thus the merchants and also the craftsmen, who were no less interested in pursuing their own advantage, were subject to supervision by the political authorities. Their activities were hobbled by interminable regulation. *Narh* was the pivotal Ottoman instrument for regulating the market. Its goal was to maintain internal equilibrium by means of government-regulated price controls, so as to ensure that the military class, the *askeri*, would continue to exceed market forces in power and importance. In other words, the goal was to establish the rule of pure "politics" over the instinct-driven "economy."[51] Yet the fact that well into the nineteenth century *narh* continued to be seen as the linchpin of a just and functional ordering of economic life is enough to make us sit up and take notice.

The institution of fixed maximum prices, that is, the policy of regulated profit margins, makes clear the importance of monetary stability under conditions when the virtues of regulation trump the profit motive. If the currency loses value, the government cannot avoid responsibility for the state of the "economy" it has decreed. If the currency loses value because of inflation or some such form of devaluation, merchants and craftsmen, whose activities are already restrained by fixed price ceilings, will either cease selling their commodities and services, which would gravely affect cities in need of provisions, or resort to a practice common in times of historical crisis and sell their commodities illegally, possibly taking them outside the country—that is, they would escape the bureaucracy's and the military's demands by resorting to smuggling.

Another option was to focus on foreign exchange. Merchants stopped accepting the Ottoman currency, the *akçe*, and demanded instead that their commodities be paid for in one of the foreign currencies circulating in the country—especially Venetian gold ducats or the internationally used Austrian silver groschen.[52] This ploy led to unrest among functionaries whose salaries were paid in the Ottoman currency. Their income no longer let them buy commodities, and they had to line up at money changers' offices in order to convert their bad money into good at unfavorable rates.

The state bureaucracy, the *kuttab*, was not the only authority involved in controlling prices and profits. Religious officials, guardians of the religious order—the *qadis*, who were responsible for issuing legal judgments, and the *muhtasib*, an authority that can be described as a kind of police enforcing the ethics of market behavior—also saw to it that the traditional rules of vocational conduct were observed.[53] The *muhtasib* made sure the market followed both the commercial and the religious rules—from product control and price fixing to prayer regulations. Thus economic life was invested with "liturgical" significance.[54]

The interspersing of sacred and profane aspects in economic life is shown by the fact that a guildlike vocational group elected a sheikh, that is, a religious authority, as its head.[55] In commercial disputes this religious dignitary acted as arbiter, and his decision was binding on the parties. Here too, religious authorities exercised their prerogatives.

The saturation of economic life by the religious, which is so self-evident a part of Muslim civilization, was also manifested spatially. The Ottoman institution of the *imaret*, or public soup kitchen, was significant in this regard. In this urban complex, commercial facilities and religious institutions not only were located in close proximity, but were pledged to provide mutual support. Reflecting the religious coloring of trade and business, the *imaret* complex was legally established as a pious endowment. There mosques, religious schools (madrassas), scriptoria, hospices, and hospitals stood side by side, along with commercial facilities such as caravansaries, khans, and bazaars, giving architectural expression to the fusion of sacred and profane elements.[56] Similar commercial complexes, so-called *bedestans*, or covered markets where precious commodities were sold, were located along trade routes and formed nuclei for the cities that then grew out of them.

Guilds and other vocational bodies were also subject to the religiously guided control of state-certified organs whose function was to supervise prices and quality and also to prevent competition and violations of labor-hiring rules. In order to monitor the use made of raw materials and handicrafts, special storehouses were built in the cities. The materials stored in them were measured, weighed, taxed, and subjected to quality control.

As well, the production of goods had to comply with regulatory measures. All efforts to produce goods in the countryside and so escape oversight by the state supervisory organs were eradicated. With such strict controls in place, the prospects for a system of production characteristic of the early stages of industrialization were poor. In Europe, merchants had begun to circumvent the guilds by establishing cottage industries in rural areas to take advantage of cheaper labor.[57] Illegal operations of this kind got nowhere in the Middle East at the time; they were tracked down by the guilds and reported to the Sublime Porte, the seat of imperial government. Concerned to ensure balance and order between the vocational groups, the government acted to stop what were viewed as dishonest practices. In the eighteenth century, merchants increasingly attempted to bypass the guilds by hiring craftsmen directly.[58] These efforts were restricted in scope, however, and could not develop the dynamics of proto-industrialization—in which businessmen use their capital to produce goods directly in the countryside using rural labor—which might have set up an unstoppable trend.[59]

Nowhere was the melding of religious, governmental, and commercial symbolism better expressed than in the Ottoman currency. Traditionally, *sikka* (minted coin) and *khutba* (Friday prayer for the ruler) were seen as twin symbols of sovereign power. The Ottoman bureaucrat and historian Mustafa Ali (1541–1600) interpreted *sikka ve khutba* as the expression of a "divine gift." The community looked on *sikka* and *khutba* as the pillars of stability and trust. *Khutba* gave expression to the sublimity of the ruler's prestige. In prayers, believers recalled the divine injunction to obey the ruler, an act of submission rooted in religious belief. *Sikka*, the minted coin of the realm, carried, along with the engraved insignia of wealth and dominion, the aura of the sultan's sublime power. Since coin circulated in the community, passing from person to person, from hand to hand, the value marked on it as corresponding to a certain weight in silver testified to a religiously legitimated power to rule. Thus two kinds of belief commingled in the currency: belief in divine power and belief that the value stamped on it was backed by a due measure of precious metal—hence *sikka ve khutba*. Also, the sacred dimensions of the currency constituted a constant demand to do business in ways pleasing to God. If one dabbled on the side in business deemed dishonorable, it was better to use foreign currency.[60]

The sacred symbolism impressed on the coin of the realm and validated by prayer conveyed the ruler's promise to back its value in precious metal. Inflation and devaluation, as manifested in cutting the precious metal content in coins, were accompanied not only by a drop in respect for the ruler's authority, but also by an impaired ability on the part of the currency to inspire trust imbued with religious belief. This is exemplified by the 1589 rebellion, an episode that occurred on the eve of the year

1000 according to the Muslim calendar (1591/92), a magical number that had given rise to apocalyptic expectations. Janissaries and craftsmen joined with other groups to violently protest the devaluation of the akçe and the Porte's fiscal policies, which they saw as draconian.[61] As in the case of other disturbances relating to monetary values, the Jewish quarter was burned and plundered.

Long before it came to this, the janissaries, who were paid in the national coin, had been upset about the devaluation. In the markets, merchants were already refusing to accept the akçe. And since its plunging value necessarily affected the legitimacy of the government—*sikka ve khutba*—Sultan Murad III (ruled 1574–1595) saw no other way to guarantee his authority than by sacrificing the official in charge of the mint, the *beylerbeyi* (governor) of Rumelia (the Ottoman possessions in the Balkans), Mehmet Pasha, as well as the head of the state treasury, the *defterdar* Mahmud Efendi. They were both executed, and the insubordinate rebels were placated by means of payments from the reserves of the internal treasury.[62]

The *beylerbeyi* rebellion resulted from the massive devaluation of the currency carried out in 1586—inaugurating an inexorable decline in value. Within ten years, prices for basic goods under the gold standard doubled.[63] Worse, no end to this process was in sight. Contemporary observers interpreted the precipitous decline in the currency's value as expressing a general decline—in morals, ethics, and institutions. The elites were infected with a sense of omnipresent decadence, fearing their empire was slipping into inflexibility, stagnation, and decay. The resultant unease led to an increased output of writings, contributing to the traditional dramatization of this period as having been one of great crisis. Later it was said that these sources were but the ramblings of overexcited bureaucrat-intellectuals to a man whose sense of the times reflected more their own mood than it did the facts.[64]

What the causes of Ottoman stagnation were, and, indeed, whether there was a decline at all or simply a quickly resolved crisis, are still debated.[65] In fact, the Ottoman Empire recovered after the catalytic events of 1589, while in the seventeenth century, a time the chroniclers portray as equally dire, the economy stabilized, and the eighteenth century experienced a noticeable recovery. This was reflected in a positive balance of trade.[66] That there had been an overreaction to the *beylerbeyi* rebellion, probably because those witnessing it still recalled the earlier "golden age," may be gleaned from the fact that later rebellions by dissatisfied janissaries in 1622 and 1623, which actually led to the sultan being overthrown, attracted less attention than the one in 1589—the year in which the inexorable decline began.[67]

Mustafa Ali, the bureaucrat and historian mentioned earlier, offered a paradigmatic image of the imperial decline (*ihtilal*) sensed from the end of the sixteenth century on. Between 1591 and 1598—with the apocalyptic expectations of the Muslim millennium just behind him—he wrote his magnum opus, *Künh ül-ahbar* (*The Nature of History*). This work is considered the standard Ottoman study of the paradigm of decay and decline. The images of the lamentable state of the Ottomans and their empire that were passed down from generation to generation essentially were taken from this book. It became the indispensable guide to Ottoman self-perception.[68]

The image of decay and decline was underscored when at just this point in time—the year was 1598—a copy of Abd ar-Rahman ibn Khaldun's *Muqaddima (Prolegomenon)* was discovered in Cairo and accorded a reception in the Ottoman Empire. Although this did not occur overnight, the influence of his cyclical theory of history, which is based less on God and more on the anthropological constants of the rise and fall of dynasties and empires, was the more thoroughgoing for that.[69]

Among the more discerning readers of the *Muqaddima* was the traveler and scholar Katip Çelebi.[70] The peripatetic encyclopedist of his time, he was considered an inexhaustible source of knowledge and experience of the crisis to which the *beylerbeyi* rebellion had drawn attention. His works were seen in their reflective authenticity as diagnostic icons. They provided a barometer of the spirit of the age and the community's sufferings. And they tried to affect the politics of the day by means of good advice, which did not stop at calling for urgently needed reforms. Thus the dissemination of Çelebi's insights had a huge influence on the bureaucrats running the state, an influence that Mustafa Ali, that prototypical Ottoman intellectual-cum-bureaucrat, had also felt called to exercise.

Whereas Mustafa Ali's historical and political diagnosis of the decline had proceeded from his own experiences, Çelebi's prognostication was infused with the authority of Ibn Khaldun's theory of history. The fourteenth-century Tunisian scholar's analogies between the human body and the body politic, together with his remarks on the five stages of the dynastic state and the tension between the nomadic and sedentary ways of life that is intrinsic to government proved enlightening to Ottoman scholars centuries after Ibn Khaldun's death. Mustafa Naima (died 1716), one of Çelebi's successors, also based himself on Ibn Khaldun, as when he complained about the condition of the Ottoman Empire and suggested ways of ending the decline. We should also mention Mehmed Sahib Pirizade (died 1749), who translated the *Muqaddima* into Turkish and was later appointed to the important office of *sheikh-ul-islam*.[71] From then on, Ibn Khaldun's cyclical theory of history would be deeply anchored in Ottoman consciousness—and never more so than when it was invoked to help understand crises seen as evidencing decline.

The application of Ibn Khaldun's theory to the Ottoman context led to attempts by intellectual bureaucrats and scholars to overcome the crisis by restoring the traditional, proven institutions of what they considered a glorious past. The key to recovery was not so much to introduce the new as to restore the old. They looked to the past as a better, because more pristine, time. Nor can this be dismissed as an exercise in nostalgia, as it answered to a certain view of history. Because history seemed to move in cycles, the "golden age" could be restored by returning to the point where the cycle began.

The Ottomans' golden age (*medine-i fazile*) had lasted around a hundred years, beginning with the conquest of Constantinople in 1453 and culminating in the mid-sixteenth century with the reign of Suleyman the Lawgiver. In this construction of history, the Ottomans—devout Muslims though they were—did not situate the ideal past so much in the time of the Prophet and the four righteous caliphs, which was the standard religion-imbued Islamic reading of history, as in the time when Ottoman power was at its peak. Ottoman intellectuals—from Mustafa Ali to Katip Çelebi to Mustafa Naima and the scholars who followed them— all concurred on this point. This deviation from classical Islamic tradition is explained by the fact that when running their empire, the Ottomans did not rely solely on Islamic law—the Sharia—but also on their own legal code, the *kanun*. And it was the tradition of a more secular-oriented *kanun*, in contrast to the revealed Sharia, that allowed a view of history that, though turned toward the past, was not fixated on the ideal age of Islam.

What about the image of decline itself? Does it reflect, as many think, the disconsolation of intellectual elites, who—like Mustafa Ali—could not come to terms with their own waning influence in that dramatic or dramatized age, to the point where their difficulties become a leitmotif in works purporting to diagnose the times? Or is it, as an impression, actually confirmed by the reality of the Ottoman situation?

Mustafa Ali's personal misfortunes—he was upset about being assigned to posts he did not much like and by the execution of his patrons, Mehmet Pasha and Mahmud Efendi, to calm the people during the unrest surrounding the *beylerbeyi* rebellion—do not suffice to explain his persistently pessimistic diagnosis of the troubles of his time.[72] It was generally accepted toward the end of the sixteenth century that all was not well in the Ottoman Empire. Here efforts undertaken in connection with the so-called Köprülü restoration (1654–1691) are significant. Yet opinions differ as to the proper description of the situation and how to diagnose its causes.[73]

Concerning the causes of the Ottoman Empire's arrested development, commonly perceived as a decline, two main trends can be discerned. One ascribes the increasing weakness of this last Muslim empire—obvious by the nineteenth century at the latest—to external factors; the other ascribes it to the empire having a conservative internal structure, inimical to the demands of modernity. Not that external and internal factors cannot overlap; even making a sharp distinction between them is problematic. Thus, for instance, the inflationary phases that racked the Ottoman Empire in the late sixteenth century can be understood as both exogenous and endogenous: exogenous in that such phases were caused by the influx into Europe of precious metals from America; endogenous in that the tendency to cling to traditional structures—in marked contrast to Europe—hindered adoption of mercantilism.[74]

Resolving this issue is not easy, not least because contemporary discourse on the grounds for the decline, stagnation, and decay of the Ottoman Empire is tendentiously loaded. It is striking, for instance, that those opting for external causes have the crisis begin relatively late, whereas those opting for internal causes tend to have it begin quite early, notable in the problematic latter part of the sixteenth century. Such temporal alignments can be tendentious on both sides of the debate, because they are commonly associated with efforts to assign blame. The later the decline-inaugurating crisis, the more likely it was due to outside factors. If the onset of the crisis is brought forward—say, to a point in the nineteenth century—the territorial, political, and economic losses incurred by the Ottoman Empire (and by Islam) at that time can be linked to the obvious fact of European military supremacy over the Ottomans. Such an explanation can then make optimal use of theories of colonialism and imperialism. If, however, the crisis is pushed back into the more distant past, into the critical early modern period, then other reasons, chiefly internal ones, will preponderate.

Moreover, the tug-of-war between endogenous and exogenous explanations is not disconnected from the general political climate, or from scholarly fashion. Thus, from the 1930s on, Kemalist historians of the newly founded Turkish Republic took to deprecating everything having to do with the Ottomans. Therefore they were all the more prepared to concur with the judgments of earlier Ottoman historians, geographers, and chroniclers such as Mustafa Ali, Katip Çelebi, and their followers, or even to take them one step further.[75] A crisis in the late sixteenth and seventeenth centuries accords well with the dominant theories of the 1970s concerning the emergence of a capitalist world system—theories whose allure by now has faded—according to which the West, as economic center of the world, marginalized the Ottoman Empire and degraded it to a source of raw materials.[76]

Since the 1980s, a new kind of shift can be sensed. Postcolonial interpretations in the humanities and social sciences have discredited talk of decline. Discredited too is all mention of a price revolution in the early modern period, long regarded as historically proven. We are now told that it did not occur.[77] Distinctions between Europe and the Orient based on culture and geography are being repudiated and cast aside as expressions of Western dominance and Western presumption in defining concepts. As in the theories of European imperialist expansion, the causes making for the decomposition of the Ottoman Empire are shifted far forward into the nineteenth century. These ideas have since made deep inroads in the canon of Ottoman studies.[78] For all that, at present we can diagnose an interregnum in interpretation. Although older explanations based chiefly on endogenous causes no longer convince, more recent ones have nothing to say about the reasons for this undeniable, unmistakable stasis—or, to say the least, failure to develop—especially as Western development had plotted such a different course. At any rate, plausible answers are called for and have yet to be tendered.[79]

One that is worth canvassing, though it is very general, looks at the parameters that shaped Western accelerated development. These point back to the Reformation and the rise of secularization, the time of the printing press, and the "discovery" of America; or to the social discipline induced by mercantilism, the morally condoned striving for profits, the separating of the functional spheres of domination and wealth, of state and society, of public and private. The changes associated with these parameters were apparently so enduring that even events of catastrophic proportions in Western civilization—for example, the religious wars of the seventeenth century with those twin scourges, demographic decline and a massive drop in production—were not able to arrest the transformation wrought by this dynamic.

In the Orient, on the other hand, all development seemed hostage to a strong central state regulating the social fabric. If tendencies seemingly analogous to Western development can be perceived—one thinks of incipient decentralization in the late seventeenth century, or the emergence in the eighteenth century of a much talked-about new stratum of notables, the *ayan*, reminiscent in some ways of a bourgeoisie—these were terminated from on high at the beginning of the nineteenth century, as central rule set about ensuring its total control of the social environment.[80]

A kind of repetition compulsion in which the central power constantly sought to reestablish control can be observed through the centuries. If the military and bureaucracy proved receptive to European innovations in technology and institutions, it was in order to strengthen the central power's grip on society. This structural conservatism, manifested and religiously legitimated in the form of the central state, posed an insurmountable obstacle to substantial change. Hence such modernity as managed to seep into the Ottoman Empire brought changes that not only did not benefit the community, but helped to destroy it.

The extent to which tendencies toward modernity gnawed at the traditional premodern structures of the Ottoman Empire can be gauged from the latter's transformation during the nineteenth century. More than anything, it was the principle of a horizontally conceived equality, constitutive of the new age, that undermined the foundation of the millets—vertically divided, self-governing religious groups based on religious law.[81] Not only did the millets increasingly see themselves as nations and nationalities, but, because of the principle of representation that was carrying all before it, they began to distinguish themselves from one another by invoking emblems of belonging in either the majority or in the minorities. It took only the territorial claims that soon followed to tear the Ottoman Empire apart.[82]

After the Greek War of Independence in the first third of the nineteenth century, the signs of a new age unfavorably disposed to the Ottomans could be observed. Thus began a new development that reduced the empire in its premodern form to the symbols of the sultan and the caliph. Meanwhile, the contours of the nation-states of the future were taking shape. This transformation was attended by powerful cataclysms, especially interreligious and interethnic unrest and bloodshed. These appeared first in the Balkans, later in eastern Anatolia, and culminated in the Armenian genocide of 1915. In 1923, the Turkish Republic emerged out of the ruins of the Ottoman Empire. It had virtually nothing in common with the old empire of the Ottomans.

5 POLITICAL POWER AND ECONOMIC BENEFIT

Muslim Social Environment in the Classical Age

Desert and Steppe—Tribute and Tax—Central Power and Urban
Culture—Umayyads and Abbasids—Mercenaries and Traders—Polis and
Medina—"Public" and "Private"—Benefices and Capital—Labor and
Property—Time and Liturgy—Ethics and Morals—Sacred and Profane

THE GREAT MUSLIM HISTORICAL THINKER Abd ar-Rahman
ibn Khaldun (1332–1406) described recurring patterns in the rise and fall
of states in the Middle East. The *Muqaddima* to his book *Kitab al'Ibar*
(*The Book of Examples*) became lauded, casting a spell over Ottoman
chroniclers and historians of the seventeenth century, not to mention the
viziers and great administrators of the eighteenth century and later. For
them, the *Muqaddima* was both an implacable oracle of what was to
come and a key to understanding their own present.[1] This was also the
judgment of later generations, who likewise admired Ibn Khaldun's theory of history, which set out the forms and modes of gaining and losing
power—doing so in its own terms, without reference to God.

Ibn Khaldun was in fact a cultural anthropologist avant la lettre. His
understanding of the genesis of power, state, and rule in the Middle East
and the circumstances of its decline derived from his activities as a scholar
and advisor to the courts of several Muslim rulers. His career took him
from his birthplace, Tunis, to Granada, and from there to Algeria and
later Egypt—to mention only the most important way stations. His proximity to power taught him its logic and grammar—and how to protect

himself from its reach. Yet all his insights could not preserve him from some unpleasant encounters with authority.

Ibn Khaldun's thought and fate remind us of Machiavelli (1469–1527). With a fine eye for the political, Machiavelli observed the essence and nature of power—if only for the Italian city-states of the premodern era. He too described the ways in which power was gained and lost; he too sought proximity to it as an adviser; he too suffered painful personal consequences. Both the Maghrebian Ibn Khaldun and the Florentine Machiavelli saw power as ultimately rooted in human nature. For Ibn Khaldun, power originates in the *asabiyya*, the energy of the fighting spirit expressed in the cohesion of a community, such as is found among the nomads of the desert, but even more among the nomads of the steppe. For Machiavelli, power arises from *virtù*, the political energy and resolve that is required of a ruler. It is important to note that for Ibn Khaldun, the will to power among the desert and steppe nomads is a collective phenomenon, whereas Machiavelli is concerned with the resoluteness of the individual.[2]

Ibn Khaldun lived in a twilight zone, a time of transition in Muslim and Middle Eastern history between the fall of the Abbasids and the rise of the Ottomans.[3] The Abbasid caliphate in Baghdad succumbed to Mongol invasion in 1258. The most important urban center of the Muslim world was then plundered and destroyed.[4] Mesopotamia's irrigation system, which needed a functioning central administration to maintain it, fell into disrepair. Without the shaping force of the central authority, in the arid landscape agriculture receded. Desert nomads moved in, transforming the cultivated plains into pastureland—an example of how civilization and nature constantly oscillate in arid zones.

The Mongols' advance faltered at Ayn Jalut, north of Jerusalem, where they were defeated by the Mamluk army. The Mamluks were a military caste that first rose to power in the Nile Valley and was renewed by a continual influx of slaves from the Caucasus and Black Sea areas. It was their steadfastness that kept the architectural and cultural Islamic treasures in Cairo from destruction at the hands of the Ilkhans, which had wreaked havoc farther north.[5]

Devastation by the Golden Horde was followed, in the fourteenth century, by the scourge of the Black Death. It would be a long time before a metropolis such as Cairo would regain its earlier population. True,

Europe also had to endure the ravages of the Black Death and lost no less of its populace than the Orient did. But in the West, the distances and geographical barriers separating communities were such that it was easier to overcome the effects of the plague. In the Orient, on the other hand, a combination of factors—the concentration of power, the central role of the state, the geographically unprotected plains—slowed recovery.[6]

Ibn Khaldun came to Damascus with the Mamluk sultan of Egypt, whom he served as an advisor, in 1400–1401, at a time when the city was under siege by the Mongol conqueror Timur (Tamerlane). The scholar was unable to prevent the destruction of the city, but he did have a long conversation with the Mongol ruler famed for his cruelty, and flattered him by evoking his aura as world conqueror. Ibn Khaldun thought he perceived in the nomads of the steppes a model, or ideal type, of the kind of group that might lead to formation of a *dawla*, or ruling dynasty—the core of his theory of the rise and fall of rule in the Middle East.[7]

The Mongol invasion and the Black Death mark a period of devastation in Arab-Muslim civilization lasting from the mid-thirteenth to the fifteenth century. This time of crisis may allow deep insight into the civilization's fabric. This situation is reflected in Ibn Khaldun's theory of rise and fall of power, rule, and domination in the Middle East. The time and the person of Ibn Khaldun met in a way that allowed him to decipher the foundations of his own culture. This conjunction may explain why Ibn Khaldun remains intellectually unrivalled.[8] His theory stands alone, outside of tradition, interpreting the emergence, waxing, and waning of power entirely through culture and society, without invoking God's will. This may be why for centuries the *Muqaddima* was such a key text for Ottoman chroniclers, historians, and administrators. Translated into French in the mid-nineteenth century, it had a remarkable impact on sociological and anthropological discourse concerning the Middle East and beyond.[9]

Ibn Khaldun's observations focused on the role of nomadism in the emergence of power and rule—a phenomenon that led modern historians to reflect on this issue. Arnold Toynbee, the great scholar of Byzantium and universal historian of the first half of the twentieth century, juxtaposes the lifeworld of the nomads of the steppe with that of the nomads of the desert.[10] On the steppe, with such concentrations of people and livestock moving over vast spaces, constant monitoring by a tightly unified, hierarchically organized leadership was imperative. The khan, the despotic central ruler, imposed the unification necessary for the survival of large groups and their herds (*ra'iya*) moving over the extensive steppe pasturelands like a ship at sea.[11] Obedience to the leader, mutual loyalty among members of the group, and taking care of the livestock were indispensable for travel on the steppe.[12] Nomads of the desert, in contrast, moving from oasis to oasis in small tribal groups, are of a different social cohesion.

The energy derived from the *asabiyya* allowed the nomads of the stepped and the nomads of the desert to establish rule over agrarian as well as urban cultures.[13] The ruling power provided protection and security in return for its privileged position. Without this protection, the urban centers where culture and civilization flourished would have been vulnerable to attack from the surrounding wilderness. Without the armed might of the militarized nomads lodged in its midst as the ruling power, urban culture would have been doomed. In addition, the central power protected foreign trade moving through the vast hinterland it controlled. Thus did the Pax Mongolica reach its zenith in the thirteenth and fourteenth centuries.[14]

In the absence of a central power, secure transportation, specifically across the steppes of Central Asia and the arid zones of the Middle East, would scarcely have been possible; commodities would have become too expensive to sell. That would have had a negative impact on economic life, bringing prosperity to an end. This suggests a symbiotic link between the merchants and the ruling power. Such a symbiosis was characteristic also of early Islam's military campaigns. Whereas the nomads, experienced warriors to a man, chiefly lusted after booty, merchants strove to harness the nomads' warlike energy to the task of securing the overland routes. This was associated with a kind of monopolization of the use of force—that is, with a civilizing of force. Thus the Prophet Mohammed's Tabuk expedition, which was conducted in 630 and would be his northernmost military campaign, was directed against Byzantium's allies, the Ghassanids, with the goal of wresting control of the main trade routes to the north.[15] Military protection by the Bedouins and urban trade were thus allied.[16]

For Ibn Khaldun, rule was characterized by the fact that nomadic peoples predisposed to wield power, through an *asabiyya* specific to them, subjugated rural and urban populations. In his historical model, this process is constantly repeated. But after setting up their *dawla*, their state and rule, in urban centers, the warlike nomads soon accommodate themselves to a life of comfort and leisure, thus losing the cohesion that equipped them to rule. They then lose power to other nomads emerging from the desert or steppe, invaders still possessing their *asabiyya*. A new dynasty is established. The cycle of power and its loss repeats itself.

However convincing Ibn Khaldun's overall theory of civilization may be, concerning the environmental and social conditions of the Middle East it can hardly be challenged. Indeed, state rule as established by a nomadic dynasty was independent of society, detached from it, so to speak. Government and rule did not reflect local conditions on the ground or emerge from them; dominance was imposed from above and from the outside. Nevertheless, this dominance was not just parasitic but necessary for the survival of the social fabric on which it was superimposed. Such was the topography that without the protection of outsider-imposed rule, agriculture and urban culture would have been defenseless against violent intrusions and threats from humans and nature alike. The irrigation systems would have deteriorated or been seized by other nomads little inclined to live in cities or in the agricultural areas around them—a process that would have seen the permanent use of force and brought destruction. In short, strong, centralized rule made up for the arid zones' deficiencies in cultural geography.

In order to discharge their protective function and other administrative responsibilities, the authorities regulated trade, crafts, and agriculture. These are the traits of a fiscal and military state.[17] Here there is no need to invoke the theory of "Oriental despotism" developed more than a half century ago by Karl-August Wittfogel, based on the idea of the central state regulating agriculture by means of irrigation.[18] The regulatory activity of a central administration was no doubt important in the Nile Valley. In Iraq, centralized management was also needed to maintain the drainage system. But at that point the hydraulic theory of state centralism in the Middle East runs out of steam. The rest of the region consists, essentially, of arid zones. No matter how much the geological and cultural geography varies, there is one constant: lack of water. Thus Ibn Khaldun's theory of the origins of power in the Middle East takes us further than

Wittfogel's—yet even this cannot explain that great enigma in the East: the superabundance of the sacred in all domains of Muslim civilization.

The presence of the sacred in all areas of life—in private life, in the marketplace, in government—raises central questions. Just how is the sacred regulated? Why can't it be given its own domain and thus kept on a leash? Why does the sacred pervade such disparate spheres as politics, economics, social and private life, even relations between the sexes? Could it be that the sacred has the function of checking the "foreign" web of power that holds society in its grip, of reconciling superimposed rule with the social environment of agriculture, urban life, and long-distance trade by means of a complex regulatory system consisting of religious commands and prohibitions? Is it possible that the omnipresence of the sacred is necessarily linked to the material facts of cultural geography and habitat? Could it be that the religious guidelines enshrined in an all-pervasive sacred later became functional for a deceleration of social time?

These questions are especially pertinent when the achievements of Arab-Muslim civilization in its classical age, the so-called Islamic Middle Ages, are considered. There we find all the phenomena commonly associated with bourgeois society: urbanization, domestic and foreign trade, finance and credit, science and technology, intensive agriculture, flourishing architecture, art and literature—in short, everything that came to the fore only much later in Europe. The East, and Muslim civilization with it, was off to a head start, but then ground to a halt, without ever having evolved its specific "modernity." Why did this happen? That is the perennial question. We can, of course, point to causes injected from the outside: the Mongols, for sure, but also the disastrous inroads of the plague. They enlighten us as to why the devastation occurred, but they do not tell us why, at their peak in the Muslim Middle Ages, the Arabs' civilized achievements did not enhance an internal dynamism that would have counteracted the inroads made by the forces of destruction—a kind of acceleration of social time like the one that took hold of the West several centuries later.

The answer to the question raised by the Western comparison may lie in the confluence of two mutually reinforcing factors: the autonomy and primacy of the central state as the sine qua non of civilization in zones characterized by aridity and nomadism; and the omnipresence of the sacred. What impeded social dynamics, therefore, seems to have been a striking fusion of political power, economic utility, and the sacred—a nexus so tight as to virtually rule out separation of these spheres and functions, which is the precondition of development and the modes of secularization.

So what was the situation in the Middle East—in its "Golden Age" from the eighth to the tenth century, but afterward as well—with regard to the separation of the key domains of state and society, politics and the economy, public and private? How did things stand with regard to predictability and calculability in the domain of production and distribution, with regard to personal security, and especially with regard to property rights? Could something akin to a general political will evolve, a public awareness capable of influencing the ruling power? After all, in the Middle East we have to do with highly evolved urban cultures, such as might very well have developed what in the Western tradition we would call bourgeois society.[19]

It all starts with the genesis of the state founded by nomads. It developed out of the historical succession of various institutions that can be interpreted in terms of legal anthropology and cultural sociology as designed to appropriate surplus production. These are booty, tributes, taxes, and rents. These means of appropriating surplus production are based on power—whether direct or indirect, whether in the form of threats, the use of force, or asserting of control to extract the items in question. All these forms of appropriation include, to varying degrees, an eminently extra-economic, political element. That is to say, they are based not on exchange but rather on relationships of precedence and subordination.

These habits of appropriation were rooted in the hierarchical nature of relationships established among the desert nomads, the Bedouins. This hierarchy was one of directly wielded power and forced subjugation. It was marked by a significant difference in status—between stronger and weaker, between tribes that fought and those that paid.[20] The weaker tribes had to pay tribute, protection money known as *khawa*, to their stronger patrons. Subordination of this kind was classically evidenced by peasants living in the oases. Tilling made them feel at one with the earth; therefore they were hardly able to mobilize effective force against the nomads surrounding them, who had the advantage of unlimited mobility in unleashing violence. There was nothing left for the peasants to do but submit to the predators around them. In return, they would be afforded protection against other nomads. This contract based on natural superiority could be said to reflect a fundamental relationship between nomads and peasants.

Raiding, or *ghazu*, is the basic form of appropriation practiced by the Bedouin. It is based on the old Arab law of plunder, the *ghanima*, which applied to moveable goods not acquired by one's own labor—anything that could be hauled off on the backs of pack animals such as horses and camels.[21] The institution of the *fai* was more complex. It was concerned with booty in the form of land and everything on it, including the inhabitants. Since land could not be carried off, it was ceded back to its former owners in return for tribute.[22] This institution first arose in Mohammed's time, and was a form of appropriation that evolved in agricultural areas as a result of conquest.

When *fai* branched off from *ghanima*, the original institution relating to moveable booty was transferred to the context of real estate. This yielded a constant stream of monetary payments. This shift in what constituted booty—from movables to immovables—was a product of the Muslims' campaigns of conquest in the Fertile Crescent—Iraq and Syria and the surrounding lands.

The military subjugation of agriculture to Bedouin rule made long-term regulation of surplus production necessary. Arbitrarily determined tribute gave way to regulated tax payments. Specifically, taxes of two kinds were imposed on "unbelievers" living in the agricultural areas to the north of the Arabian peninsula: a poll tax (*jizya*) and a land tax (*haraj*). The latter was never less, and mostly more, than a quarter of the value of the harvest. This furnished an essential part of the government's revenues; it could represent as much as 40 to 50 percent of its total income.[23]

Those who converted to Islam, or Muslims who appropriated land previously held by Byzantine or Sassanid owners, mainly officials and dignitaries who had fled the country, had to pay only a tenth part of the income—the so-called profits tax (*usr*). Faced with such disparities, large numbers of non-Muslims converted to Islam clearly for fiscal reasons. The conquerors were interested mainly in the lucrative land taxes, and only secondarily in making proselytes. The more new converts among the rural population were refused exemption from the land tax, the more they took advantage of the fluid new situation to move into the garrison towns built by the Arabs, which promised an easier lot.

This trend was most evident in Iraq, where farmers during the Sassanid era were still bound to the soil or forced to perform unpaid labor. Their situation was not much better than that of slaves. Thus they experienced the Muslim conquest as a liberation.[24] The encroaching flight from the countryside, however, could not be accepted by the land-owning Arab aristocracy, if only on the ground of lost tax revenues. The story of the Umayyad governor of Iraq at the end of the seventh and the beginning of the eighth century, Ibn Yusuf Hajjaj (ruled 694–714), is notorious in this regard.

An administrator under Caliph Abdel Malik (ruled 685–705), Ibn Yusuf Hajjaj was known for being both competent and ruthless. In order to put a stop to this flight from the land, which he felt was getting out of hand, he had peasants who had settled in the garrison towns rounded up and forcibly returned to their villages; and when necessary he even prohibited conversion to Islam. In the long term another solution equally favorable to the state treasury was found, as when the tributary land taxes were made independent of whether the owner was Muslim or non-Muslim. Taxation would henceforth be determined by the land alone and no longer by the owner's status. New converts had to pay as well. State revenues had to be secured, irrespective of the effect of unforeseen transfers of property.[25]

Under Caliph Omar II (ruled 717–720), non-Arab converts were granted exemption from the poll tax but not from the land tax. The agrarian situation was not finally resolved until the reign of Caliph Harun ar-Rashid during the Abbasid period. He assigned the judge and jurist Abu Yusuf Yakub al-Kufi (died 798) to compose a "Book on Land Tax"; this codified once and for all the idea that the land belonged to the caliph, God's trustee. Thus a kind of state ownership of the land was put in place, ensuring a constant stream of land taxes for the state treasury. The idea that the land belonged first and foremost to the ruling power was not a specifically Muslim invention. It had deep roots in the Middle East and was a function of the region's morphology, ecology, and cultural geography, all of which favored the primacy of the central power.

The transformation of Bedouin booty into tribute and then taxes began under the Umayyads (661–750) and was completed under their Abbasid successors. The changes involved in this transition were such that the Muslim empire shifted its capital from Damascus to Baghdad. But underlying this shift was an even deeper transformation. The Abbasid revolution of 749–750 can be said to have "catholicized" Islam, embracing non-Arabs, sundering Islam from Arab tribal tradition, and equipping it with certain aspects of the "Asiatic"—Iranian-Persian or Byzantine—tradition of a centralizing ruling power.[26]

Dislocations also occurred in the accumulation of wealth. Although agriculture did not lose its importance as a contributor to the state treasury, there was a marked increase in income deriving from foreign trade. This was a product of more centralized rule and, with it, improved security. By moving east, the Muslim empire took control of the ancient central trade routes passing from the Indian Ocean through the Persian Gulf and on to the north and the Mediterranean.[27] Thus the principal artery of world trade now ran from Hormuz through Basra to Baghdad, probably the most prosperous city of the age, and then branched out in various directions.[28]

Under the Abbasids prosperity grew apace. Increasing urbanization boosted mass consumption, which, in turn, further shaped and expanded a regional division of labor already shaped by tradition and natural factors. Wheat was shipped downstream from northern to southern Iraq; olive oil was sent to Egypt from Syria, Palestine, and Tunisia; Iraq was the principal producer of dates; sugar was imported from Khuzistan and far-off Yemen; Bukhara and Samarkand provided textiles and the Caspian provinces silk; and Egypt specialized in linens.[29] An informal but highly functional system of banking and credit made long-distance exchange possible without any need for cash to change hands, and this was backed up by a monetary policy that took the broader market into account.[30]

Just how much money was circulating in the Abbasid empire can be seen from the low interest rate charged. Whereas in the European urban centers of the eleventh and twelfth centuries interest rates on loans ran to some 20 percent, in the Middle East money could be borrowed for a paltry 4 to 10 percent.[31] Moreover, by threatening to confiscate tradesmen's cash reserves, imperial tax policy provided an incentive for further investment. Idle capital fell to the state, as did treasures found in ancient tombs or newly discovered lodes of precious metals.[32] This pattern of subordinating commerce to the demands of the state, which was typical in the Middle East, in no way altered the growing importance of trade under the Abbasids.[33]

The transition from the Umayyads to the Abbasids was accompanied by changes not only in social lifeworlds but also in the modes of exercise of power, which became increasingly detached from society. The literature speaks of a "Asiatic" transformation in the nature of the ruling power. This went hand in hand with a thorough restructuring of the army, in which a force consisting of slaves—the Mamluks—was set up under the direct command of the ruler.[34] Their undivided loyalty was guaranteed by denying them all forms of direct income.[35]

This trend toward greater autonomy for the ruling power, beginning in the early ninth century, corroborates Ibn Khaldun's observation of a dynasty newly established by the nomads of the desert and especially of the steppe—with the difference that this particular dynasty did not result from external conquest but rather from a local ruling power transforming itself. This kind of process was already present in embryonic form in the archaic tribal culture of the desert nomads. Mercenaries or slaves, who remained outside tribal loyalties, would be inducted into the tribal organization to ensure the ruler's security. From this derived later practice of maintaining standing armies in the service of the ruler.[36]

The military slaves operated in a social no-man's-land outside kinship ties. As an instrument of power, they were absolutely dependent on the ruler—ethnically different from the host culture and therefore alien to it. They were descended from the steppe nomads, in this case Turkish tribes from Transoxiana.[37] To ensure their unwavering loyalty, they were spatially isolated from their new environment. And to prevent this isolation from breaking down, new military slaves were constantly being brought into the ranks of the mercenaries. This constant restocking was necessary because the descendants of Mamluk soldiers were automatically excluded from the ranks of the caste. Otherwise, their isolation could not have been guaranteed. In any case, precisely because of their ostracism from wider society, these military slaves were an instrument potentially dangerous to the ruler and could easily rebel.[38] Thus, al-Mutawwakil (ruled

847–861) was the first caliph to be murdered by his own praetorian guard. His immediate successors did the bidding of their slave soldiers, who, in 865, did not hesitate to riot through the whole of Baghdad.

Mamluks were but the most obvious manifestation of alien rule being imposed on the social environment. The consequences are predictable: because urban culture was not able to generate its own forms of political representation, the vacuum was filled by the power of the ruler—meaning, in this instance, by governors chosen among the tribal military slaves.

Moreover, this gravitation of rule toward increased autonomy altered the urban architecture. Thus in 763, Caliph al-Mansur (ruled 754–775) founded Baghdad in symbolic proximity to the Persian city of Ctesiphon, ranging himself in a topographical tradition where the Tigris served as a natural barrier against possible attack. At the same time, he was responding to Mesopotamia's dependence on irrigation, the regulation of which favored a centralized, autocratic power that was "Asiatic" in kind.[39]

The increasing distance between the ruler and his milieu is illustrated symbolically by a particular episode. It is said that Caliph al-Mansur was persuaded by an envoy from Caesaropapist Byzantium to banish the market, and so urban life per se, from his immediate environment. The suggestion was made when the caliph and the envoy were conversing in the palace apartments; they were surprised to see a fleeing cow pass by, closely pursued by a butcher. The envoy, steeped in the autocratic tradition of Byzantium, remarked to the caliph that such proximity to the people and everyday life rendered impossible a degree of secrecy befitting the ruler. Impressed by the envoy's sagacity, al-Mansur is said to have ordered that the market be moved to the suburb of al-Karkh.[40]

The circular layout of Baghdad, with the centrally positioned caliph's palace, attested to the distance separating the people—mere subjects—from the ruler. The ruler's ability to reach every person at will was symbolized by the equidistance of all parts of the periphery from the hub.[41] Such architectonics were a continuation of Mesopotamian, possibly Sassanid, tradition. By the time Caliph al-Mutasim (ruled 833–842) created a bodyguard of Turkish slaves and, in 836, with the help of the Samarra garrison, established a new residence more than a hundred miles from Baghdad and the urban life concentrated there, the distance between government and social environment characteristic of the "Asiatic" mode of domination was realized. The tradition of the old Orient had absorbed the tribal legacy of the aristocratic desert Arabs.[42]

A city's layout is an external expression of its internal order. Thus the "Oriental city" (or, as others would call it, the "Islamic city") reveals the foundation on which the social and religious order of Muslim civilization is established. Above all, the merger of modes of power and modes of economic benefit by means of religious rules of conduct offers an insight into the social fabric of the traditional Middle East. Thus from the Oriental city's plethora of dead-end streets—a consequence of the fragmentation of urban relationships—the absence of a planning authority for the urban public sphere can be inferred.[43] Thoroughfares are as rare as public squares. A cul-de-sac ending at the door of a house is a symbol of private interest trumping public space.

The constraints of public space stand in marked contrast to the expansiveness of the inner courtyards. The house's very seclusion from the outside world, its existence as an autonomous domestic community separated by a high wall from the street and facing inward, stresses family solidarity and intimacy above all else.[44] The private and the intimate weigh down any demands directed at the public sphere. At the same time, the dominant inner public sphere of the extended family is inimical to any individual privacy. This is mirrored in the smallest architectural details. To ensure the cloistering of domestic space, windows and roofs were built in such a way that neighbors could not peer inside. For the same reason, house doors were not allowed to face each other on a street.[45]

How far is the mode of urban life peculiar to the Oriental city a reflection of Muslim culture? Can one speak at all of an ideal type of the Islamic city—an attribution that has been unanimously accepted by experts for many decades? As evidence for the existence of such a questionable ideal type, characteristics are highlighted that allegedly show the transformation of a world of belief into a material way of life. And the point is made that right from the outset, Islam was an urban phenomenon. The flight of the Prophet and his followers from Mecca to Medina—that is, the Hegira—was nothing if not a flight "to the city" (*al-Medina*).[46] And it was city dwellers from Mecca and Medina who led the conquests of early Islam, while Bedouins supplied the troops. The basic structure of the

Islamic city, with its different neighborhoods separated from one another, its agglomeration of cells, is said to result from tribal culture and its loyalties being reconstituted in an urban milieu.

In addition there is the notion that Muslim religious prescriptions required urban space for their performance. To begin with the fundamental importance of the mosque and its central location: the liturgical and political meaning of the Friday prayer, the administration of justice, and religious instruction all are necessarily city-based. This identifies Islam as an urban religion; the very gestalt of the city reflects the primary ingredients of Muslim belief. What we do not find are the self-governing institutions so integral to Western urban life: privileges that became freedoms, the emergence of corporate bodies such as guilds and trade associations, and, not least, a gradually emerging public domain.[47]

Since the 1970s, this notion of the "Islamic city," which had been widely accepted since the nineteenth century, has been questioned. According to its critics, the image of the Islamic city was a mere fabrication of Orientalists passed down from generation to generation; hence its canonical status. Based on a few examples, chiefly relating to Maghreb practices, this construct failed to allow for the multiplicity of urban cultures in the Muslim world. And it was alleged that this construct served as a foil to Max Weber's ideal type of the European city and the corporate institutions so central to it.[48]

Whether the Islamic city was indeed an architectonic expression of a genuinely Muslim way of life is doubtful.[49] The decline of the urban structure of the polis, which was widespread in the Middle East in late antiquity, began long before the rise of Islam. The broad streets became narrower, major public squares were filled in with new buildings. What is thought to be so characteristic of the social fabric of the Muslim city, the pattern of dead-end streets and the medley of caravansaries, madrassas, and khans, appeared only in the eleventh and twelfth centuries.[50] So, in reality, there was a slow process of transformation that beyond and before the conquest of Islam changed the culture of open public squares and broad avenues into the impenetrable urban maze the West thought typical of urban life in the Middle East.

How did the cities of late antiquity—say, Damascus or Aleppo—make the transition from polis to *medina*? What changes in the social fabric led to the disappearance of public space, the metamorphosis of broad avenues into narrow alleys? These questions touch on the basic theme of city life: the preservation, or creation, of urban space as an expression of corporate community—meaning the public domain or its antecedents. After all, space that is accessible to all does not simply happen. It requires the active cooperation of the population, not to say the citizenry. It requires the elements of civil self-management and an urban authority prepared to take responsibility for its actions. By the time of the Muslim conquest, such elements no longer existed. Muslims adopted what they encountered and incorporated it into the Islamic order.

Public space is exposed to constant pressure to be appropriated by private interests. Only a clear legal distinction between public and private property, such as that enshrined in Roman law, can prevent such encroachment. By firmly excluding private claims to public property, Rome shaped the very appearance of its cities. Only in this way can government prevent private individuals from laying claim to public space.[51]

Islamic law, in contrast, was based on different notions, its primary aim being to protect domestic space and the property enclosing it. But that was not all: it granted the private home a kind of morally privileged status. Public interests were secondary. City government did not regulate the construction of private buildings. The settlement of disputes among neighbors was a matter for the parties involved, not a governmental judiciary. If a neighbor felt he had been harmed, it was up to him to pursue his complaint. Even the responsibility of maintaining public access to private houses devolved on those concerned. The tendency was unmistakable: private space trumped public space.

Similarly the spacious marketplace did not survive the transition from polis to *medina*. The ancient colonnades gave way to a dense accumulation of stalls. Crowding let the largest possible number of merchants operate in the privileged space of the market (and so in proximity to the mosque). To be a merchant was to enjoy high standing among Muslims. The fact that the narrowing of the once broad streets of late antiquity was constrained only by a Muslim ruling that a street should be wide enough for two pack animals to pass each other, is suggestive of the transformation of transportation logistics that swept over the Middle East at the end of late antiquity and achieved visible expression in the transition to Muslim rule: the gradual disappearance of wheeled vehicles. Between the fourth and the eighth centuries, the more efficient pack animals—especially camels bred for the purpose—came into general use for long-distance transportation through arid regions. Broad roads and streets were unnecessary and therefore were taken over for private needs, especially when, as a result of a flight from the land during the Muslim period, urban space was becoming more densely populated and more precious.[52]

In the Muslim context, private buildings took precedence over those intended for public or even governmental use. Sumptuous buildings were thought to express unwarranted extravagance and scorned accordingly. Mosques were no exception. The Jewish Talmud also deems excessive magnificence in synagogues inappropriate and reprehensible. The general disapproval of public building projects was based on financial and moral factors. In any case, it was up to the merchants and craftsmen to pay the lion's share of the bill. In addition, for some representative ventures forced labor could be raised. The costs, in such cases, were not paid from a calculable and publicly controlled budget; rather they were arbitrarily imposed on the population. So, for example, the inauguration of a caliph had to be celebrated with due pomp and ceremony. The people were therefore urged to erect suitable buildings, a demand that could lead to unrest. Some rulers sought to do away with this practice, as did the Umayyad caliph Jasid III, who came to power in 744 following the murder of his predecessor, by promising to refrain from "putting one brick on another." Thus was Jasid able to pacify his subjects, who had bridled at the excessive building undertaken by his predecessor.

A century later, the Abbasid caliph Mutawakkil (ruled 847–861) would commit to no such limits on building projects. Rule in Baghdad had by then, in any case, taken an autocratic, if not "Asiatic," turn. Mutawakkil built nineteen palaces in various places, spending on them the sum—then considered exorbitant—of 247 million silver dirhams and 100 million gold dinars. It is not surprising that such behavior met with scant approval in the juristic writing of the time, reflecting chiefly the merchant way of life and mindset. On the other hand, spending large sums of money on one's own house was considered perfectly acceptable.[53]

The special place accorded private matters cannot obscure the fact that private property was not at all secure. A weak, inchoate public sphere suggests an equally weak notion of private property, delivered over to the ruler's whims. It was one thing for merchants to amass capital, quite another for this to be safe from seizure by the authorities—especially when it could easily be turned into cash. In addition, government officials were not above entering into partnership with merchants, drawn by the prospect of easy money. Conversely, from the first century of the Muslim calendar merchants sought appointment to such desirable offices as governor and tax collector.[54] Later, merchants would pursue administrative appointments with equal zeal.[55] It is no surprise, then, that during their term in office they accumulated great wealth. But if they were so imprudent as to lose their post, they could also lose their property. This taught a lesson: that it was less capital per se than one's skill in acquiring benefices that led to wealth. In the absence of a separation between the domain of economic benefit and that of government, we cannot speak of capitalist endeavor in any meaningful sense.

So constant was the threat to capital holdings that merchants scurried to protect what they had—for example, by investing in land. One document reports that a young man with security worries invested 50 percent of his inheritance in land, so as to live off the rents it generated; he buried 25 percent to preserve it for any eventuality; he set aside 20 percent to refurbish his dwelling; and the remaining 5 percent he invested in a partnership with another merchant. Whether this example represents a general trend is unclear. But the fact that he opted for a major investment in land and a small investment in business says much about the young man's calculation of risk.[56]

The credit system at the height of the Arab-Muslim Middle Ages suggests a rather different conclusion. Credit was well developed and widespread. For long-term transactions covering great distances, networks of merchants banded together to share the risk (Max Weber's *organisierte Risikogemeinschaften*). The agreements and deals they struck provided a security of sorts for their capital. Credit transactions, which were not covered by the provisions of Islamic law, were standard practice throughout the region. Centuries before the credit system began to spread in Europe, it was a flourishing part of the Muslim world.[57]

That Islamic restrictions on the credit system could be handled so pragmatically can be ascribed to the fact that legal and religious scholars were extremely active in economic life. It was not that these scholars engaged in illicit transgressions; rather, in order to have enough to live on, they were obliged to supplement their highly respectable activities with another source of income. In the classical age of Islam, religious and legal activity was not seen as an independent line of work. All were expected to participate in the preservation and administration of Islamic law as well as the interpretation of tradition. Authority was based solely on prestige so acquired.

The pressure to fend for oneself had two results. First, the practice of a profession and the sense of the realities of life this generated brought a pragmatic influence to bear on the development of the law. This can be seen in the credit system so problematic for Islam. Some scholars and legal officials were, as it happened, also bankers and money changers.[58] The jurists who interpreted and applied Islamic law were not at all remote from everyday life but fully involved in it. Most religious and legal scholars were merchants or craftsmen; hence Islamic law's flexibility and closeness to life. This also explains why religious treatises sing the praises of trade and the merchants who engage in it. The idea that money and sagacity go hand in hand was widespread. Second, and as a consequence of the first, the interpretive constraints of Islamic law penetrated directly into the fabric of life. Therefore the absence of a barrier between worldly things and liturgical stipulations nipped in the bud all attempts to secularize the social environment. The imprint of the sacred was too deep. The prohibition against excessive acquisitiveness was a religious injunction.[59]

The fusion of economic culture and religious observance can also be diagnosed from the symbiotic proximity of ulema and urban elites, especially the great merchant families. Apart from the fact that rich merchants needed the ulema to draw up complex contracts, regulate legal relationships, mediate lawsuits, and divide up a deceased person's property, close relationships with high-ranking legal scholars, cemented if possible by marriage, provided the weak institution of private property with protection backed by religious authority against the arbitrary hand of the state. The transfer of property to the *waqf*—religious charitable foundations protected by divine law—offered the donor more security, though at the price of restricted access.[60] The more sacred the institution, the greater the legal protection—but the property was then tied up. Limits were set on the convertibility of resources. If these had ever been capital, that capital was now capital of the dead hand.

The prerequisite for capital formation is ownership. Only security of possession, the assurance that one has control over one's resources, can transform money into capital. Predictability and calculability are its elixir; they alone confer the certainty of law. Only then can capital command labor on a grand scale, adapting it to its needs, measuring it, bending it to its rationality—in short, generalizing it so as to yield wage labor.

Subjection of labor to a rational production process does not leave the motion of social time unchanged. By generalizing the form of labor, time too is standardized, rationalized, rendered abstract. Thus labor and time are formally related in what can be called an elective affinity—and precisely this is characteristic of modernity.

How does this apply to labor in the Muslim East in its classical age, when the likes of money, credit, and trade are found in such abundance as to suggest "bourgeois" development? What were the forms of labor at the time? And could labor remake time and bend it to its own rhythms—secularizing it in the process?

That is a rhetorical question. We cannot speak of a "capitalist" economic culture in the classical age, the multiplicity of exchange phenomena and a highly developed urban social life notwithstanding. Labor was not standardized or rationalized, nor was time secularized. Time remained essentially religious, while labor took diverse forms—slave labor, independent labor, and wage labor—all existing side by side.[61] Thus various "modes of production" coexisted, with none predominant. They were held together and regulated by the primacy of the central power and by a differentiated legal system that regulated complicated combinations.[62] Not that the state kept its distance from production, or involved itself only in governing, or was indifferent to turning a profit. In fact it maintained, in various sectors and at various locations, factories that were quite impressive for the period. The weaving mills in the Mediterranean town of Tinnis are thought to have been owned largely by the state.

Nor was there any separation between capital and labor such as typifies the capitalist mode of production; rather, mixed modes prevailed, obscuring the distinction, of such crucial importance for the later course of

European capitalism, between those who own capital and those who own only their labor.[63] The producer therefore does not have to be separated from his tools or from access to the raw materials necessary to manufacture a product. The most diverse combinations of access to money, labor, material, and tools for the manufacture of a product are conceivable— and with a high degree of division of labor.[64] Characteristic of this "unseparated" (compared with capitalist contexts) economic configuration is the partnership in labor.[65]

In the partnership in labor, or *comenda* (*mudaraba/muqarada*), people's skills and whatever else is needed to carry out a project are pooled for the benefit of all concerned; profits are then shared, once the work is completed, in accordance with rules the parties have negotiated. This is done not on the basis of a presumed "objective" value of the labor involved, but rather based on subjective notions of the value of the individual labor that has gone into the product. Here all the aptitudes and means required to make the product, whether tools, raw materials, or labor, are counted as capital. Thus in the production process there is no superordination or subordination resulting from access to the means of production on the one hand, and from mere labor performed for a wage on the other. Now, we must bear in mind that this holds chiefly for so-called qualified—that is to say, skilled—labor. For simple jobs, there was always the option of forced or slave labor. Because of the constantly replenished supply of such workers, unskilled labor was never a problem. This, in turn, made technical innovation unnecessary, which explains why economic life remained undisturbed by revolutionary technological changes—a circumstance that appears to have made this already strikingly static civilization even more rigid.[66] Under such conditions no temporal order regulating economic life, much less standardizing it, could be expected to emerge.

Not much later, in the European high Middle Ages, signs of an emerging standardization of both labor and time could be discerned. We can, with hindsight, say that these were the industrial harbingers of abstract time's entry into the world. That they were closely connected with Christianity is perhaps less apparent.[67]

For first indications we must look to the fourteenth century, chiefly to the textile mills of Flanders, where a system of bells was introduced.[68]

Working hours were set for day laborers, who, as the name suggest, were paid on a daily basis. Every mill set its own working hours, and these were announced by bells. The practice caught on. To avoid conflicts regarding time and the value of work measured in units of time, other businesses started using bells to summon and dismiss their workers. Soon the sound of bells had come to signal the hours of work for all within earshot.[69] Thus could the organization of the work process and social life in the towns be brought into close alignment.

The unification of time and space by regulating working hours was anticipated by the mechanical clocks that began appearing on church towers at the end of the thirteenth century. These clocks were the technological expression of abstract time. Their origins lie in the conversion of sacred, liturgical time into mechanical processes by monastic *regula*, the liturgy of prayer times, in particular by the *officium nocturnum*, which had to be conducted precisely at midnight. In northern latitudes it was no small challenge to perform the midnight prayer punctually, especially since on cold nights neither sundials nor water clocks functioned. Time could be measured only by mechanical means independent of natural conditions.[70]

Abstract measurement of time therefore has its origins in Christian liturgy, which, in turn, arose in the Orient: in the fourth century, monasticism supplanted individual hermitage; from then on, living together under monastic rules would require a standardized daily routine. Around the middle of the sixth century in the West, the Benedictine order began dividing the day up precisely, hour by hour. Having the daily schedule regulated by clock time detached the act of worship from natural processes; as a result, the monastic *horarium* and the temporal discipline associated with it became part of the liturgy. Nothing mattered more than that the mass—an act of prayer chanted in unison—should be celebrated exactly on time.

The delicately adjusted parts of the liturgy constituted a collective work of art. Any deviation from the temporal orchestration of the liturgy injured the sacred. Especially the nightly mass required great self-discipline from the monks. To oversleep was tantamount to a sin of the flesh. The abbot was responsible for ensuring that discipline was strictly upheld. This fixed religious ordering of time, culminating in the notion of the canonical hours, spread throughout Western Christianity and became generally accepted.

This religion-based economy of time also spilled over into the secular world. From the late Middle Ages on, we find it regulating urban work life. For monks in cloisters, in any case, there was no distinction between the demands of the world and those of religion. Work was seen as prayer, as a form of worship—*laborare est orare*. The Cistercian order, whose reach was enormous in its time, was at once a spiritual and an economic enterprise. And in both domains, spiritual and economic, time was meticulously partitioned liturgically: there was a time for prayer, a time for work, a time for study, a time for getting up in the morning, a time for going to bed in the evening. The changing of the times was marked by the ringing of bells, by ringing "the changes." Thus bells became acoustic signs. That the hours they rang out were audible everywhere is what collectivized time. The same held for the working day. And so, we can trace the origins of mechanical, abstract time—created by humans and controlling humans— to religious stipulations.

In contrast to Christian practice, the liturgical time of Muslims and Jews is not abstract but bound to natural events. The day begins at sunrise and ends at sundown, and among Jews animal sounds could even serve as markers—the cock's crow, for instance, partitioned day from night. Seasonal changes in the hours of sunrise and sundown thus led to constant shifting. Thus the daily prayers—five times a day for Muslims, three for Jews—are not performed at specific times, as in Christian practice, but are spread over the span of available time. Hence it is evident that the fixed liturgical time of Western Christianity spawned the abstract time so integral to Western civilization. Converted into secular terms, it becomes global time.

Because their liturgical time is constrained by natural events, neither Muslims nor Jews can construe time as consisting of fixed (and so universally transferable) units. Nor does it stop there. Calendrical time is also highly complex and not at all suited to temporal abstractions—the Muslim calendar is exclusively lunar, so the year is a lunar year, whereas the Jewish calendar manages to combine lunar and solar time. Because there are 12.37 lunar, or "synodic," months in a solar year, the Muslim holy days move forward through the seasons. Ramadan, for instance, can and does occur at any time in the solar year. Things are a bit different in Judaism, where major holidays are linked to seasonal events like sowing and harvesting. Hence the combined use of lunar and solar calendars. The Julian-Gregorian calendar, in contrast, is purely solar.

The Muslim calendar is not at all suited to fixing recurrent events. And for purposes of business and management, especially the taxing of agricultural products, it is worse than useless. Thus right from the outset, in Islam the date for delivery of the harvest tithes, under the prevailing system of land taxes, needed constant resetting. To this end, time planners were brought in who were versed in the solar cycle.[71] During the Muslim Middle Ages, a number of attempts were made to reform the calendar. Later on, in 1677 a "fiscal year" was introduced by the Ottomans—being made binding for all in 1789, the year of the French Revolution. It commenced on March 1 and followed the Julian calendar. Thus Muslims lived with several parallel calendars, which, like the changing times of prayer during the day, did not exactly conduce to developing a sense for abstract time.

In Islam, not only is time put beyond human control, but also religious constraints pervade social life. This leads to liturgically determined precautions being taken, especially in those places where economic life, because of its physical, instinctive aspects, is most in need of monitoring: in the marketplace. The world of commodities, of things, poses, it would seem, a danger to morality that impugns and threatens the omnipresence of God.

Control of the marketplace—where anonymous encounters are transacted through commodities—was vested in the office of the *muhtasib*—a kind of market inspector. This individual was responsible not only for monitoring the weights and measures used in places of business, but also for carefully checking the quality of the goods offered for sale. But that was not all: he had to keep a watchful eye on the conduct of craftsmen and traders, and also ensure that the religious obligations and ethical norms were observed. These included performing the required rituals and liturgical duties at the appropriate time and place; then there was the delicate matter of separating the sexes and watching over the *dhimmi*—the protected "unbelievers," Christians and Jews, whose conduct was subject to lower standards in line with their inferior status.

The *muhtasib* was a moral authority, his task being to see that no religiously sanctioned norms were infringed in a place that, by the nature of the activities performed there, guaranteed anonymity. Through his presence, his sharp eye, and, if necessary, his physical disciplining of culprits, the *muhtasib* prevented any free space from opening up in the confusion of the marketplace.

Both the *hisba*, the body that supervised trade and exchange, and its enforcement officer, the *muhtasib*, were visible manifestations of the fusion, the liturgical oneness, of economic, governmental, and religious functions. By upholding the Islamic canon of duties, morals, and ethical standards, they erected a powerful barrier against any possible separation of the spheres of the public and the private. In place of these, the *muhtasib* offered the most striking expression of a religiously imbued form of communication. That this came into play in the marketplace, where the individual was removed from domestic care—or rather, domestic supervision—lay in the nature of things. As a monitor of decency and good behavior, the *muhtasib* stood on the threshold separating domestic from social order. And since the *muhtasib* was appointed by the authorities, he represented, almost more than any other example, the visible proximity—indeed fusion—of the ruling power, economic life, and religious authority. His office symbolized the extent to which liturgically rationalized religious taboos suffused Muslims' lived experience.

The Islamic canon of duties and morals, which regulated all conduct in the public sphere, is based on Surah 3, verse 104, of the Koran, which insists that Muslims command right and forbid wrong. This not only calls on the individual Muslim to behave ethically and morally; it also urges him to hold others to the same standard. The cut and thrust of the sacred can be inferred from this canon of duties and its zealous practical enforcement.

The revealed call to encourage right conduct and to ban wrongdoing is addressed to state authorities (*umara*), scholars (*ulema*), and common people (*amma*) alike. All are instructed to drive out the false, the unjust, and the sinful from their midst. Officials complied with this demand by wielding the "hand" (i.e., by physical force); scholars by wielding the "tongue" (i.e., by castigating sinful conduct in speech and writing); and the common people by wielding the "heart" (i.e., by being vigilant both for themselves and for others).[72] Thus God's presence was upheld in all walks of life.

For individuals, this may seem to involve trivialities—the bans on playing chess, for instance, on drinking alcoholic beverages, on playing musical instruments, on unmarried couples or couples not suitably related appearing in public together. Yet to offend was not trivial; it was to shake the foundations of the divine order. No exceptions could be made—because to violate these duties and commands was not just an individual failing; rather, it reflected on the community of the faithful as a whole. The concern was less to protect the individual against sin than to preserve the religious integrity of the *umma*. Therefore, all were expected to act against sinful behavior.

The Koran's summons to encourage what is right and to forbid what is wrong is the key to understanding Islamic ethics. It is also the key to understanding what counts as public and private in Muslim life. In the context of Muslim culture, one can hardly speak of a distinct private sphere in the Western sense, because proper conduct, conduct as decreed by Islam's ethical and religious canon, is expected to the same degree everywhere.[73] According to Islam's ethical doctrine, what does make a difference is the protection granted to the intimate against the demands of the canon of duties. Thus, when the need to protect the enclosed sphere of the intimate collides with the imperatives of ethical control, the former takes precedence. What was being protected was not a person's private sphere, but rather a sin to be concealed and not to be dragged into the light of day. The ethical monitor was therefore not to engage in preventative spying in order to deter possible transgressions. So long as the offense in question was not manifest, so long as it remained invisible and inaudible to others, no damage was deemed to have been done. Only when the incriminating act became a matter of public knowledge, leaving the private realm behind, as it were, was it necessary to act.[74]

So the demand for social control was not a demand for mutual surveillance. Persons who could not contain their zeal might be punished. Thus in 1357 the Mamluk authorities of Damascus led a group of overzealous monitors in chains through the city, showing what fate awaited those who pried into intimate matters not concerning them.[75] Such action by the authorities did not necessarily correspond to "public opinion," that is, to the feelings these processions evoked in those who witnessed them. After all, everyone had to obey Surah 3, verse 104, and defend the sacred. when one punished an offense to morals and proper conduct, one was acting on behalf of a higher—or rather, the highest—power. In performing duties imbued with the sacred—as in jihad—one was prepared to give one's all.

Through the duty to encourage right conduct and to ban wrongdoing, a fine-spun veil of the sacred was laid over Muslim life. It penetrated Muslims' social behavior so as to obliterate, in view of God's omnipresence, any distinction between public and private—the very spheres that in the West have historically diverged. In more recent times, the government challenged such sacred omnipresence. Muslim reformers of the late nineteenth and early twentieth centuries strove to bring the Islamic corpus into line with the exigencies of modernity. Such changes were repudiated by some as offensive forms of Westernization. Restrictive interpretations of how to apply the canonical duty to prevent wrongdoing draw on al-Ghazali (1058/59–1111). His reading of Surah 3, verse 104, was excessive, not only because he expanded the office of *muhtasib*—who, as we have seen, was traditionally responsible for ethical supervision of the local marketplace—to encompass a wider span of social events, but also because he granted to the common people the right, normally vested in the authorities alone, to lay "hand" on presumptive offenders.[76] When they saw immoral conduct, al-Ghazali maintained, the people had the right to respond instantly, breaking wine glasses or musical instruments.[77]

The duty, enshrined in the Koran, of every Muslim to command what is right and forbid what is wrong is diametrically opposed to Western custom. Whereas Islam regulates people's lives down to the minutest detail, the Western way of life leaves it to the individual to find his own path. Sayyid Qutb, the twentieth-century theoretician of a radical brand of Islam, loathed this Western notion of individualism and self-direction. He rejected it as incompatible with the Islamic canon of duties. In a world that has fallen away from God, vices and sins are treated, he said, as "personal matters," beyond the reach of the transcendental and sublime.[78] The conduct of one who thinks himself free and unaccountable, however, is a blot on all who have to witness such publicly flaunted sinning: taking public transportation while scantily clad, poking fun at religion, gambling, drinking alcoholic beverages, or enjoying the blessings of Western free speech, which—horror of horrors—allows one to say whatever one thinks. In contrast, the Muslim canon of duties provides only for the protection of "good opinions."[79]

The Western notion that a person's personal integrity has to be protected from injury by immediate public intervention, and the Muslim command to encourage what is right and forbid what is wrong—these seek to protect different goods. In the first, harm to a person must be prevented; in the second, a sin against God must be averted. In the context of Western civilization, intervention is called for when a person or thing is threatened. In the Muslim context, it is less a matter of the person than of preventing damage to the *umma*. Damage is even considered to have been inflicted when no concrete harm to a person results. The fact that in Islam conduct can be harmful, even if no one has been concretely harmed by it, can mean only one thing: God is present among men. It is the presence, or rather the omnipresence, of God that leads to Muslim social life being steeped in the sacred.

6 HISTORICAL THOUGHT AND DIVINE LAW

Converting Sacred into Profane Time

Acceleration or Deceleration—Law and History—Cyclical versus Linear Time—Ibn Khaldun and Giambattista Vico—Past Utopias and Future Worlds—Islam and Judaism—Leo Strauss and Moses Maimonides—Dual Law and Dual Time—Muhammad Asad and Moses Mendelssohn—Law of the Land and Secularization

A SCHOLARLY INVESTIGATION OF THE Koranic verse on commanding right and forbidding wrong (Surah 3, verse 104)—the backbone of Islam's ethical canon—considers three legal rulings concerning how Muslim women should behave in public.[1] The first dates from the ninth century, the second from the fourteenth century, and the third from the early twentieth century. The author, a leading expert in his field, apparently finds nothing incongruous about lumping together such disparate rulings on the public behavior of Muslim women, as if the fact of their great separation in time were a matter of no import. This should make historians—alert as historians invariably are to boundaries between eras—sit up and take notice.

Are we to conclude that this learned scholar believes that the object of his scrutiny has remained untouched by the hand of time, and that a *historically* relevant distinction between the three cases, taking change into account, deserves no further attention? An approach that ignores the passage of centuries would seem to suggest that over massive tracts of time no change occurred. Our scholar, it seems, sees no problem in lumping together legal rulings from the ninth, the fourteenth, and the early twentieth centuries—as if time makes no difference.

What are we to make of this? Does ignoring change over time in observing a phenomenon of Muslim life stand for a perception of the other that is open to the charge of "Orientalism"? Does this expert on the Orient and Islam implicitly claim that Muslim society is immutable, static, recalcitrant to change? Or does it mean that the Western concept of history, based on the movement of time, is not indigenous to Muslim culture?

Perhaps we should not make too much of these Muslim rulings, because legal traditions can retain their validity across lengthy tracts of time—particularly in view of the proverbial conservatism of Muslim jurists and the fact that this particular legal tradition is based on a code imbued with the sacred.[2] And a code is sacred, indeed, when it ignores time or seeks at every turn to arrest it.

Time can be sealed off by law, especially when the law is steeped in the sacred. If law proves impervious to time, this spills over into other domains. As a result, law penetrates all areas of lived experience, with the goal of regulating social life in its entirety. Law, as it were, stands for everything. Thus the fact that sacred, sublime law retains its validity over long periods allows us to presume that it is not all that interested in change. In any case, we should not expect change in the direction of secularization, as was the case in the West, change that via the process of secularization engenders a self-reflective awareness of the flow of time—and it is this very awareness that in the West came to be associated with the concept of *history*. But to conclude this would seem to land us in highly problematic terrain. This would evoke, for instance, the questionable assumption that people in the Muslim world lack an idea of history. It would even evoke the idea that Muslims have no historical understanding of the world, as indeed Hegel's and von Ranke's perceptions of the Orient suggest.[3]

It would be wrong to draw such a conclusion. An abundance of historical representations have emerged in various Muslim cultures and in their principal languages—Arabic, Persian, and Turkish.[4] In Arabic, for instance, there are many subtly differentiated names for what is understood as history. Thus history in the sense of a mere report, a simple account of what happened, is known as *al-akhbar*. The term *tarikh* is used for history as measured in units of time. *Tarikh* also strives for a common memory, drawing together dates into a connected narrative. In view of the enormous body of works by Arab and Muslim historians, chroniclers, and travelers accumulated over the centuries, to claim that Muslims lack historical understanding would be uninformed at the very least.[5]

We cannot rest content, however, with a mere reference to the corpus of Arab historiography. That would be to evade a latent problem: in the West, at least since the early modern period, history has adopted a meaning rather different from that of the word *tarikh* in the Arab and Muslim context. When in the early modern period, through the Renaissance, printing, the Reformation, and the "discovery" of the New World, Christendom was converted into the West, history adopted the meaning of change through time. And in the eighteenth century, the age of Enlightenment, this understanding of history evolved into the notions of movement, acceleration, and development.[6]

History in its own right—not the history *of* something, but rather history per se—is the expression of modern experience. The discovery of "history" as such (*Geschichte überhaupt*), of history as a "collective singular" (if I may invoke Reinhart Koselleck's *Kollektivsingular*) is an outgrowth of the Enlightenment. The word used first in this sense can be traced back to the mid-eighteenth century.[7] According to such an understanding, history was no longer seen as the manifestation of a higher providence, but as made by mankind. Thus God withdrew from history. This change was first perceived by Giambattista Vico (1668–1744) in his *Scienza Nuova* (*New Science*), published in 1725. His book transferred the Copernican revolution from the world of things to that of consciousness—in the process, rewriting the fundamental categories of matter, time, movement, and infinity.[8]

The transformation of the view of the physical world in the seventeenth century brought with it a shift from the divine to the earthly.[9] This did not leave historical thinking untouched. What was earlier expressed in words and images of divine promise underwent a profane transformation. This shift reshaped in worldly terms the older salvational notion of a self-fulfilling future. Thus the form of the historical process remained ensconced in the image of divine promise, even if "the finger of

God" gave way to the metaphor of the "invisible hand."[10] Eschatology became history. Like eschatology, history had a direction and a goal; it had a telos. The eschatological template, secularized, brought about a forward-directed motion of time. This way of conceiving time later gave birth to the idea of progress. Its operation was held to determine human action; it triggered "development."[11]

The notion that progress could take the place of Providence presupposed the religious idea of salvation. The notion of the future imposed on the flow of time has its roots in the Judeo-Christian tradition of the prophet as seer, the progenitor of history.[12] Among the pagan Greeks, however, history related only to the past. It was enacted on the political and military stage—and in a cyclical form. Hubris and nemesis, wanton overreaching and chastising justice, followed each other in constant succession. What the cyclical movement in the ancient Greeks' conception of history shows is that the cosmic course of the immutable had not been shaken by deep changes in the social environment that would remind people that transformations are under way. Greek historical dynamics were too weak to cross a threshold beyond which real change might have been discerned. There was—to stay with the metaphor—a "deficit of history" (in Christian Meier's phrase).[13] In other words, there was no development.

The Western concept of history is problematic in its Eurocentrism. Its commitment to temporality and spatiality makes this obvious. The division of history into meaningful periods is bound up with the spatial environments associated with them. Thus antiquity is located around the Mediterranean; the Middle Ages move to northwestern Europe and then advance toward the south and the east; and the beginning of the modern era is marked by European expansion into the Atlantic and beyond. The division of historical time into antiquity, the Middle Ages, and the modern era—a tripartite segmentation reminiscent of the Christian trinity—is transplanted into the general meaning of history. Since the beginning of the early modern era, other cultures and communities, and the Muslim civilization especially, have produced no comparable interpretation of what Western civilization has chosen to read into the concept of history.[14]

Also problematic is the application to non-European contexts of the terminology of time and temporal sequences developed in Western thought—as in, for example, talk of a Muslim "Middle Ages," a dubious analogy if ever there was one. We must acknowledge that temporal sequences in different civilizations—in this case, Western and Muslim—are not compatible. If they are nonetheless compared, the resultant asymmetries set up tensions. What we end up with, then, is the invalidation of the culture deemed weaker in terms of Western timelines. This holds especially for talk of the "modern era" and the historical speculations this has generated.[15] From a European perspective, this period is associated with a transformation beyond the reach of other civilizations at the time. Unless we reflect on the asymmetries of simultaneous nonsimultaneity in the periodization of history, and so agree to relativize the impact of European-cum-Western periodizations on historical thought, the construction of world history as a universal timeline accommodating different cultures and civilizations and their multiple reciprocities will be difficult to achieve.[16]

In view of rampant European-Western claims to know the meaning of history, how do things stand with the parameters of periodization applicable to the Arab-Muslim understanding of history? Can Muslim civilization point to a periodization of its own? And if so, then to what end? Is it only a matter of prying apart the various dynasties, of chronicling their rise and fall, of—at best—inquiring into their respective legitimacies?[17] Or are themes of change and development implicit, and if so, which ones? But this question is skewed by a Western perspective that is predicated on Western concepts of movement of time. The suggestion is that history per se began only in the early modern era. This epistemic stance is one in which the Orient is repeatedly asked why it has not fulfilled Western expectations of development. To ask this is not unproblematic. But is there another question?[18]

To ask about the traditional idea of history in the Middle East is to seek to discover whether its historical conceptions of time, and the way in which time is experienced as a result, are the expression and consequence of stasis—or whether it is not the case that the material reality of social life in the Middle East is associated with a conception of time's flow (and of the awareness of such) that is incompatible with Western models, a conception that is rationalized as history. This distinction is not insignificant if we are to understand the condition of Muslim, and particularly Arab, countries, a condition currently adjudged lamentable—and especially if we are postulating an inherent nexus between the diagnosed stasis in Muslim social life and the arresting of time by the sacred.

Let us look more closely at how the sacred arrests time and how this affects material life. Can we assume that belief, or religion—more precisely, the conspicuousness of the sacred taboo—is so strong that it shapes the material world? Or is it the case that the prevailing specific material conditions of the ecology and social environment give birth to such a strict taboo?

It would be useless to try to resolve such a question. Instead of seeking to establish the primacy of one over the other, it seems preferable to speak of an affinity between material conditions and their sacred underpinnings. Thus it is not that the one produces the other; rather their relationship is one of convergence, with each strengthening the other.

Given this assumption of an affinity between the material social environment and the immutability expressed in the sacred, it is appropriate to return to Ibn Khaldun's idea of history. The Tunisian scholar should not, however, be lauded as if he were a protosecular historical thinker, a prime witness for some Arab protomodernity that, for reasons unknown, has still not managed to blossom into full modernity. Instead, we shall focus on the cyclical nature of Ibn Khaldun's narrative, considering it as a template; in particular, we shall ask what it shares with the sacred interpretation of the world.[19]

Ibn Khaldun is an icon of discourse on the Middle East. But to concede the iconic character of his work and person is to concede a certain uneasiness. For one thing, this Tunisian scholar–cum historical thinker–cum judge is thought somewhat overresearched; for another, respectful Western references to him are immediately suspected of "Orientalism." Thus Ibn Khaldun—whose arguments look secular enough against the background of the sacred world he inhabited—is often cited as standing apart from his civilization. The more clearly his interpretations appear to differ from those of his environment, imbued as the latter was with the numinous, the more he seems to have earned praise from Western scholars.[20]

But Ibn Khaldun can in no way be considered a secularizer avant la lettre. As the *qadi*, or chief judge, of Cairo, he was constantly concerned with religious issues. Moreover, it is far from clear that he stood apart in his thinking from the cultural milieu of his day, or that he contradicted it in his secular interpretations of the course of events. The cyclical theory of history set out in *The Science of Culture* differs from standard perceptions less than is generally assumed.[21] His investigation of how the historical process moves along is consonant with the religion-imbued narrative of Muslims. Furthermore, his famous prolegomenon, the *Muqaddima*, must be distinguished from his "world history," the *Kitab al'Ibar*, bearing the opulent subtitle *The Book of Cautionary Examples and the Archive of Earlier and Later History, Treating of the History of the Arabs, Non-Arabs, and Berbers*. If in his prolegomenon he appears as the historical thinker par excellence, his compiled narrative history does not differ essentially from that of other contemporaneous Arab-Muslim historians. He avoids all attempts to apply his thinking about history to the actual writing of history.

Ibn Khaldun wrote his history in North Africa, near the Algerian city of Oran, during the last third of the fourteenth century. The dramatic crises of his time were what impelled him to write. Among these was the plague that broke out in 1348; and in the same year, Abu al-Hassan, the Marinid sultan of Morocco, met defeat at the hands of Arab tribes advancing from the desert.[22] These events gave Ibn Khaldun the final impetus to address the rise and fall of dynastic power.

Dynastic succession in Arab-Muslim tradition is seen as a kind of historical periodization. Chronicles and reports invariably use dynastic markers when narrating events and episodes. Thus, each dynasty can be said to function as a self-contained cosmos of historical movement. This model also underpins Ibn Khaldun's explanatory and interpretive procedures. Taking this as his point of departure, he examines the circumstances of his day to see what they can tell him about the rise and fall of rule and power.

Ibn Khaldun traces with great care the way in which power is established, flourishes, and then succumbs to ineluctable decline. Yet what interests us here is less the empirical description of historical events than the historical mold in which they are cast.[23] For all the rigorous causality in the sequence of events leading to the rise and fall of dynastic rule, history, for this thinker, moves in cycles. No other pattern of motion is conceivable. Vainly do we look to lived reality, or to transcendentally founded inspiration, for an inkling that history might, indeed, be strung out along a line, that history might move forward and, in so doing, break through the constant need for repetition. Because of the nearly immutable realities of life in Ibn Khaldun's day, no breakthrough to a linear conception of time, based on the idea of progress, was possible.

To grasp this conception of history, we need not fall back on the religious content of Islam, though, to be sure, Islam by constantly invoking both its foundational myth and the religious law it has put in place certainly promotes the repetition model. We need but recall the cultural-geographic realities of the Middle East. The fact is, the morphological, climatic, and ecological conditions in arid zones are such as to make centralized rule indispensable for civilization. And the latter's collapse is inexorable as soon as urban refinement of morals causes the feeling of solidarity (which is the sine qua non of power for Ibn Khaldun) among the nomads of the deserts or steppes—the *asabiyya* that constitutes the rule or dynasty—to grow weaker, whereupon the dynasty succumbs to a new cycle of nomadic domination. By being constrained to repeat itself, history moves in a circle, hostage to formal laws.

In the Middle East, power rises and falls in never-ending cycles. Civilization is subject to a natural law of sorts, and it is this that Ibn Khaldun expresses in his writings. The sheer endlessness of this process well suits an idea of time in which a sense of eternity is inscribed. Does this imply that the endlessness enshrined in the image of the circle generates a feeling for the sacred? Does the idea of transcendence merely reflect a process of constant repetition?

It would be presumptuous to interpret Islam and its rituals, based as these are on repetition of the Prophet's central act in founding the Muslim community, as mere reflex, or even transcendental rationalization, of living conditions in arid regions. For eons, the Arabs of the desert had lived in a polytheistic religious world, until the Prophet Mohammed was able to unite them religiously and politically in the name of the "one and only God." Reference to the revolutionary breakthrough to monotheism in the guise of Islam signals that the sacred possesses a power of its own to convince. The fact that, formally speaking, the idea of sacred time accords with the material circumstances under which time passes into history presupposes no causal relationship as prevailing between the two, even if the affinity is striking.

As salvational history, the traditional Islamic conception of historical time is transcendental. There can be no separating the inner world from the outer world. Ultimately, history is based on revelation.[24] Islamic revelation differs from that of the other revealed religions in terms of its temporal orientation: the state of human affairs deemed ideal, and to be striven for, lies not in time moving along a temporal axis; rather—and here we have a paradox—it lies in the past.[25] And not in just any past either, but in an ideal past of the Muslims' own making—the few decades stretching from the Hegira, the Prophet's flight from Mecca to Medina in 622, to the time of the four righteous caliphs, which ended in 661. Thus the sacred narrative is based on a *past* utopia, one situated in the time of the "best community that ever existed among men." It tells of a "precedent" set aside for emulation, the expression of a divine "economy of salvation" in which God himself has at His disposal the spatial-temporal fabric of the universe.[26]

What, then, are the core features of this historical narrative framed in terms of the sacred? And how are these features applied to the realities of whatever turn future events may take? Above all, how do they contribute to the cyclical interpretation that matches the material conditions prevailing in the Middle East?

Ideally, what has to be done is to preserve the sacred dimensions of the time of origin, that is, to reproduce it. This time of origin is invested with normative significance under all circumstances. All changes and innovations depart from this ideal condition, and therefore carry the stigma of retrogression. Present events are interpreted against the template of the sacred narrative and the salvational episodes related therein. There is nothing in the eventful history of the Muslims that does not have some antecedent; everything is necessarily a repetition of the past. Thus current events hark back to an originary time steeped in the sacred.[27] This religiously founded model of eternal return is very much inherent in Ibn Khaldun's interpretation of history, whatever its similarity may be to later secular or cultural-anthropological models. In his work, there is no shortage of assertions such as that the past resembles the future as one drop of water resembles another.[28] The sequencing of events as constant repetition is independent of the semantic content—whether expressed in the language of sacred or profane discourse.

An eschatological aspect is also revealed in the methodology of the Arab-Muslim historians of the classical age.[29] Because this aspect is revealed, it can only be handed down unchanged, not explored in its own terms. As is the case with legal scholars and other religious authorities, historians who combine the writing of history with the discharging of a judicial office constitute part of the chain of tradition. Verifiability in the form of an assertion having been handed down from one generation of scholars to another is the benchmark of how much truth that assertion contains. This epistemological qualification means that the historian must abstain from innovative interpretations. What remains is the task of compilation. Ultimately, history is also a traditional branch of inquiry, through its religious narrative and, especially, through the hadiths (the individual records of Mohammed's sayings) that have entered into it. As such, it has to obey the standards of the sacred.[30] This was so with the great historian Abu Jafar at-Tabari (839–923), who lived centuries before Ibn Khaldun. Tabari sought to abstain from all interpretation, rejecting even rational deductions going beyond immediate eyewitness reports.

In contrast, Ibn Khaldun interprets historical events with the goal not only of seeing things as they are, but of "understanding why they are as they are."[31] In so doing, he goes far beyond traditional compilation. His approach, based on a theory of history, is thus able to escape the exigencies of eschatological narration. In addition, because he focuses on causalities, he perceives the nature of history as a process. This caveat holds, however, only for the theoretical *Muqaddima*. In the practical aspects of his historical work, he remained faithful to the tradition of compilation. He too respected and fully accepted the sacred ur-narrative. Moreover, Ibn Khaldun was quickly forgotten until the Ottomans rediscovered him in the late sixteenth century, thinking they glimpsed in his theory a rationale for their own perception of decline. Not until the twentieth century did he become the secular prophet of a future Arab modernity. Such delays in the recognition of an author's achievement should not be used to fan Western arrogance, however. Giambattista Vico, after all, had to await the advent of the progress-obsessed nineteenth century for the West to accord him proper respect. In his own lifetime Vico was barely noticed—like many others whose thinking was ahead of their time.

The cyclical movement of history is not entailed by the sacred ur-narrative, even if it exhibits formal affinities. Such affinities can offer support and meaning, in that the notion of an ideal community of Muslims (as a theocratic state) contrasts unfavorably with currently experienced reality, so much so as to constantly prompt efforts at renewal. But each new beginning tends to end in the evils of the past being repeated. Thus decline in the Muslim community can always be glossed as proceeding from conduct that violates the strict letter of what is pleasing to God, and for this very reason is doomed. Thus transition to a new dynasty can be seen as yet another attempt, yet another cycle within the salvational scheme whose goal is the renewal of righteousness, the reconstruction of the ideal community.

The way to restore the ideal Muslim community is to imitate the past, and the way to do that is to strictly obey divine law. It is the Sharia, the body of law combining the Koranic with extra-Koranic teachings of the Prophet, the Sunna, that points the way. Thus it is not history, conceived as an onward movement in space and time whose course is subject to interpretation, but rather law that regulates the conduct of Muslims and is the lodestar for all striving and action. History so construed is realized in the scrupulous observance of the law. And observance of the law stops time in its tracks—it arrests acceleration. Furthermore, the law as divine will is fulfilled in that realm where the reach of Islam is absolute, the *dar al-islam*, or House of Islam—the realm subject to Muslim rule where the Sharia holds undisputed sway. Not that the Sharia does not itself have a universal horizon: indeed, it is in principle valid worldwide.[32] But only under Islamic rule can sacred time (as regulated by the Sharia) truly apply in the sacred space it articulates. Only there can it hope to arrest self-devouring historical time and turn it into sacred (and so eternal) time.[33] Thus the geographical validity of the law places limits on its unrestricted, conscientious observance. And the observance of Islamic law is guaranteed by Muslim power. Therefore in the House of Islam space and time are united in the law.[34]

The space imbued with religious law (and so with eternal time) has neither center nor periphery. This is evidenced in the topography of ritual.

While it is true that the whole world is subject to sacred time in the form of religious law and ritual, areas and places differ in the intensity of the indwelling sacred, especially if visited during the holy time of pilgrimage.[35] Thus the Kaaba shrine is a spatial node of sacred time that spreads outward to all of Mecca and Medina too. From these towns, sacred space then radiates to the whole of the Arabian peninsula. But other areas also fall within the domain of the sacred, especially if the holiness ascribed to them is thought endangered, or if Muslims are, or think they are, prevented from discharging their religious duties there. The Arabic name for Jerusalem voices just such an absolute predicate. As *al-Kuds*, "the holy," its sacredness spills over onto the land, turning it into *al-ard al-muqaddasa*, or sacred soil.

Religious law pervades Muslim life—from everyday affairs to politics. Ultimately, Islam is a religion of the law, a "nomocracy."[36] Its agency is best strengthened in a territorially guaranteed Muslim community, that is, when Muslims live under Muslim rule. For in the House of Islam, the sacred trumps the political. That other religion of the law—Judaism—has historically been spared this fate. Judaism's holy canon too traditionally pervades all areas of lived experience and insists, no less, on the performance of ritual, with the difference that because of Diaspora existence, it has not been possible for Jews to adhere solely and exclusively to their religious law, the Halakhah. Because the Diaspora has become a way of life, sacred Jewish time as summed up in the Law cannot be realized in a political space that is as exclusively Jewish as its Muslim counterpart is Muslim.[37] Jews of course are subject to their religious law, but the area where they happen to live does not fall under it. Thus Judaism recognizes a division between power and the social life. To that extent Diaspora Judaism, unlike Islam, is not political.[38]

One of the principles enshrined in Jewish law points to a fundamental distinction between Jewish law and Islamic law, for all their evident similarity. This distinction is found in a principle written in Aramaic, a preamble of sorts to Jewish religious law: *dina demalkhuta dina*, "the law of the land is the law."[39] This applies to all principal legal issues. It developed out of an earlier exilic tradition and was adapted to the reality of Jews living in the Diaspora, who were subject simultaneously to religious law and to local law, that is, the law of the ruling power. This replicating of their existence in exile (in the words of Franz Rosenzweig) meant that they had to align themselves with two different calendars—an exclusively Jewish one, measuring religious time; and a worldly one, measuring profane time. Thus they lived in two temporal orders and the legal domains appertaining to these.[40] It was essential that they be made compatible through interpretation and exegesis. An initial attempt to combine Jewish and Gentile chronologies and to construct a hybrid timeline was undertaken by David Gans's *Tsemahk David* (*Scion of David*), written in 1592.[41] It is no accident that this came at a time of great upheaval—an era in which a "world time" born of European expansion was beginning to emerge, its function being to join all and everything.

Because of their Diaspora existence, Jews were not able to obey their law exclusively, whereas Muslims developed for their part, by dint of the political nature of their religion and their successful establishment of power, a historically sanctioned way of life, based on the oneness of rule and religion. That is to say, the claimed conflation of Islam and power was corroborated by historical reality. Thus the two monotheistic religions of the law—Judaism and Islam—came to be specified in terms of two opposing principles: that of *din va-daula* (Arabic for the oneness of religion and rule), which later became part of Muslim tradition, and the *dina demalkhuta dina* of the Jewish legal tradition.

So it is a fact that Jews can live under non-Jewish rule without violating their religious law—a concession to life in the Diaspora. Muslims, on the contrary, are expected to submit to the rule of Islam in two ways: they are to obey Islamic law in everyday life and also to obey laws that guarantee Muslim rule. If the territories of *dar al-islam* fall under the control of infidels, God-fearing Muslims are expected to leave. In modern times, this first occurred in 1774 when, following the Ottoman defeat in a war with Russia, areas inhabited by Muslims were ceded to Russian rule. There is a clear rationale behind this expectation: only by living under Muslim rule can Muslims fulfill the demands of Sharia. Thus sacred space and sacred time coincide in their law. Only on the basis of this overlap can the ideal Muslim community be reproduced.

As a religion of the law, Judaism differs from its Islamic counterpart in its principles as well as in many of its details. In their conceptions of the relationship between sacred time (which is expressed in religious law) and secular history, however, we can discern similarities between the two religions. Thus the Jewish transition to modernity was marked by controversy, in which the relationship to the law was discussed in terms of the so-called Jewish entry into history.[42] The issue was whether Jews could accept a mode of historical thinking that relativized all traditional certainties, a mode that culminated in historicism as an intellectual movement and as a way of understanding the world, and one that threatened Judaism's very essence as a religion of the law. Religious law and secular history turned out to be contraries nestling together at the heart of Judaism.[43]

Historical thinking posed a threat to traditional Judaism. From the mid-eighteenth century on, there were many attempts to read the Jews' sacred book, the Bible, as a historical text, even if one pursuing a moral mission. Such undertakings, which were spawned by the early Jewish Enlightenment or *Haskalah*, ran into fierce resistance. Opponents of such undertakings grasped that a historical reading of the biblical narrative would undermine the sacredness of the Torah.

Paradoxically, the great Enlightenment thinker Moses Mendelssohn adopted a similar attitude. In his commentary on the Torah, the *bi'ur*, he noted that he deemed historical time to have no theological significance. For God, there can be no past and no future, only the present, an eternally enduring present—or sacred time. Moreover, it is the hand of God, not human will, that determines events. According to Mendelssohn, for Jews the Bible has no meaning whatsoever as history. Its only use is for studying the commandments, which is the highest duty incumbent on Jews. Hence history has no relevance either to issues of faith or to the preservation of Judaism. It has no relevance to efforts at ethical improvement or self-perfection that Jews must make in obedience to the commandments (and therefore the law). Indeed, for Mendelssohn ethical questions are ahistorical.[44]

Because Diaspora Jews inhabited two temporal worlds, they were unable to escape the historical thinking taking shape around them or historical interpretations of the social environment in which they found themselves. Hoping for emancipation and civic equality, they created a historical narrative that brought them into conformity with their surroundings. Yet it would take some time for Jews to establish a historically sanctioned canon for themselves. When the legendary Society for Culture and Science of Judaism was founded in 1819, its name pointedly failed to include a reference to history. Such a reference would have aroused suspicions of a profane, or even Christian, worldview. By taking refuge in the semantic world of philologically oriented "Wissenschaft," the founders thought they had found a way to shield themselves, at least in part, from straying too far into a secularized intellectual environment.[45]

The fact that history, the historical interpretation of past social environments, nonetheless made its way into Judaism, thereby putting heavy pressure on the validity of Jewish law as the guardian of sacred time, may be taken as a leitmotif of Jewish inner conflict in the modern era. Two paths beckoned: either Judaism could blend in with the ambient, profane world and thus turn religion into mere belief—that is, shift religion inward, realign it with the inner life, "privatize" it—or Judaism could draw a clear distinction between the demands of sacred law and the expectations of the profane world. The first alternative meant a "Protestantizing" of Judaism, what may be understood as a secondary conversion that extended to ritual and liturgy. The overarching nature of sacred law and the strict observance of the commandments were to be softened. The tendency to Protestantize Judaism culminated spiritually in the thought of Hermann Cohen (1842–1918), the founder of the neo-Kantian Marburg school of philosophy, who stressed ethical perfection as opposed to ritual observance.

The other alternative, embracing the notion of two worlds—the world of strict observance of Jewish law and the world of profane knowledge, *thora im derehk erez*—was advocated by the neo-Orthodox school founded in Frankfurt-am-Main by Samson Raphael Hirsch (1808–1888).[46] By simultaneously dwelling in two different worlds, one steeped in the sacred and the other in the secular, the acolytes of neo-Orthodoxy could keep the commandments while still concerning themselves with issues of philosophy, ethics, and even literature and music. In this way, they did not have to fear becoming estranged from their faith.

Judaism exposed to the conflicts of modernity was therefore caught between sacred law and profane history. It anticipated, in the cultural arena of Western Christianity undergoing secularization, the very issues with which Islam, that other religion of the law facing rampant modernity—only this time on a global scale—has now to deal. The evident proximity of Judaism and Islam has impelled some Jews working out their dilemmas vis-à-vis modernity to "discover" Islam. This can be seen in the works of certain nineteenth- and twentieth-century Jewish scholars of Muslim thought and life.[47]

In his dissertation "Was hat Mohammed aus dem Judenthume aufgenommen?" ("What Did Mohammed Take from Judaism?"), Abraham Geiger (1810–1874) rejected Europeans' harsh judgments of the Prophet.[48] For example, the founder of modern Arabic studies, Antoine-Isaac Silvestre de Sacy (1758–1838), considered Mohammed a mere charlatan.[49] Other writers were no more restrained in their derogatory opinions about the Prophet.[50]

The early research of Ignaz Goldziher (1850–1921), published in his *Muhammedanische Studien* (1888–1889), was a breakthrough in Islamic studies. This important scholar of Islam first earned his living as secretary of the Budapest Reform Jewish community. As a child, he had received a thorough grounding in the Torah and Talmud, entailing a scholar's virtuosity in Hebrew as well as in Aramaic, the closer of the two ancient tongues to Arabic. Goldziher detected an epistemic affinity between the Jewish Halakhah and the Sharia in the Koran and Sunna, as well as between the Aggadah (the nonlegal, narrative part of the Talmud) and the narrative parts of the Hadith.[51] The fundamental affinity between Judaism and Islam affected him so deeply that during a visit to Damascus he was overcome by the sense that he was a Muslim. In Cairo, where Goldziher became the first European to study at the Al-Azhar religious academy, he participated in the Friday prayers, lost in reverie among the thousands of Muslim believers.

A different case is that of Leopold Weiss (1900–1992), who converted from Judaism to Islam in Berlin in 1926; taking the name Muhammad Asad, he embarked on a career as a Muslim scholar, politician, and Pakistani diplomat.[52] Weiss, a former correspondent of the *Frankfurter Zeitung* in the Orient and probably the most important Jewish convert to Islam in the twentieth century, had in his Galician homeland received a classical Jewish education in Hebrew and Aramaic. He saw his conversion to Islam as a return to the Abrahamic origins of the Jews—and he persuaded himself that in the desert Arabs he had found a distant reflection of the ancient Hebrews.[53] Islam attracted him as a universalization of the religion of the Israelites, whom he saw as captive to a narrow tribal particularism. In addition, during a stay in Palestine in the 1920s, he formed a quite realistic assessment of the irreconcilable conflict between Arabs and Jews. A sharp critic of Zionism, he took the part of the Arabs.[54] Although Weiss was not an academic in the formal sense, his contribution to the Islamic canon, especially his work as a translator and commentator, marks him as a great reform-oriented Muslim scholar.[55]

The large number of Jewish Orientalists and students of Islam during the nineteenth and twentieth centuries, most of whom had an Orthodox or similar religious background, saw their task as presenting Islam as it was seen by Muslims themselves.[56] Hardly any Islamic scholar of Jewish descent came closer to realizing this goal than Paul Kraus, who was born in Prague in 1904 and died in Cairo in 1944.[57] While still a student in Berlin, where he attended lectures by C. H. Becker and Hans Heinrich Schaeder, Kraus made his mark as an outstanding philologist. Franz Rosenthal, who later translated Ibn Khaldun's *Muqaddima* into English, cut his teeth on Arabic under Kraus's tutelage. Kraus also knew the ancient Oriental languages, could write in Akkadian (an ancient Mesopotamian idiom), and shone in Arabic poetry. In addition, he had mastered the history of "medieval" Arab science.[58] Based in Paris during the 1930s as a young collaborator of Louis Massignon, an Orientalist who focused on the history of religion, he did research on Sufism. Massignon, who had studied under Goldziher, saw Kraus as an avatar of Goldziher.[59] On Massignon's recommendation, Taha Husain, the worldly Egyptian minister of culture and science, appointed Kraus as a university lecturer in Cairo. It was there that Kraus committed suicide.

Paul Kraus was the brother-in-law of Leo Strauss (1899–1973), who, like Kraus, escaped from Berlin to Paris. At the École des Hautes Études, they participated in the legendary seminar on Hegel taught by Alexandre Kojève (1902–1968). Earlier, as a research assistant at the Hochschule für die Wissenschaft des Judentums, Strauss had developed an interest in the Muslim rationalist Alfarabi (870–950), whom he saw as an intellectual harbinger of the great Jewish philosopher, jurist, and medical doctor Moses

Maimonides (1135–1204), and Kraus helped him with the Arabic text. It would be Leo Strauss who raised anew, in light of the upheavals of modernity, the issue of what the law actually means in Judaism.

Confronted by the crisis of the period between the two World Wars, and with relativism encroaching on all sides, Strauss sought refuge in a philosophy with a restored absolute at its core. The absolute, for him, was expressed in the law, the expression of revelation—or more precisely, the *form* of the revelation of Sinai.[60] It was not religious belief that was central, but rather unconditional acceptance of the law that counted. Strauss, who considered himself an atheist—or rather, a "cognitive theist" or Epicurean—turned himself, by dint of the theological-political problems he posed anew, into a defender of Orthodoxy, an Orthodoxy insistent on man's need for divine illumination.[61] It is not given to man to find truth by his own unaided efforts. Since man by nature is sinful, the law has to be revealed to him. Confronted with this normative exigency, he struggles incessantly to meet it. Thus, revealed religion is the utopian form of law, whereas opposition to the moral utopia of the fulfilled law takes the form of the Enlightenment's critique of religion.[62]

In his critique of Spinoza and Spinozism, which he dedicated to Franz Rosenzweig, Strauss already saw the Enlightenment as digging Judaism's grave.[63] The Enlightenment had ridiculed revelation as superstition, but was unable to refute it philosophically. In reality, revelation could fend for itself. Enlightenment and revelation ultimately moved in wholly different spheres. To that extent, the truth of Judaism was less irrational than super-rational. It did not so much contradict rationality as bypass it, orienting itself toward what rationality, by its very nature, cannot grasp. Siting himself in this tradition, Strauss rejected any application of rationalism to ontological questions. He repudiated belief in history, in progress, in the ultimate ability of science to control nature, and in everything that claimed to be a historically necessary process. In any case, the Hegelian system had irretrievably broken down, a collapse that renewed the call for revelation and biblical truth.

In the crisis of the 1930s, which he saw as both a crisis of the West and a crisis of Judaism, Strauss wrestled with the same problem that ten years later, faced with the disintegration of Western concepts, Max Horkheimer and Theodor W. Adorno took up in their *Dialektik der Aufklärung*

(*Dialectic of Enlightenment*). For him as for them, the question was how it could happen that rationality and rationalism had destroyed reason. Almost in the same words, though earlier than Horkheimer and Adorno, Strauss wrote of the "self-destruction" of rational philosophy as the great crisis facing the West. Whereas Horkheimer and Adorno despairingly characterized the destruction of reason as the Enlightenment dialectically turning on itself, Strauss believed he had found in medieval rationalism an answer to the enigma of modernity. Ultimately, medieval rational philosophy was bound to the law as the form of revelation—and this law was valid for Jews and Muslims alike. The path to medieval rationalism that began with the philosophers Al-Farabi and Ibn Sina (or Avicenna, 980–1037), both much admired by Strauss, led straight to Maimonides.[64] In Maimonides, whom Hermann Cohen called "the classical exponent of rationalism in Judaism," Strauss thought he had found his model.[65] In Maimonides as in the ancient Greek philosophers, Strauss detected a possible answer to Spinoza.[66] The good human order, the "ideal city," was a prophetic revelation, supported by Platonic and Aristotelian thought and enshrined in the essence of the law, as the formalized will of God.[67] As such, there is nothing more to be said. There can be no argument over the reality of revelation and the duty to obey the law. A Jew with eyes to see sees from the superhuman wisdom and justice of the Torah that revelation is real; and a Muslim with eyes to see knows from the superhuman beauty of the Koran that revelation is real.[68]

Strauss recognizes that Maimonides' principal philosophical treatise, *Moreh Nevukhim* (*The Guide for the Perplexed*), was situated in the Muslim intellectual currents of his time, in particular the movement of the enlightened theologians. The latter opposed traditional theology (*kalam*) as concerning itself more with the roots of religion (*usul ad-din*) than with the law itself (*fiqh*).[69] For Strauss, however, *Moreh Nevukhim* was still a work of *kalam* in both spirit and intention, for it was written to defend the law against the philosophers.

Maimonides is therefore not the unbelieving Jew the rabbis have made of him. But he is not a believer in the traditional religious sense, either.[70] Rather, he argues for the law as an expression of revelation. In law revelation is formalized.[71] And by conversion of revelation into the form of law, the question of belief no longer arises as such. What remains essential is observance of the law.[72] The ideal law thus becomes the foundation of the ideal order. And the law is just as political as the prophet who promulgates it as a statesman. Thus the founder of the Platonic ideal city is the Prophet.[73]

Strauss bases his thought on Maimonides because the latter supplies a key, in the form of the law, to ethical action in the conflict between reason and revelation, between morality and knowledge. The resulting open process of interpretation between the absolute and the relative, between the principled and the historical, also fits with Maimonides' allegorical interpretation of the Bible.[74] Because he refuses to accept literal interpretation, he targets the epistemic motif of unreconciled contradiction. Strauss interpreted this way of deliberately leaving interpretation open as Maimonides' "esoterics"—an esoterics of rationalist philosophy constrained by the law.[75]

Strauss's mistrust of the Enlightenment and Spinozism did not spare those Jewish representatives of the Enlightenment who operated within religious constraints. He accuses Moses Mendelssohn of "religious liberalism," citing his translation of the Bible as evidence. Strauss also distanced himself from the neo-Kantian Hermann Cohen. When asked what role remained in his philosophy for the *bore olam*, the Creator of the world, Cohen had been forced to admit, despairingly, that the gulf between his views and traditional belief was unbridgeable.[76]

Strauss distinguished two kinds of laws and two lawgivers in the tradition of medieval Jewish rationalism. The first kind of law had no function other than to enable people to live peaceably in a community. In Strauss's language, its goal was the "hallowing of the body." The goal of the second kind of law was the "hallowing of the soul," achieving its perfection. The first kind of law is made by humans, while the second kind of law, law that seeks the perfection of the soul (and thus also the understanding), is a divine law. It can be promulgated only by a prophet.[77]

Faced with the crisis of Western civilization, Strauss sought to bar man from having full authority over himself. He rehabilitated revelation at the Enlightenment's expense by "divinizing" the law. This was a reaction to an overreaching modernity. Leopold Weiss, who like Strauss had taken issue with modernity in 1920s Berlin, had devoted himself, under the name Muhammad Asad, to a very different enterprise. Whereas Strauss, the atheist, had traced the crisis of the West and Judaism back to the Enlightenment and taken refuge in medieval rationalist philosophy, Weiss, as we have seen, converted to Islam. In this religion the law was absolute. It needed no "divinizing"; on the contrary, it needed what Strauss, proceeding from the opposite direction, from the secular world, had demanded for the law: its partition. In his Indian period, Muhammad Asad was concerned with doing just this, albeit within Islam. Together with other reform-minded Muslims, he tried to change the Islamic legal tradition so as to fence off the "eternal" (and thus immutable) law from merely time-bound norms that changed with history. The problem was how to effect this and set up two temporal worlds—the same problem that had confronted Judaism from the onset of the Enlightenment.

In the early 1930s Asad was invited to British India by Muhammad Iqbal, the great Indian Muslim scholar, poet, politician, and philosopher whose vision of an independent state for Muslims in India inspired the creation of Pakistan. Asad had previously spent many years in Arabia at the court of Ibn Saud, where he served as an adviser. In India he became involved, together with other Muslim scholars and intellectuals, in efforts to reform the Islamic conception of law. The distance he had to overcome was by no means short. The Saudi kingdom had been heavily influenced by its pact with Wahhabism, while on the Indian subcontinent Muslims were grappling with issues of orthodoxy as well as reform. These debates were linked to the idea, even then under consideration, of creating a Muslim state on Indian soil—the state that later became Pakistan. The issues related to this future event: what kind of law should the Muslim community then adopt? Should it be based entirely on Sharia, as supporters of an Islamic state desired? Or should the goal be a Muslim community strongly oriented toward secular values? Muhammad Asad took part in these controversies over the character of the future Pakistan, especially the debate over how its constitution should be framed.[78]

It was among Indian Muslims that debates over reform and orthodoxy in Islam were probably most advanced. The role of the law was central in these debates. Muhammad Iqbal and other reformers attributed the stasis in the Muslim world to the static nature of its legal thinking. Ultimately, strict observance of the law meant arresting time. But the world was subject to change, and this change entailed the opposite of what was implied by the law: an acceleration of time. In order to accommodate such a demand, the reformers toyed with partitioning the law. Thus, based on a codification of the Koran and the prophetic tradition, rules regarding the obligatory and the forbidden were to be derived and given a timeless character (*nusus*). As eternal Sharia, they would be sacred, and therefore "divinized." Everything else would be left up to parliamentary decisions, made by a legislature following a so-called open path (*minhaj*).[79]

Partitioning the law meant embracing two kinds of sovereignty: the eternal sovereignty of God, and the time-bound sovereignty of a representative organ of the people. This can certainly be compared, in its effects, with the solution adopted by the other religion of the law, Judaism: namely, to live under two differently founded but equally valid legal codes—one sacred, the other profane. That this seemingly liberal idea would cause opponents to enter the fray was entirely foreseeable. Thus the founder of the radical Jama'at-i Islami, Abu'l-'Ala' Mawdudi, distinguished himself in debates over the constitution by opposing the proposals of the reformers. To him these proposals were anathema. In his correspondence with Maryam Jameelah, who was born as Margret Marcus to Reform Jewish parents in New York and who had flirted with Jewish Orthodoxy before converting to Islam, Mawdudi compared the progressive Muslims he so reviled with adherents of Reform Judaism. In his opinion, both had failed to grasp the meaning of divine law.[80]

The constitutional debate in the early days of Pakistan was all the more important for the development of Islamic legal thinking as it took place within a Muslim community that had no identity beyond Islam. Thus it was obvious that Muslim space and Muslim time would coincide in the law here as they did nowhere else. Right from the outset, the question of the law in Pakistan acquired political-theological overtones unmatched elsewhere in the Muslim world. That is why the question was so pressing there—and could have gone either way, toward reform or toward orthodoxy.

A similar question, albeit arising from opposite circumstances, arises with regard to the Muslim diaspora that has happened in the meantime. For in a diaspora situation, where right from the start Islamic law cannot be an expression of the ruling power and where the political tradition is built on Western—that is, secularized Christian—foundations, Muslims are challenged to make their sacred law compatible with non-Muslim social environments. This leads to a splitting along the lines proposed by the Indian Muslim reformers: "divinization" of the timeless on one side, and embracing the mutability of the time-bound on the other. In the diaspora, it is no less obligatory to observe one's own religious law than it is to observe the law of the land. This is tantamount to fostering a "Protestantization" of Islam, especially since what would then result is a separation of the spheres. The sacred would be confined to its own sphere and time. The performance of religious duties and the mundanities of everyday life would go separate ways. This would amount to accepting a situation-appropriate secularization. Muslims in the diaspora would be called on to observe the same separation that the other religion of the law, Judaism, already observes. Judaism has succeeded—though not without internal conflict—in adapting to the yardsticks of an inexorable modernity. In this way, enlightened Jewish Orthodoxy has been able to live according to the principle: Jews at home, ordinary people in the world.

Not only in the context of the Pakistani constitutional debate was Muhammad Asad on the side of the reformers. In the area of exegesis and translation of the Koran, he also challenged Islamic orthodoxy. In his work of translating the Koran, the analogy with Moses Mendelssohn's translation of the Bible is striking. Not that we should draw too close a parallel between Mendelssohn and Muhammad Asad, especially with regard to their significance and historical impact. After all, the Jewish community instantly recognized Mendelssohn's achievement, whereas Muhammad Asad, as a Jewish convert to Islam, still evokes suspicion. But the similarities in their projects cannot be dismissed. In translating their respective holy scriptures, Mendelssohn and Asad both sought to align them with the circumstances of modernity. From this arose no small share of problems. In the Koran, the sacred was inscribed into the very text itself. Any allegorical translation would impugn its divine nature; any metaphorical interpretation was bound to encounter resistance from traditional and radical believers alike. But allegory and metaphor rather than literality accorded with Asad's quest to ground faith in reason based on the sources of Islam. No wonder the Muslim World League rejected his credentials. In contrast, because he was conditioned by prior Diaspora life, Mendelssohn could straddle two antithetical legal orders. This gave him a free hand in dealing with the rabbinical authorities. In translating the Bible, he simply bypassed them—*dina demalkhuta dina*, as it were!

As a Muslim adherent of the Enlightenment, Muhammad Asad bestrode two worlds. In approaching the divine scriptures he wanted to achieve two things. First, by translating and interpreting the Koran, he sought to communicate its message. Second, by circumventing a literal reading, he wanted to remove from the Muslims' holy book the white heat of the sacred. In adopting such an attitude, Asad stood alone—doomed to isolation. Not unjustly, he was dismissed as a wanderer between the poles of knowledge and faith: as a "Muslim Orientalist" plying his trade by hermeneutically penetrating and analytically dissecting the text, and as an "Islamic scholar" who took the text to be the absolute word of God.[81] Mendelssohn, as the outstanding Jewish figure of the Enlightenment, can be viewed in similar terms. He also sought to straddle two worlds—the world of literal interpretation and the world of allegory, that of sacred time and that of historical time. To be sure, Asad's and Mendelssohn's quests have had different outcomes so far.

Changes are on the horizon, however—especially where the Muslim diaspora is concerned, and in particular in the United States, where a unique brand of religious pluralism and ethnic diversity prevails, and that in distinction to the European domain. This prevailing pluralism contributes to no small extent to the current phenomenon of initial attempts among American Muslims to establish their own existence as a diasporic population, trying to accommodate Islamic law and the law of the land. The newly established tendency of *fiqh al-aqalliyyat*—a jurisprudence of Muslim minorities in the West based on the principle of Islam as a global religion—intends to develop rules for Muslims' everyday life in a non-Muslim environment. This ought to be done by the interpretive efforts of a new *ijtihad*—namely the procedure of promoting legal decision by independent interpretation of the legal sources, the Qur'an and Sunna. This tendency is represented by the U.S.-based Muslim legal authority Taha Jabir al-Alwani.[82]

Al-Alwani first made a name for himself when the American Fiqh Council, over which he presided, issued a *fatwa* in 1994 in which Muslims were allowed to vote in U.S. elections. Another *fatwa* even permitted them to serve in the American military—and to do so even if sent to Muslim countries. This reminds us again of the Jewish case, when in the era of Emancipation military service for Jews was bound up with all kinds of religious obstacles and severe complications, especially in keeping the Sabbath and *kashrut* dietary laws. Rabbi Moses Sofer, an Orthodox authority in early nineteenth-century Hungary, considered obligatory military service proper even if one had to violate *mitzvoth* (religious obligations). After all, this was an obvious case of *dina demalhkuta dina*—and not an objectionable Jewish innovation such as anticipated by Reform he intensely despised.[83] Already as early as 1798 in the Austrian military, Jews were somewhat accommodated by the introduction of a special oath for them upon induction in keeping with Jewish faith. In the Russian army, which was not too well disposed toward the Jews in its ranks, to put it mildly, military obligations and Jewish religious observance were reconciled only in 1881 by means of a recognized halakhic compendium, *mahkane yisrael*.[84]

Are there any analogous similarities between the principle of *dina demalhkuta dina* in Jewish Law and possible effects emanating from the newly established Islamic tradition of *fiqh al-aqalliyyat* as a form of collective *ijtihad*? To some extend it looks likely according to certain interpretive tendencies. According to the new minority *fiqh*, the realm beyond *dar al-islam* is no longer construed as a space alien or even hostile to Muslims. Rather the opposite. This is the case when this domain is perceived as *dar al-dawa*, where the spread of Islam can be pursued by conviction and conversion of unbelievers. This fits well with a ruling based on *fiqh al-aqalliyyat*, which allows women who become Muslims to remain married to their non-Muslim husbands so as not to frighten away women who wish to embrace Islam. This ruling prevails over traditional law according to the mode of *maslaha* (public interest, so to speak), in order to increase the number of women converts.

In any event, the regulation of the *hijra*—the Islamic religious obligation to abandon lands that came under non-Muslim rule—is obviously suspended. In a recent interview, al-Alwani suggests rethinking the narrow traditional understanding of the *dar al-islam* as a space of dominance and law of the Muslims. According to the interpretation of *fiqh al-aqalliyyat*, *dar al-islam* is to be found everywhere where Muslims can observe the duties of their faith, that is, where freedom of religion prevails. In al-Alwani's judgment, this is doubtless the case in America. Conversely, American Muslims are obligated to be loyal to their polity, their *watan*, and insofar are obligated to observe the law of the land.

Muslim desires, however, to pursue Islamic autonomy in the domain of law and justice, principally in the realm of family law, are not accepted in the West. The recent rejection of such a wish in the province of Ontario, Canada, where demands of multiculturalism are considered the most endorsed in the West, is significant in this regard.

The potential of *fiqh al-aqillayyat,* the Muslim minority *fiqh,* goes beyond mere legal interpretation, however. It enters even into the wider domain of insight and awareness. Actually, a tendency can be noticed among Muslim interpreters and commentators of the Law, who perceive the minority *fiqh* rather as an epistemic gateway for a changed and even more profane comprehension of the world. Ultimately, the original meaning of *fiqh* as a category of independent understanding, knowledge, and applied intelligence, points beyond the traditional Islamic canon while contrasting with the notion of `*ilm* as religious knowledge imbued with sacral authority. As such, *fiqh* systematically goes together with a reading of the world that is disenchanted by the modes and concepts of the social sciences—precisely the epistemic turn that the London-based sheikh Zaki Badawi speaks of, relaying an extensive interpretation of Abu Hanifah's "greater *fiqh*."[85]

That seems to be a particularly interesting way of opening the door to a culture of knowledge permeated by the modes of Western discourse. Indeed, no less than the great Oriental scholar Ignaz Goldziher identified a hermeneutic affinity between the meaning of the Hebrew *khochma* (wisdom, knowledge) and the modes of interpretation enshrined in the Arabic *fiqh*. A closer look reveals even more in common. When the Judaic canon of *khochmat yisrael,* the traditional and sacredly enshrined Wisdom of Israel, embarked on a process of transformation generated by the current of the Jewish Enlightenment, the *Haskalah,* in the early nineteenth century into the German-language *Wissenschaft des Judentums (Science of Judaism),* a painful contravention from a divinely infused understanding of the world converted into more profane, indeed secular modes of interpretation.

The experience of Muslim minorities in non-Muslim, predominantly Western surroundings might instigate a transformation of Islamic knowledge and understanding more easily than in Muslim lands, where beyond religion proper the fabric of material life is evidently more impregnated with the sacred, decelerating social time. The *Arab Human Development Report* presents a rather bleak diagnosis of the state of the Arab world. This lamentable situation, thrown into relief by the *Report*'s insistence on mere facts and figures, has evoked again, with unrestrained urgency, the question of modernity and secularization.

Such a conclusion is not self-evident. In the last few decades, public and academic discourse on the Western trinity of modernity, enlightenment, and secularization has been systematically avoided, to say the least. These values have almost lost their legitimacy. The reasons for such an ultimate rebuff are manifold and should not be discussed here further. All in all, these values have been blamed for the tribulations of humankind since the advent of the modern age. At the utmost, the phenomenon of modernity and its modes of societal acceleration became rather tolerable in its plural form. The argument is that different cultures produce different modernities. This statement cannot be otherwise than true. The universal discourse about modernity is at its core, however, not a discourse about cultural diversity and the ability of each culture to adopt the preferences of the modern world in its particular way, and therefore it is not a discourse about the various cultural forms modernity takes. It is far more a question of its specific adaptability to the modes and the accelerated pace that the attributions of development require—presupposing that beyond cultural diversity men and women strive for the fulfillment of their personalities based on anthropologically similar, if not equal, universal assumptions for the advantages and sometimes the blessings of individual and collective security, of freedom, and of material well-being for the greatest number possible. The core moment of the ability to produce and reproduce the attributes of modernity leads us into the prerequisites and requirements for the development of humankind—the political, social, and cultural environment to discover, to create, and to invent.

In the beginning is basic research in the natural sciences—even more than ability to apply its results—accompanied by the enlightening significance of the humanities and the social sciences in enchanting the world. The production of knowledge, its means, and its consequences are the outcome of the process of secularization and are accelerated by the admittedly overzealous and impatient requirements of the Enlightenment. That this course happened to start first in the domain of the West as Christianity secularized does not disclaim other cultures' paths to modernity. Indeed, modernity is a continuously ongoing universal process of transformation, conversion, and change—and all humankind has its role in this endeavor. A different way above and beyond the requirements of modernity is still not visible. That is the inescapable message inherent in the critique presented by the Arab Human Development Report.

Introduction

1. Shakib Arslan, *Our Decline and Its Causes*, trans. M. A. Shakoor (Lahore, 1944).

2. Norman Daniel, *Islam and the West: The Making of an Image* (Edinburgh, 1980).

3. Edward Said, *Orientalism* (New York, 1978); Sadiq Jalal al-Azm, "Orientalism and Orientalism in Reverse," *Khamsin: Journal of Revolutionary Socialists of the Middle East* 8 (1981): 5–26.

4. *Khamsin: Revue des socialistes révolutionnaires du proche orient*, published in Paris since 1975; in addition to Sadiq al-Azm, editors and regular authors from the Arab world include Lafif Lakdhar and Mohammed Jaffar (also known as Kanan Makiyya).

5. Dan Diner, *Israel in Palästina: Über Tausch und Gewalt im Vorderen Orient* (Königstein i. Ts., 1980).

6. Dan Diner, "Herrschaft und Gesellschaft im Vorderen Orient," unpublished manuscript from research project, University of Frankfurt am Main, 1979–1981.

7. Norman Stillman, *The Jews of Arab Lands in Modern Times* (Philadelphia and New York, 1991).

8. Mark R. Cohen and A. L. Ludovitch, eds., *Jews among Arabs: Contacts and Boundaries* (Princeton, 1989).

Chapter 1: Knowledge and Development

1. *The Arab Human Development Report* [AHDR] 2002: *Creating Opportunities for Future Generations*, sponsored by the Regional Bureau for Arab States, United Nations Development Programme (New York, 2003).

2. AHDR 2004: *Towards Freedom in the Arab World* (New York, 2005).

3. Rifa'a al-Tahtawi, *Ein Muslim entdeckt Europa: Die Reise eines Ägypters im 19. Jahrhundert nach Paris*, ed. Karl Stowasser (Leipzig, 1988). See also Daniel L. Newman, *An Imam in Paris: Al-Tahtawi's Visit to France (1826–31)* (London, San Francisco, and Beirut, 2002).

4. Pierre-Nicolas Hamont, *L'Égypt sous Méhmét Ali* (Paris, 1843).

5. James Heyworth-Dunne, "Printing and Translation under Muhammad Ali of Egypt: The Foundation of Modern Arabic," *Journal of the Royal Asiatic Society* (1940): 325–349.

6. Ibrahim Abu-Lughod, *The Arab Discovery of Europe: A Study in Cultural Encounters* (Princeton, 1963), pp. 46ff.

7. Bernard Lewis, *The Muslim Discovery of Europe* (New York, 1982), pp. 71ff.

8. Edward Said, *Orientalism* (New York, 1978).

9. Emmanuel Sivan, "Edward Said and His Arab Reviewers," in *Interpretations of Islam: Past and Present* (Princeton, 1985), pp. 133–156.

10. Martin Kramer, *Ivory Towers on Sand: The Failure of Middle Eastern Studies in America* (Washington, DC, 2001).

11. Albert Memmi, *The Colonizer and the Colonized* (Boston, 1991).

12. Emmanuel Sivan, "Colonialism and Popular Culture," in *Interpretations of Islam: Past and Present* (Princeton, 1985), pp. 157–186.

13. Ulrich W. Haarmann, "Ideology and History, Identity and Alterity: The Arab Image of the Turk from the Abbasides to Modern Egypt," *International Journal of Middle East Studies* 20, no. 2 (1988): 175–196.

14. Bassam Tibi, *Die Verschwörung: Das Trauma der arabischen Politik* (Hamburg, 1993).

15. AHDR 2002, p. 28.

16. AHDR 2003: *Building a Knowledge Society* (New York, 2004), pp. 118–119.

17. Hartmut Fähnrich, "Orientalismus und *Orientalismus*," *Die Welt des Islams* 28 (1988): 178–186; Gyan Prakash, "Orientalism Now," *History and Theory* 34 (1999): 199–212.

18. Shmuel Noah Eisenstadt, *Comparative Civilizations and Multiple Modernities*, 2 vols. (Leiden, 2003).

19. AHDR 2003, p. 67.

20. Ibid., p. 77.

21. Ibid., p. 125.

22. Ibid., pp. 70ff.

23. Ibid., pp. 72–73.

24. Afaf Lutfi as-Sayyid Marsot, *Egypt in the Reign of Mohammad Ali* (Cambridge, 1984); Ehud R. Toledano, *State and Society in Mid-Nineteenth-Century Egypt* (Cambridge, 1990).

25. AHDR 2003, p. 42.

26. Robert Hunter, *Egypt under the Khedives, 1805–1879: From Household Government to Modern Bureaucracy* (Pittsburg, 1984); Gabriel Baer, *Studies in the Social History of Modern Egypt* (Chicago, 1969).

27. Peter Malcolm Holt, ed., *Political Change in Modern Egypt* (London, 1968).

28. Khaled Fahmy, *All the Pasha's Men: Mehmed Ali, His Army and the Making of Modern Egypt* (Cambridge, 1997).

29. Anwar Abd-al-Malik, *Ägypten: Militärgesellschaft: Das Armeeregime, die Linke und der soziale Wandel unter Nasser* (Frankfurt a.M., 1971).

30. John Waterbury, *The Egypt of Nasser and Sadat: The Political Economy of Two Regimes* (Princeton, 1983); Derek Hoopwood, *Egypt: Politics and Society, 1945–1990* (London, 1991).

31. Jean Batou, ed., *Between Development and Underdevelopment: The Precocious Attempts at Industrialization of the Periphery, 1800–1870* (Geneva, 1991).

32. Jean Batou, "L'Égypte de Muhammed Ali: Pouvoir politique et développement économique," *Annales ESC* (1991): 401–428.

33. Tahtawi, *Ein Muslim entdeckt Europa*, p. 200.

34. Ibid., p. 93.

35. Bernard Lewis, *What Went Wrong? Western Impact and Middle Eastern Response* (Oxford, 2002), p. 141.

36. AHDR 2003, p. 74.

37. Ian Buruma and Avishai Margalit, *Occidentalism: The West in the Eyes of Its Enemies* (New York, 2004).

38. Norman Cohn, *Warrant for Genocide: Myth of the Jewish World Conspiracy and the Protocols of the Elders of Zion* (London, 2006); Stefan Wild, "Die arabische Perzeption der 'Protokolle der Weisen von Zion,'" in *Islamstudien ohne Ende: Festschrift für Werner Ende zum 65. Geburtstag*, ed. Rainer Brunner et al. (Würzburg, 2002), pp. 517–528.

39. Ludwik Fleck, *Genesis and Development of a Scientific Fact*, ed. Thaddeus J. Trenn and Robert K. Merton (Chicago, 1979).

40. AHDR 2003, p. 76.

41. AHDR 2002, p. 27.

42. Tahtawi, *Ein Muslim entdeckt Europa*, p. 96.

43. AHDR 2003, p. 153.

44. Ibid., p. 148.

45. Dale F. Eickelman and Jon W. Anderson, *New Media in the Muslim World: The Emerging Public Sphere* (Bloomington, 1999).

46. AHDR 2002, pp. 27–28.

47. Bernard Lewis, *The Political Language of Islam* (Chicago, 1988), pp. 111–112.

48. Bernard Lewis, *The Emergence of Modern Turkey* (London, 1968), pp. 129–130.

49. Tahtawi, *Ein Muslim entdeckt Europa*, p. 96.

50. Lewis, *The Emergence of Modern Turkey*, p. 133.

51. Helga Rebhan, *Geschichte und Funktion einiger politischer Termini im Arabischen des 19. Jahrhunderts (1798–1882)* (Wiesbaden, 1986).

52. AHDR 2003, p. 17.

53. Ibid., pp. 137–138.

54. AHDR 2002, p. 135.

55. Andreas Boeck and Peter Pawelka, *Staat, Markt und Rente in der internationalen Politik* (Opladen, 1996).

56. Kiren Aziz Chaudhary, *The Price of Wealth: Economics and Institutions in the Middle East* (Ithaca, NY, 1997).

57. Hazem Beblawi and Giacomo Luciani, eds., *The Rentier State* (London, 1987).

58. Rossein M. Mahdavy, "Patterns and Problems of Economic Development in Rentier States: The Case of Iran," in *Studies in the Economic History of the Middle East: From the Rise of Islam to the Present Day*, ed. M. A. Cook (London, 1970), p. 431.

59. Zuhayr Mikdashi, *A Financial Analysis of Middle Eastern Oil Concessions, 1901–1965* (New York, 1966), p. 27.

60. Mahdavy, "Patterns and Problems of Economic Development," p. 431.

61. Peter Pawelka, *Herrschaft und Entwicklung im Nahen Osten: Ägypten* (Heidelberg, 1985).

62. Tahtawi, *Ein Muslim entdeckt Europa*, pp. 183–184.

63. George Annesley, *The Rise of Modern Egypt: A Century and a Half of Modern Egypt, 1798–1957* (Edinburgh, 1994), p. 61.

64. Volker Perthes, *Geheime Gärten: Die neue arabische Welt* (Munich, 2004), pp. 417ff.

65. Tahtawi, *Ein Muslim entdeckt Europa*, pp. 19, 88.

Chapter 2: Geopolitics and Religious Zeal

1. Fred Halliday, *Two Hours That Shook the World: September 11, 2001: Causes and Consequences* (London, 2002).

2. Fred Halliday, *The Middle East in International Relations: Power, Politics and Ideology* (Cambridge, 2005).

3. William Roger Louis, *The British Empire in the Middle East, 1945–1951: Arab Nationalism, the United States, and Postwar Imperialism* (Oxford, 1988), pp. 103ff.

4. Bruce Robellet Kuniholm, *The Origins of the Cold War in the Near East: Great Power Conflict and Diplomacy in Iran, Turkey, and Greece* (Princeton, 1980).

5. Malcolm Edward Yapp, *The Near East since the First World War* (London/ New York, 1991), pp. 411ff.

6. Amatzia Baram, *Building toward Crisis: Saddam Husayn's Strategy for Survival*, Washington Institute for Near East Policy, Policy Papers no. 47 (Washington, DC, 1998).

7. Henner Fürtig, *Der irakisch-iranische Krieg, 1980–1988: Ursachen, Verlauf, Folgen* (Berlin, 1992).

8. Laurie Mylroie, "The Superpowers in the Iran-Iraq War," *American-Arab Affairs* 21 (1987): 15–26.

9. Anthony Arnold, *Afghanistan: The Soviet Invasion in Perspective* (Stanford, 1985).

10. Johannes Reissner, "Die Besetzung der großen Moschee in Mekka," *Orient* 21 (1980): 194–203.

11. Natana DeLong-Bas, *Wahabi Islam: From Revival and Reform to Global Jihad* (Cairo, 2004).

12. Feroz Ahmad, *The Making of Modern Turkey* (London, 1993); Udo Steinbach, *Die Türkei im 20. Jahrhundert: Schwieriger Partner Europas* (Bergisch-Gladbach, 1996).

13. Sylvia Haim, "The Abolition of the Califate and Its Aftermath," in *The Caliphate*, ed. Thomas W. Arnold (London, 1965), pp. 205–244.

14. Erwin I. J. Rosenthal, "Politisches Denken im Islam: Kalifatstheorie und politische Philosophie," *Saeculum* 23 (1972): 148–171.

15. Akdes Nimet Kurat, "Tsarist Russia and the Muslims of Central Asia," in *The Cambridge History of Islam*, vol. 1A, *The Central Islamic Lands from*

Pre-Islamic Times to the First World War, ed. Peter Malcolm Holt, Ann K. P. Lambton, and Bernard Lewis (Cambridge, 1977), pp. 503–523.

16. Hasan B. Paksoy, "'Basmachi': The Turkistan National Liberation Movement, 1916–1930," in *Modern Encyclopedia of Religions in Russia and the Soviet Union* (Moscow, 1991), vol. 4, pp. 5–20.

17. Andrew Mango, *Atatürk* (New York, 1999), p. 323.

18. Azade-Ayse Rorlich, "Fellow Travelers: Enver Pasha and the Bolshevik Government, 1918–1920," *Journal of the Royal Society for Asian Affairs* n.s. 13, no. 3 (1982): 288–296.

19. David Gillard, *The Struggle for Asia, 1828–1914* (London, 1977); Malcolm Edward Yapp, *Strategies of British India* (Oxford, 1980).

20. Edward Ingram, *The Beginning of the Great Game in Asia, 1828–1834* (Oxford, 1979).

21. Yapp, *Strategies of British India.*

22. Matthew Smith Anderson, *The Eastern Question, 1774–1923* (London, 1966).

23. David Frumkin, *A Peace to End All Peace: The Fall of the Ottoman Empire and the Creation of the Modern Middle East* (New York, 1989).

24. Roger Owen, *Lord Cromer: Victorian Imperialist, Edwardian Proconsul* (New York, 2004).

25. Ram Lakhan Shukla, *Britain, India and the Turkish Empire, 1853–1882* (New Delhi, 1973), pp. 170–171.

26. Arnold J. Toynbee, ed., *Survey of International Affairs* (London, 1925), vol. 1, p. 40.

27. Minna Rozen, "Pedigree Remembered, Reconstructed, Invented: Benjamin Disraeli between East and West," in *The Jewish Discovery of Islam: Studies in Honor of Bernard Lewis,* ed. Martin Kramer (Tel Aviv, 1999), pp. 49–76.

28. Robert William Seton-Watson, *Disraeli, Gladstone and the Eastern Question* (London, 1935).

29. William Gladstone, *Bulgarian Horrors and the Question of the East* (London, 1876).

30. Malcolm Edward Yapp, *The Making of the Modern Middle East, 1792–1923* (London, 1987).

31. Henry Sutherland Edwards, *Russian Projects against India from the Tsar Peter to General Skobeleff* (London, 1885).

32. Shukla, *Britain, India and the Turkish Empire,* p. 132.

33. Rudolph Peters, *Islam and Colonialism: The Doctrine of Jihad in Modern History* (The Hague, 1979), pp. 44–45.

34. Syud Ahmad Khan, *An Essay on the Causes of the Indian Revolt* (London, 1960).

35. Gail Minault, *The Khalifat Movement: Religious Symbolism and Political Mobilization in India* (New York, 1982), p. 5.

36. Alexander Schölch, *Ägypten den Ägyptern! Die politische und gesellschaftliche Krise der Jahre 1878–1882* (Zurich, 1972).

37. Shukla, *Britain, India and the Turkish Empire*, p. 184.

38. Minault, *The Khalifat Movement*, pp. 65ff.

39. Richard Hattemer, *Atatürk und die türkische Reformpolitik im Spiegel der ägyptischen Presse: Eine Inhaltsanalyse ausgewählter Pressereaktionen auf Maßnahmen zur Umgestaltung des politischen, religiösen und kulturellen Lebens in der Türkei zwischen 1922 und 1938* (Berlin, 1997), pp. 71–72.

40. Elie Kedouri, "Egypt and the Caliphate, 1915–1946," *Journal of the Royal Asiatic Society* (1963): 208–248.

41. Martin Kramer, *Islam Assembled: The Advent of the Muslim Congresses* (New York, 1986), pp. 110–111.

42. Gotthard Jäschke, "Die Türkei seit dem Weltkriege. Geschichtskalender für 1929 mit neuem Eintrag zu 1918–1928," *Die Welt des Islams* 12 (1930): 1–154.

43. Bernard Lewis, *The Emergence of Modern Turkey* (London, 1968), p. 428.

44. Uriel Heyd, *Language Reform in Modern Turkey* (Jerusalem, 1954).

45. Akdes Nimet Kurat, "Islam in the Soviet Union," in *The Cambridge History of Islam*, vol. 1B, *The Central Islamic Lands since 1918*, ed. Peter Malcolm Holt, Ann K. P. Lambton, and Bernard Lewis (Cambridge, 1977), pp. 627–643.

46. Joseph Castagné, "La latinisation de l'alphabet turc dans les républiques turco-tatares de l'U.R.S.S.," *Revue des Études Islamiques* 1 (1927): 321–353.

47. Stefan Wurm, *Turkic Peoples of the USSR: Their Historical Background, Their Language, and the Development of Soviet Linguistic Policy* (Oxford, 1954).

48. Peter Hardy, *The Muslims of British India* (Cambridge, 1972).

49. Hafeez Malik, *Moslem Nationalism in India and Pakistan* (Washington, DC, 1963).

50. Yochanan Friedmann, "The Attitude of the Jam íyyat-I'Ulama'-iHind to the Indian National Movement and the Establishment of Pakistan," in *The 'Ulama' in Modern History*, ed. Gabriel Baer (Jerusalem, 1971), pp. 157–183.

51. Stephen Philip Cohen, *The Idea of Pakistan* (Washington, DC, 2004).

52. Ayesha Jalal, *The Sole Spokesman: Jinna, the Muslim League and the Demand for Pakistan* (Cambridge, 1993).

53. Erwin I. J. Rosenthal, *Islam in the Modern National State* (Cambridge, 1965), pp. 209ff.

54. Charles T. Adams, "Mawdudi and the Islamic State," in *Voices of Resurgent Islam*, ed. John Espositio (New York, 1983), pp. 99–133; Ulrike Freitag, "Politische Religion im Nahen Osten: Nationalistische und islamistische Modelle," in *Politik und Religion: Studien zur Entstehung, Existenz und Wirkung des Totalitarismus*, ed. Klaus Hildebrand (Munich, 2003), pp. 139–155.

55. Abul Ala Maudoodi, *Correspondence between Mualana Maudoodi and Maryam Jameela* (Lahore, 1969), p. 68.

56. Emmanuel Sivan, *Radical Islam: Medieval Theology and Modern Politics* (New Haven, 1990), p. 22.

57. Aziz Achmed, *Studies in Islamic Culture in the Indian Environment* (London, 1964).

58. Abul Ala Mawdudi, *Jihad in Islam* (Lahore, 1976); Abul Ala Mawdudi, *Islamic Way of Life* (Lahore, 1979); Abul Ala Mawdudi, *Als Muslim leben* (Karlsruhe, 1995).

59. Dan Diner, "Politischer Islam," in *Weltordnungen: Über Geschichte und Wirkung von Recht und Macht* (Frankfurt a.M., 1993), pp. 179–220.

60. Reinhard Schulze, *Islamischer Internationalismus im 20. Jahrhundert: Untersuchungen zur Geschichte der islamischen Weltliga* (Leiden, 1990), pp. 187, 201–202.

61. Richard P. Mitchell, *The Society of the Muslim Brothers* (New York, 1969).

62. Henri Laoust, "Le réformisme orthodoxe des 'Salafiyya' et les caractères généraux de son orientation actuelle," *Revue des Etudes Islamiques* 6 (1932): 175–224.

63. Malcolm H. Kerr, *Islamic Reform: The Political and Legal Theories of Muhammad 'Abduh and Rashid Rida* (Los Angeles, 1966); Albert Habib Hourani, *Arabic Thought in the Liberal Age, 1798–1939* (Oxford, 1970).

64. Rudolph Peters, "Religious Attitudes towards Modernization in the Ottoman Empire: A Nineteenth-Century Pious Text on Steamships, Factories and the Telegraph," *Die Welt des Islams* 26 (1986): 76–105.

65. Israel Gershoni, *Redefining the Egyptian Nation, 1930–1945* (Cambridge, 1995).

66. Josef Muzikar, "Gamal Abdel Nasser and His Attitude to Islam," in *Egypt: The Revolution of July 1952 and Gamal Abdel Nasser*, ed. Martin Robbe and Jürgen Hösel (Berlin, 1989), pp. 104–113.

67. Sayyid Qutb, *Islam and Universal Peace* (Indianapolis, 1977); Sayyid Qutb, *Milestones* (Delhi, 1988); Sayyid Qutb, *Dieser Glaube—der Islam* (Munich, 1987); Sylvia G. Haim, "Sayyid Qutb," *Asian and African Studies* 16 (1982): 147–156.

68. Yvonne Haddad, "Sayyid Qutb: Ideologue of Islamic Revival," in *Voices of Resurgent Islam*, ed. John Esposito (New York, 1983), pp. 67–98.

69. Hélène Ahrweiler, *L'Idéologie politique de l'Empire byzantine* (Paris, 1975).

70. Norbert Elias, *The Civilizing Process*, 2 vols. (Oxford, 2000).

71. Dan Diner, "Universelle Rechtsform und partikulare Differenz: Islam und Völkerrecht," in *Weltordnungen: Über Geschichte und Wirkung von Recht und Macht* (Frankfurt a.M., 1993), pp. 165–196.

72. Carl Schmitt, *Political Theology: Four Chapters on the Concept of Sovereignty* (Chicago, 2006). Quotation is taken from the German edition: Carl Schmitt, *Politische Theologie: Vier Kapitel zur Lehre von der Souveränität* (Munich, 1922), p. 49.

73. Thomas Hobbes, *Leviathan*, ed. Crawford Brough Macpherson (Harmondsworth, 1968), pt. 3, chap. 43, p. 621.

74. Maudoodi, *Correspondence*, p. 19.

75. Emmanuel Sivan, "The Sanctity of Jerusalem in Islam," in *Interpretations of Islam: Past and Present* (Princeton, 1985), pp. 3–44.

76. Sivan, *Radical Islam*, pp. 96–97.

77. Dieter Groh, "'Why Do Bad Things Happen to Good People?'" in *Anthropologische Dimensionen der Geschichte* (Frankfurt a.M., 1992), p. 267.

78. Gilles Kepel, *Muslim Extremism in Egypt: The Prophet and Pharaoh* (Berkeley, 2003).

79. Gudrun Krämer, "The Integration of the Integrists: A Comparative Study of Egypt, Jordan and Tunesia," in *Democracy without Democrats: The Renewal of Politics in the Muslim World*, ed. Ghassan Salamé (London, 1994), pp. 200–226.

80. Raymond William Baker, *Islam without Fear: Egypt and the New Islamists* (Cambridge, MA, 2003).

81. Luis Martinez, *The Algerian Civil War, 1990–1998* (London, 2000).

Chapter 3: Text and Speech

1. Bernard Lewis, *The Emergence of Modern Turkey* (London, 1968), p. 274.

2. Elizabeth L. Eisenstein, *The Printing Press as an Agent of Change—Communications and Cultural Transformations in Early Modern Europe* (Cambridge, 1979), vol. 2, pp. 683–684.

3. Elizabeth L. Eisenstein, *The Printing Revolution in Early Modern Europe* (Cambridge, 1983), pp. 15–16.

4. Herschel Baker, *The Wars of Truth* (Cambridge, MA, 1952).

5. Paul Münch, "Der Buchdruck mit beweglichen Lettern," in *Meilensteine der Menschheit: Einhundert Entdeckungen, Erfindungen und Wendepunkte der Geschichte*, ed. Brockhaus Redaktion (Leipzig, 1999), pp. 138–141.

6. Johannes Burkhardt, *Das Reformationsjahrhundert: Deutsche Geschichte zwischen Medienrevolution und Institutionsbildung, 1517–1617* (Stuttgart, 2002), p. 24.

7. Michael Giesecke, *Der Buchdruck in der frühen Neuzeit: Eine historische Fallstudie über die Durchsetzung neuer Informations- und Kommunikationstechnologien* (Frankfurt a.M., 1991), p. 667.

8. Jacques Derrida, *Of Grammatology*, trans. G. Spivak (Baltimore, 1974), pp. 6–7.

9. Seyyed Hossein Nasr, "Oral Transmission and the Book in Islamic Education," in *The Book in the Islamic World: The Written Word and Communication in the Middle East*, ed. George N. Atiyeh (New York, 1995), pp. 57–70; Labib as-Said, *The Recited Koran* (Princeton, 1975).

10. Jack Goody, *The Interface between the Written and the Oral* (Cambridge, 1987); see also Jan Assmann, *Das kulturelle Gedächtnis* (Munich, 1991), pp. 259ff.

11. Franz Rosenthal, "'Of Making Many Books There Is No End': The Classical Muslim View," in *The Book in the Islamic World: The Written Word and Communication in the Middle East*, ed. George N. Atiyeh (New York, 1995), pp. 33–56.

12. Ignaz Goldziher, *Muslim Studies*, ed. S. M. Stern (London, 2006).

13. Robert Brunschvig, "Herméneutique normative dans le Judaïsme et dans l'Islam," *Atti della Accademia Nazionale dei Lincei: Classe di Scienze Morali, Storiche e Filologiche* 30 (1975): 233ff.

14. Julius Kaplan, *The Redaction of the Babylonian Talmud* (New York, 1933).

15. Birger Gerhardsson, *Memory and Manuscript: Oral Tradition and Written Transmission in Rabbinic Judaism and Early Christianity* (Uppsala, 1961).

16. Jacob Neusner et al., trans., *The Talmud of the Land of Israel* (Chicago, 1982ff.), p. 142, quoted in Michael Cook, "The Opponents of the Writing of Tradition in Early Islam," *Arabica* 44 (1997): 498–499.

17. Gershom Scholem, "Revelation and Tradition as Religious Categories in Judaism," in *The Messianic Idea in Judaism* (New York, 1995), pp. 282–303.

18. Ignaz Goldziher, "Kämpfe um die Stellung des Hadit im Islam," *Zeitschrift der Deutschen Morgenländischen Gesellschaft* 61 (1907): 869ff.

19. Josef Horovitz, "Alter und Ursprung des Isnad," *Der Islam* 8 (1918): 44–47.

20. Cook, "Opponents of the Writing" pp. 504–505.

21. Gregor Schoeler, "Mündliche Thora und Hadit: Überlieferung, Schreibverbot, Redaktion," *Der Islam* 66 (1989): 213–251, esp. p. 216.

22. G.H.A. Juynball, *The Authenticity of the Tradition Literature* (Leiden, 1969); Angelika Neuwirth, "Zur Archäologie einer Heiligen Schrift: Überlegungen zum Koran vor seiner Kompilation," in *Streit um den Koran: Die Luxemburg-Debatte. Standpunkte und Hintergründe*, ed. Christoph Burgner (Berlin, 2004), pp. 82–97.

23. Josef van Ess, *Zwischen Hadit und Theologie* (Berlin, 1975); Michael Cook, *Early Muslim Dogma* (Cambridge, 1981).

24. Cook, "Opponents of the Writing," p. 481.

25. Ibid., pp. 478–479.

26. Gregor Schoeler, "Weiteres zur Frage der schriftlichen oder mündlichen Überlieferung der Wissenschaften im Islam," *Der Islam* 66, no. 1 (1989): 38–67, esp. pp. 66–67.

27. Ibid., p. 65.

28. Schoeler, "Mündliche Thora und Hadit," p. 221.

29. Talal Asad, *The Idea of Anthropology of Islam*, Center for Contemporary Arab Studies, Occasional Papers (Washington, DC, 1986), p. 14.

30. Edward Said, *The World, the Text, and the Critic* (Cambridge, 1983), p. 46.

31. Dale F. Eickelman, "The Art of Memory, Islamic Education and Its Social Reproduction," *Comparative Studies in Society and History* 20 (1978): 485–516.

32. Rainer Brunner, *Die Schia und die Koranfälschung* (Würzburg, 2001).

33. Brinkley Messick, *The Calligraphic State: Textual Domination and History in a Muslim Society* (Berkeley and Los Angeles, 1993), p. 26.

34. Gerhard Endress, "Herkunft und Entwicklung der arabischen Schrift," in *Grundriß der arabischen Philologie*, ed. Wolfdietrich Fischer (Wiesbaden, 1982), pp. 165ff.

35. Messick, *Calligraphic State*, p. 252.

36. [Baruch] Benedict de Spinoza, *Theologico-Political Treatise*, in *The Chief Works of Benedict de Spinoza*, trans. R.H.M. Elwes (New York, 1955), vol. 1, p. 109.

37. Scholem, "Revelation and Tradition as Religious Categories in Judaism."

38. Messick, *Calligraphic State*, p. 21.

39. Derrida, *Grammatology*, p. 37.

40. Ibid., p. 62.

41. Ibid., p. 66.

42. Ibid., p. 67.

43. Ibid., p. 120

44. Walter Benjamin, "The Work of Art in the Age of Mechanical Reproduction," in *Illuminations: Essays and Reflections* (New York, 1969), p. 221.

45. Ibid.

46. Benedict Anderson, *Imagined Communities: Reflections on the Origin and Spread of Nationalism* (London, 1991), p. 21.

47. Sheldon Pollock, "India in the Vernacular Millennium: Literary Culture and Polity, 1000–1500," *Daedalus* 127, nos. 3–4 (1998): 41–74.

48. Giesecke, *Buchdruck in der Frühen Neuzeit*, p. 166.

49. Ibid., p. 176.

50. Ibid., p. 177.

51. Ibid., pp. 182–183.

52. Rudolf Hirsch, *Printing, Selling, and Reading, 1450–1550* (Wiesbaden, 1974).

53. Dagmar Glass and Geoffrey Roper, "Arabischer Buch- und Zeitungs-druck in der arabischen Welt," in *Middle Eastern Languages and the Print Revolution: A Cross-Cultural Encounter*, ed. Eva Hanebutt-Benz et al. (Westhofen, 2002), pp. 177–226.

54. Ekmeleddin Ihsanoglu, "Some Remarks on Ottoman Science and Its Relation with European Science and Technology up to the End of the Eighteenth Century," in *Science, Technology and Learning in the Ottoman Empire: Western Influence, Local Institutions and the Transfer of Knowledge*, ed. Ekmeleddin Ihsanoglu (Burlington, 2004), pp. 45–73, esp. p. 47.

55. André Demeerseman, "Une etape décisive de la culture et de la psychologie islamique: Les données de la controverse autour du problème de l'imprimerie," *Institut de Belles-Lettres Arabes* 17 (1954): 1–48, 101–141, esp. pp. 31–32.

56. Lehrstuhl für Türkische Sprache, Geschichte und Kultur, Universitätsbibliothek Bamberg, Staatsbibliothek Bamberg, ed., *The Beginnings of Printing in*

the Near and Middle East: Jews, Christians and Muslims (Wiesbaden, 2001), pp. 9–10.

57. Ittai Joseph Tamari, "Zu den hebräisch-schriftlichen Drucken vom 15. bis 19. Jahrhundert," in *Middle Eastern Languages and the Print Revolution: A Cross-Cultural Encounter*, ed. Eva Hanebutt-Benz et al. (Westhofen, 2002), pp. 33–52.

58. Lutz Berger, "Zur Problematik der späten Einführung des Buchdrucks in der arabischen Welt," in *Das gedruckte Buch im Vorderen Orient*, ed. Ulrich Marzolph (Dortmund, 2002), pp. 15–28, esp. p. 17.

59. Reinhard Schulze, "The Birth of Tradition and Modernity in 18th- and 19th-Century Islamic Culture—The Case of Printing," *Culture and History* 16 (1997): 29–72, esp. p. 42.

60. George N. Atiyeh, "The Book in the Modern Arab World: The Case of Lebanon and Egypt," in *The Book in the Islamic World: The Written Word and Communication in the Middle East*, ed. George N. Atiyeh (New York, 1995), pp. 233–253, esp. p. 235.

61. Hartmut Bobzin, "Von Venedig nach Kairo: Zur Geschichte arabischer Korandrucke (16. bis frühes 20. Jahrhundert)," in *Middle Eastern Languages and the Print Revolution: A Cross-Cultural Encounter*, ed. Eva Hanebutt-Benz et al. (Westhofen, 2002), pp. 151–176.

62. Geoffrey Roper, "Faris al-Shidyaq and the Transition from Scribal to Print Culture in the Middle East," in *The Book in the Islamic World: The Written Word and Communication in the Middle East*, ed. George N. Atiyeh (New York, 1995), pp. 209–231, esp. p. 213.

63. Atiyeh, "The Book in the Modern Arab World," p. 244.

64. Salaheddine Boustany, *The Press during the French Expedition in Egypt, 1798–1801* (Cairo, 1952), p. 11.

65. Schulze, "The Birth of Tradition and Modernity in 18th and 19th Century Islamic Culture—The Case of Printing," p. 50.

66. Bobzin, "Von Venedig nach Kairo," pp. 170–171.

67. Terence Frederick Mitchell, *Colloquial Arabic: The Living Language of Egypt* (London, 1962).

68. Charles Albert Ferguson, "Diglossia," in *Sociolinguistic Perspectives: Papers on Language and Society, 1969–1994*, by Charles Albert Ferguson, ed. Thom Huebner (New York, 1996), pp. 25–39; Joshua Fishman, "Bilingualism with or without Diglossia; Diglossia with or without Bilingualism," *Journal of Special Issues* 23 (1967): 29–33.

69. Niloofar Haeri, *Sacred Language, Ordinary People: Dilemmas of Culture and Politics in Egypt* (New York, 2003), pp. 31–32.

70. Ibid., p. 39.

71. Bassam Tibi, *Nationalismus in der Dritten Welt am arabischen Beispiel* (Frankfurt a.M., 1971).

72. Haeri, *Sacred Language*, p. 18.

73. Yasir Suleiman, *The Arabic Language and National Identity: A Study in Ideology* (Washington, DC, 2003).

74. Haeri, *Sacred Language*, p. 150.

75. Ibid., pp. 78, 126.

76. Benjamin Harshav, *Language in the Time of Revolution* (Berkeley and Los Angeles, 1993), pp. 81–132.

77. Werner Weinberg, "Language Questions Relating to Moses Mendelssohn's Pentateuch Translation," *Hebrew Union College Annual* 105 (1984): 197–242.

78. Alexander Altmann, *Moses Mendelssohn: A Biographical Study* (Philadelphia, 1973), p. 374.

79. Weinberg, "Moses Mendelssohn's Pentateuch Translation," p. 206, n. 36.

80. Altmann, *Moses Mendelssohn*, pp. 381–382.

81. Nils Römer, *Tradition und Akkulturation: Zum Sprachwandel der Juden in Deutschland zur Zeit der Haskalah* (Münster, 1995), p. 116.

82. Charles Albert Ferguson, "Diglossia," *Word* 15 (1959): 325–340.

83. Haeri, *Sacred Language*, p. 18.

84. Israel Gershoni and James P. Jankowski, *Egypt, Islam and the Arabs: The Search for Egyptian Nationhood, 1900–1930* (New York, 1987).

85. Roel Meijer, *The Quest for Modernity: Secular Liberal and Left-Wing Political Thought in Egypt, 1945–1958* (London, 2002).

Chapter 4: Rise and Decline

1. *The Oldest Map of America, Drawn by Piri Reis*, presented by Leman Yolac (Ankara, 1954); Svat Soucek, "Piri Reis and Ottoman Discovery of the Great Discoveries," *Studia Islamica* 79 (1994): 212–142.

2. Thomas D. Goodrich, *The Ottoman Turks and the New World: A Study of Tarih-i Hind-i Garbi and the Sixteenth-Century Ottoman Americana* (Wiesbaden, 1990), p. 15.

3. Bernard Lewis, *The Muslim Discovery of Europe* (New York, 1982), p. 196.

4. John Munro, "The Medieval Origins of the Financial Revolution: Usury, *Rentes*, and Negotiability," *International History Review* 25 (2003): 505–562.

5. David Hackett Fischer, *The Great Wave: Price Revolutions and the Rhythm of History* (Oxford, 1996), pp. 65ff.; Douglas Fisher, "The Price Revolution: A Monetary Interpretation," *Journal of Economic History* 49 (1989): 883–902.

6. Jan de Vries, *The Economy of Europe in an Age of Crisis, 1600–1750* (London, 1976), pp. 21ff.

7. Joseph Alois Schumpeter, *History of Economic Analysis* (Oxford, 1954), pp. 311–312.

8. Earl Jefferson Hamilton, *American Treasure and the Price Revolution in Spain, 1501–1650* (Cambridge, MA, 1934); Fernand Braudel and Frank Spooner, "Prices in Europe from 1450–1750," in *The Cambridge History of Europe*, ed. E. E. Rich and C. H. Wilson, vol. 4, *The Economy of Expanding Europe in the Sixteenth and Seventeenth Centuries* (Cambridge, 1967), pp. 374–486.

9. Halil Inalcik, "The Ottoman State: Economy and Society, 1300–1600," in *An Economic and Social History of the Ottoman Empire, 1300–1914*, ed. Halil Inalcik and Donald Quataert (Cambridge, 1994), pp. 9–410, esp. pp. 98–99.

10. Benjamin Braude, "International Competition and Domestic Cloth in the Ottoman Empire, 1500–1650: A Study in Underdevelopment," *Review* 2, no. 3 (1979): 437–454.

11. Cemal Kafadar, "The Question of Ottoman Decline," *Harvard Middle Eastern and Islamic Review* 4 (1997/98): 30–75.

12. Eli F. Heckscher, "Mercantilism," in *Revisions in Mercantilism*, ed. Donald C. Coleman (London, 1969), pp. 19–34, esp. p. 32.

13. George A. Moore, ed., *The Response of Jean Bodin to the Paradoxes of Malestroit and The Paradoxes* (based on the 2d French edition, Paris, 1578) (Washington, DC, 1946).

14. Cemal Kafadar, "Les troubles monétaires de la fin du XVIe siècle et la prise de conscience ottomane du déclin," *Annales ESC* 43 (1991): 381–400.

15. De Vries, *Economy of Europe in an Age of Crisis*, pp. 84ff.

16. Bruce A. Masters, *The Origins of Western Economic Dominance in the Middle East: Mercantilism and the Islamic Economy in Aleppo, 1600–1750* (New York, 1988), pp. 186ff.

17. Inalcik, "The Ottoman State," pp. 48, 52–53.

18. Sevket Pamuk, *The Ottoman Empire and European Capitalism, 1820–1913: Trade, Investment and Production* (Cambridge, 1987), pp. 41ff.

19. Huri Islamoglu and Caglar Keydar, "Ein Interpretationsrahmen für die Analyse des Osmanischen Reiches," in *Kapitalistische Weltökonomie: Kontroversen über ihren Ursprung und ihre Entwicklungsdynamik*, ed. Dieter Senghaas (Frankfurt a.M., 1979), pp. 201ff.

20. Ömer Lütfi Barkan, "The Price Revolution of the Sixteenth Century: A Turning Point in the Economic History of the Near East," *International Journal of Middle East Studies* 6 (1975): 3–28; Holm Sundhaussen, "Die 'Preisrevolution' im Osmanischen Reich während der zweiten Hälfte des 16. Jahrhunderts," *Südost-Forschungen* 42 (1983): 169–181.

21. Janet L. Abu-Lughod, *Before European Hegemony: The World System, A.D. 1250–1350* (Oxford, 1989), pp. 137–138.

22. Eliyahu Ashtor, *Levant Trade in the Later Middle Ages* (Princeton, 1983).

23. Subhi Labib, *Handelsgeschichte Ägyptens im Spätmittelalter, 1171–1517* (Wiesbaden, 1965).

24. Daniel Goffman, *The Ottoman Empire and Early Modern Europe* (Cambridge, 2002), pp. 137–138.

25. Suraiya Faroqhi, *The Ottoman Empire and the World Around* (London, 2004), p. 52.

26. Klaus Kreiser, *Der osmanische Staat, 1300–1922* (Munich, 2001).

27. Aaron J. Gurjewitsch, *Das Weltbild des mittelalterlichen Menschen* (Munich, 1980).

28. Carl Schmitt, *Nomos of the Earth in the International Law of Jus Publicum Europaeum* (New York, 2003).

29. Abbas Hamdani, "Columbus and the Recovery of Jerusalem," *Journal of the American Oriental Society* 99, no. 1 (1979): 39–48.

30. Pauline Moffitt Watts, "Prophecy and Discovery: On the Spiritual Origins of Christopher Columbus's Enterprise of the Indies," *American Historical Review* 90 (1985): 73–102.

31. Carlo M. Cipolla, *Guns, Sails and Empires: Technological Innovation and the Early Phases of European Expansion, 1400–1700* (New York, 1965).

32. Dieter Rothermund, *Europa und Asien im Zeitalter des Merkantilismus* (Darmstadt, 1978), p. 58.

33. Bailey Wallys Diffie and George Davison Winius, *Foundations of the Portuguese Empire, 1415–1580* (Minneapolis, 1977).

34. Halil Inalcik, "The Ottoman Economic Mind and Aspects of the Ottoman Economy," in *Studies in the Economic History of the Middle East: From the*

Rise of Islam to the Present Day, ed. M. A. Cook (London, 1970), pp. 207–218, esp. p. 212.

35. Abbas Hamdani, "Ottoman Response to the Discovery of America and the New Route to India," *Journal of the American Oriental Society* 101 (1981): 323–330.

36. Niels Steensgaard, *The Asian Trade Revolution of the 17th Century: The East India Companies and the Decline of the Caravan Trade* (Chicago, 1974).

37. Abu-Lughod, *Before European Hegemony*, p. 131.

38. Inalcik, "The Ottoman Economic Mind," p. 215.

39. Abu-Lughod, *Before European Hegemony*, p. 201.

40. Inalcik, "The Ottoman State," p. 345.

41. Halil Inalcik, "The Heyday and Decline of the Ottoman Empire," in *The Cambridge History of Islam*, vol. 1A, *The Central Islamic Lands from Pre-Islamic Times to the First World War*, ed. Peter Malcolm Hold, Ann K. P. Lambton, and Bernard Lewis (Cambridge, 1977), pp. 324–353, esp. p. 329.

42. Inalcik, "The Ottoman Economic Mind," p. 215.

43. Charles Issawi, "The Ottoman Empire in the European Economy, 1600–1914: Some Observations and Many Questions," in *The Ottoman State and Its Impact in World History*, ed. Kemal H. Karpat (Leiden, 1974), pp. 107–117.

44. Matthew P. Anderson, *The Eastern Question* (London, 1972).

45. Suraiya Faroqhi, "Crisis and Change, 1590–1699," in *An Economic and Social History of the Ottoman Empire, 1300–1914*, ed. Halil Inalcik and Donald Quataert (Cambridge, 1994), pp. 433ff.

46. Halil Inalcik, "Military and Fiscal Transformation in the Ottoman Empire, 1600–1700," *Archivum Ottomanicum* 6 (1980): 283–337.

47. Halil Inalcik, "The Socio-Economic Effects of the Diffusion of Fire-Arms in the Middle East," in *War Technology and Society in the Middle East*, ed. Vernon John Parry and Malcolm Edward Yapp (London, 1975), pp. 195–217.

48. Inalcik, "The Ottoman State," p. 47.

49. Inalcik, "The Ottoman Economic Mind," p. 207.

50. Inalcik, "The Ottoman State," p. 46.

51. Cemal Kafadar, "When Coins Turned into Drops of Dew and Bankers Became Robbers of Shadows: The Boundaries of Ottoman Economic Imagination at the End of the Sixteenth Century" (Ph.D. diss., McGill University, 1986), pp. 153ff.

52. Sevket Pamuk, *A Monetary History of the Ottoman Empire* (Cambridge, 2000).

53. Inalcik, "The Ottoman Economic Mind," pp. 216–217.

54. Inalcik, "The Ottoman State," p. 47.

55. Gabriel Baer, "Administrative, Economic and Social Function of Turkish Guilds," *International Journal of Middle Eastern Studies* 1 (1970), pp. 28–50.

56. Inalcik, "The Ottoman Economic Mind," pp. 207–208.

57. Peter Kriedke, Hans Medick, and Jürgen Schlumbohm, *Industrialisierung vor der Industrialisierung: Gewerbliche Warenproduktion auf dem Lande in der Formationsperiode des Kapitalismus* (Göttingen, 1977).

58. Masters, *The Origins of Western Economic Dominance*, pp. 209–210.

59. Timur Kuran, "Islamic Influences on the Ottoman Guilds," in *Ottoman-Turkish Civilisation*, ed. Kemal Çiçek (Ankara, 2000), vol. 2, pp. 43–59.

60. Kafadar, *When Coins Turned into Drops*, p. 88.

61. Ibid., pp. 76ff.

62. Ibid., p. 89.

63. Pamuk, *A Monetary History*, p. 135.

64. Cornell H. Fleischer, *Bureaucrat and Intellectual in the Ottoman Empire: The Historian Mustafa Ali (1541–1600)* (Princeton, 1986), p. 242.

65. Faroqhi, "Crisis and Change."

66. Pamuk, *A Monetary History*, p. 162.

67. Stanford Jay Shaw, *History of the Ottoman Empire and Modern Turkey*, vol. 1, *1280–1808* (Cambridge, 1979), pp. 193–194.

68. Bernard Lewis, "The Ottoman Observers of Ottoman Decline," *Islamic Studies* 1 (1962): 71–87.

69. Cornell H. Fleischer, "Royal Authority, Dynastic Cyclism, and 'Ibn Khaldunism' in Sixteenth-Century Ottoman Letters," *Journal of Asian and African Studies* 18 (1983): 198–220, esp. p. 199.

70. Gottfried Hagen, *Ein osmanischer Geograph bei der Arbeit: Entstehung und Gedankenwelt von Katib Çelebis Gihannüma* (Berlin, 2003).

71. Franz Babinger, *Die Geschichtsschreiber der Osmanen und ihre Werke* (Leipzig, 1927).

72. Fleischer, *Bureaucrat and Intellectual*, p. 133.

73. Faroqhi, "Crisis and Change," pp. 419–420.

74. Timur Kuran, "The Islamic Commercial Crisis: Institutional Roots of Economic Underdevelopment in the Middle East," *Journal of Economic History* 63 (2003): 414–446.

75. Büsra Ersanli, "The Ottoman Empire in the Historiography of the Kemalist Era: A Theory of Fatal Decline," in *The Ottoman Empire and the Balkans: A Discussion of Historiography*, ed. Fikret Adanir and Suraiya Faroqhi (Leiden, 2002), pp. 115–154.

76. Immanuel Wallerstein, *The Modern World System, Capitalist Agriculture, and the Origins of the European World Economy in the Sixteenth Century* (New York, 1974).

77. Pamuk, *A Monetary History*, pp. 112ff.

78. Suraiya Faroqhi, "In Search of Ottoman History," *Journal of Peasant Studies* 10, nos. 3–4 (1991): 211–241; Faroqhi, "Crisis and Change," pp. 411–636.

79. Cemal Kafadar, "The Question of Ottoman Decline," *Harvard Middle Eastern and Islamic Review* 4 (1997/98): 30–75.

80. Bruce McGowan, "The Age of the Ayans, 1699–1812," in *An Economic and Social History of the Ottoman Empire, 1300–1914*, ed. Halil Inalcik and Donald Quataert (Cambridge, 1994), pp. 637–758.

81. Kemal H. Karpat, *An Inquiry into the Social Foundations of Nationalism in the Ottoman State: From Social Estates to Classes, from Millets to Nations*, Princeton University Research Monograph no. 39 (Princeton, 1973).

82. Roderic H. Davidson, "The Advent of the Principle of Representation in the Government of the Ottoman Empire," in *The Beginnings of Modernization in the Middle East*, ed. William R. Polk and Richard L. Chambers (Chicago, 1968), pp. 93ff.

Chapter 5: Political Power and Economic Benefit

1. Cornell H. Fleischer, "Royal Authority, Dynastic Cyclism, and 'Ibn Khaldunism' in Sixteenth-Century Ottoman Letters," *Journal of Asian and African Studies* 18 (1983): 198–220.

2. Erwin Rosenthal, *Ibn Khalduns Gedanken über den Staat: Ein Beitrag zur Geschichte der mittelalterlichen Staatslehre* (Munich, 1932).

3. Cemal Kafadar, *Between Two Worlds: The Construction of the Ottoman State* (Berkeley and Los Angeles, 1995).

4. Bertold Spuler, *Geschichte der Mongolen: Nach östlichen und europäischen Zeugnissen des 13. und 14. Jahrhunderts* (Zurich, 1968).

5. David Ayalon, "Aspects of the Mamluk Phenomenon," *Der Islam* 53 (1976): 196–225, and 54 (1977): 1–33.

6. Michael Dols, "The General Mortality of the Black Death in the Mamluk Empire," in *The Islamic Middle East, 700–1900: Studies in Economic and Social History*, ed. Abraham Udovich (Princeton, 1981), pp. 397–428.

7. Walter Joseph Fischel, *Ibn Khaldun and Tamerlane: Their Historical Meeting in Damascus, 1401* (Berkeley, 1952); Tilman Nagel, *Timur der Eroberer und die islamische Welt des späten Mittelalters* (Munich, 1993), pp. 336–337.

8. Gustav E. v. Grunebaum, "Die islamische Stadt," *Saeculum* 6 (1955): 138–153, esp. p. 153.

9. Antoine Isaac Silvestre de Sacy, *Les Prolegomenes* (Paris, 1863–1868).

10. Arnold J. Toynbee, "The Ottoman Empire's Place in World History," in *The Ottoman State and Its Place in World History*, ed. Kemal H. Karpat (Leiden, 1974), pp. 15–16, 24–25.

11. Lawrence Krader, "Qan-Qayan and the Beginning of Mongol Kingship," *Central Asiatic Journal* 1 (1955/56): 17–18.

12. Toynbee, "The Ottoman Empire's Place," p. 25.

13. Krader, "Qan-Qayan and the Beginning of Mongol Kingship," p. 19.

14. John Andrew Boyle, *The Mongol World Empire, 1206–1370* (London, 1977).

15. Xavier de Planhol, *Kulturgeographische Grundlagen der islamischen Geschichte* (Zurich, 1975), p. 26.

16. Henry Rosenfeld, "The Social Composition of the Military in the Process of State Formation in the Arabian Desert," *Journal of the Royal Anthropological Institute of Great Britain and Ireland* 95 (1965): 75ff., 174ff., 185.

17. John Haldon, *The State and the Tributary Mode of Production* (London, 1993), pp. 75ff.

18. Karl August Wittfogel, "Die natürlichen Ursachen der Wirtschaftsgeschichte," *Archiv für Sozialwissenschaften und Sozialpolitik* 67 (1932); Karl August Wittfogel, *Oriental Despotism: A Comparative Study of Total Power* (New Haven, 1957).

19. Arthur Herman, *How the Scots Invented the Modern World: The True Story of How Western Europe's Poorest Nation Created Our World and Everything in It* (New York, 2001); Jonathan I. Israel, *Radical Enlightenment: Philosophy and the Making of Modernity, 1650–1750* (Oxford, 2001).

20. Joseph Henninger, "Das Eigentumsrecht bei den heutigen Beduinen Arabiens," *Zeitschrift für vergleichende Rechtswissenschaft einschließlich ethnologischer Rechtsforschung und des Kolonialrechts* 61 (1956): 6ff.

21. Hans Kruse, *Islamische Völkerrechtslehre* (Bochum, 1979), p. 118.

22. Julius Wellhausen, *Das arabische Reich und sein Sturz* (Berlin, 1902), p. 20.

23. Abdelaziz Duri, *Arabische Wirtschaftsgeschichte* (Zurich, 1979), p. 33.

24. Ibid., p. 188.

25. Carl Heinrich Becker, "Die Entstehung von Usr- und Harag-Land in Ägypten," in *Islamstudien* (Leipzig, 1927), vol. 1, pp. 218ff., 226.

26. Carl Heinrich Becker, "Der Islam als Problem," in *Islamstudien* (Leipzig, 1927), vol. 1, pp. 1ff., 18.

27. Janet L. Abu-Lughod, *Before European Hegemony: The World System, A.D. 1250–1350* (New York, 1989), pp. 185–186.

28. Gaston Wiet, *Baghdad: Metropolis of the Abbasid Caliphate* (Norman, OK, 1971), pp. 75–76.

29. Eliyahu Ashtor, *A Social and Economic History of the Near East in the Middle Ages* (London, 1976), p. 90.

30. Abraham L. Udovitch, *Partnership and Profit in Medieval Islam* (Princeton, 1970), pp. 190–191.

31. Andrew P. Ehrenkreuz, "Studies in the Monetary History of the Near East in the Middle Ages," *Journal of the Economic and Social History of the Orient* 2 (1959): 139; Maurice Lombard, *Monnaie et histoire d'Alexandre à Mohamet* (Paris, 1971), pp. 158–159.

32. Claude Cahan, *Der Islam* (Frankfurt a.M., 1968), vol. 1, p. 113.

33. Duri, *Arabische Wirtschaftsgeschichte*, p. 107.

34. Daniel Pipes, *Slave Soldiers and Islam: The Genesis of the Military System* (New Haven, CT, 1981).

35. Henry Rosenfeld, "The Social Composition of the Military," pp. 178–179.

36. Alois Musil, "Arabia Deserta," *American Geographic Society, Oriental Exploration Studies* 2 (1972): 162ff.

37. Patricia Crone, *Slaves on Horses: The Evolution of the Islamic Polity* (Cambridge, 1980), pp. 74ff.; Wilhelm Hoenerbach, "Zur Heeresverwaltung der Abbasiden," *Der Islam* 29 (1950): 157ff.

38. Crone, *Slaves on Horses*, p. 79.

39. Bryan P. Turner, *Weber and Islam* (London, 1974), p. 86.

40. Charles Wendell, "Baghdad: *Imago Mundi* and Other Foundation-Lore," *International Journal for Middle East Studies* 2 (1971): 99–129, 107.

41. Jacob Lassner, "The Caliph's Personal Domain: The City Plan of Baghdad Re-examined," in *The Islamic City*, ed. Albert Habib Hourani and Samuel Miklos Stern (Oxford, 1970), pp. 103–118.

42. Becker, "Der Islam als Problem," p. 13.

43. Reinhard Stewig, *Der Orient als Geosystem* (Opladen, 1977), p. 168.

44. Stefano Bianca, *Architektur als Lebensform im islamischen Staatswesen* (Zurich, 1979), pp. 98–99.

45. Grunebaum, "Die islamische Stadt," p. 146.

46. Hans Kruse, *Islamisches Völkerrecht* (Bochum, 1979), p. 118.

47. Claude Cahan, "Y a-t-il eu des corporations professionelles dans le monde musulman classique?" in *The Islamic City*, ed. Albert Habib Hourani and Samuel Miklos Stern (Oxford, 1970), pp. 51–63.

48. Janet L. Abu-Lughod, "The Islamic City—Historic Myth, Islamic Essence, and Contemporary Relevance," *Journal for Middle Eastern Studies* 19 (1987): 155–176.

49. Oleg Graber, "The Architecture of the Middle Eastern City," in *Middle Eastern Cities*, ed. Ira M. Lapidus (Berkeley and Los Angeles, 1969), pp. 19–46.

50. Hugh Kennedy, "From *Polis* to *Medina:* Urban Change in Late Antique and Early Islamic Syria," *Past and Present* 106 (1985): 3–27.

51. Dietrich Claude, *Die byzantinische Stadt im 6. Jahrhundert* (Munich, 1969), pp. 54–55.

52. Richard W. Bulliet, *The Camel and the Wheel* (Cambridge, MA, 1975), pp. 216ff., 227.

53. Shlomo Dov Goitein, "The Bourgeoisie in Early Islamic Times," in *Studies in Islamic History and Institutions* (Leiden, 1966), pp. 217–241, esp. pp. 225–226.

54. Shlomo Dov Goitein, "The Rise of the Middle-Eastern Bourgeoisie in Early Islamic Times," in *Studies in Islamic History and Institutions* (Leiden, 1966), pp. 239ff.

55. Ashtor, *A Social and Economic History*, pp. 136, 134.

56. Maxime Rodinson, *Islam and Capitalism* (London, Beirut, and San Francisco, 2007).

57. Udovitch, *Partnership and Profit*, pp. 249ff.

58. Goitein, "The Rise of the Middle-Eastern Bourgeoisie," p. 236.

59. Hayyim J. Cohen, "The Economic Background and the Secular Occupation of Muslim Jurisprudents and Traditionalists in the Classical Period of Islam," *Journal of the Economic and Social History of the Orient* 13 (1970): 16–61.

60. Albert Habib Hourani, *A History of the Arab Peoples* (Cambridge, MA, 1991), pp. 115–116.

61. Rodinson, *Islam and Capitalism.*

62. Ann K. P. Lambton, *State and Government in Medieval Islam* (Oxford, 1981).

63. Maya Shatzmiller, *Labour in the Medieval Islamic World* (Leiden, 1994).

64. Shlomo Dov Goitein, "The Main Industries of the Mediterranean as Reflected in the Records of the Cairo Geniza," *Journal for the Economic and Social History of the Orient* 4 (1961): 168–197.

65. Abraham L. Udovitch, "Labor Partnership in Early Islam," in *The Formation of the Classical Islamic World*, vol. 12, *Manufacturing and Labour*, ed. Michael G. Morony (Aldershot, 2003), pp. 307ff.

66. Gaston Wiet, Vladimeer Elisseeff, and Philippe Wolff, "The Development of Techniques in the Medieval Muslim World," in *The Formation of the Classical Islamic World*, vol. 12, *Manufacturing and Labour*, ed. Michael G. Morony (Aldershot, 2003).

67. Johannes Fabian, *Time and the Other* (New York, 1983).

68. Jacques Le Goff, "Labor Time in the 'Crisis' of the Fourteenth Century," in *Time, Work, and Culture in the Middle Ages* (Chicago, 1980), pp. 45–46.

69. David P. Landes, *Revolution in Time: Clocks and the Making of the Modern World* (Cambridge, MA, 1983), pp. 73–74.

70. Ibid., pp. 60–61.

71. Bernard Lewis, *What Went Wrong? Western Impact and Middle Eastern Responses* (Oxford, 2002), pp. 125–126.

72. Michael Cook, *Forbidding Wrong in Islam: An Introduction* (Cambridge, 2003), p. 26.

73. Ibid., p. 62.

74. Ibid., p. 63.

75. Ibid., p. 94.

76. Michael Cook, *Commanding Right and Forbidding Wrong in Islamic Thought* (Cambridge, 2001), pp. 506ff.

77. Ibid. p. 515.

78. Ibid., p. 514.

79. Ibid., p. 115.

Chapter 6: Historical Thought and Divine Law

1. Michael Cook, *Forbidding Wrong in Islam: An Introduction* (Cambridge, 2003), pp. 14–15.

2. Robert Brunschvig, "Le culte et le temps dans l'Islam classique," *Revue de l'histoire des religions* 177 (1970): 183–193.

3. Ernst Schulin, *Die weltgeschichtliche Erfassung des Orients bei Hegel und Ranke* (Göttingen, 1959), pp. 125ff., 270ff.

4. Bernard Lewis and Peter Malcolm Hold, eds., *Historians of the Middle East* (London, 1962).

5. Franz Rosenthal, *A History of Muslim Historiography*, 2nd revised ed. (Leiden, 1968), pp. 8–9; Ludwig Ammann, "Kommentiertes Literaturverzeichnis zu Zeitvorstellungen und geschichtlichem Denken in der islamischen Welt," *Die Welt des Islams: International Journal for the Study of Modern Islam* 37, no. 1 (1997): 28–87, esp. p. 45; Ulrike Freitag, "Notions of Time in Arab-Islamic Historiography," *Storia della Storiografia* 28 (1995): 55–68; R. Stephen Humphreys, *Islamic History: A Framework for Inquiry* (Minneapolis, 1988); Aziz al-Azmeh, "Histoire et narration dans l'historiographie arabe," *Annales ESC* (1986): 411–431; Tarif Khalidi, *Arabic Historical Thought in the Classical Period* (Cambridge, 1994).

6. "Geschichte, Historie," in *Geschichtliche Grundbegriffe: Historisches Lexikon zur politisch-sozialen Sprache in Deutschland*, ed. Otto Brunner, Werner Conze, and Reinhard Koselleck (Stuttgart, 1975), vol. 2, pp. 593–717.

7. Ibid., p. 648.

8. Karl Löwith, *Meaning in History: The Theological Implications of the Philosophy of History* (Chicago, 1949), pp. 107–108.

9. Hans Blumenberg, *The Legitimacy of the Modern Age* (Cambridge, 1985).

10. Amos Funkenstein, *Theology and the Scientific Imagination* (Princeton, 1986), p. 207.

11. Löwith, *Meaning in History*, p. 7.

12. Hermann Cohen, *Die Religion der Vernunft aus den Quellen des Judentums* (Leipzig, 1919), pp. 307ff., quoted in Löwith, *Meaning in History*, pp. 17–18.

13. "Geschichte, Historie," p. 603.

14. Jack Goody, *Capitalism and Modernity: The Great Debate* (Cambridge, 2004).

15. Blumenberg, *The Legitimacy of the Modern Age*.

16. Ulrich Haarmann, "Ein Missgriff des Geschicks," in *Muslimische und westliche Standpunkte zur Geschichte der islamischen Welt im 18. Jahrhundert, Geschichtsdiskurs*, ed. Wolfgang Küttler, Jörn Rüsen, and Ernst Schulin, vol. 2, *Anfänge modernen historischen Denkens* (Frankfurt a.M., 1994), pp. 184–201; Reinhard Schulze, "Das islamische 18. Jahrhundert. Versuch einer historiographischen

Kritik," *Die Welt des Islams* 30 (1990): 140–159; Bernd Radke, "Erleuchtung und Aufklärung: Islamische Mystik und europäischer Rationalismus," *Die Welt des Islams* 34 (1994): 48–66; Reinhard Schulze, "Was ist islamische Aufklärung?" *Die Welt des Islams* 36 (1996): 276–325.

17. Werner Ende, *Arabische Nation und islamische Geschichte: Die Umayyaden im Urteil arabischer Autoren des 20. Jahrhunderts* (Beirut, 1977), pp. 191ff.; Rainer Brunner, *Islamic Ecumenism in the 20th Century: The Azhar and Shiism between Rapprochement and Restraint* (Leiden, 2004), pp. 1ff.

18. Tilman Nagel, "Identitätskrise und Selbstfindung: Eine Betrachtung zum zeitgenössischen muslimischen Geschichtsverständnis," *Die Welt des Islams* 19 (1984): 74–97.

19. Angelika Hartmann, "Zyklisches Denken im Islam. Zum Geschichtsbild des Ibn Haldun," in *Europas islamische Nachbarn*, ed. Ernstpeter Ruhe (Würzburg, 1993), pp. 125–158.

20. Aziz al-Azmeh, *Ibn Khaldun in Modern Scholarship: A Study in Orientalism* (London, 1981).

21. Heinrich Simon, *Ibn Khalduns Wissenschaft von der menschlichen Kultur* (Leipzig, 1959).

22. Peter von Sivers, *Khalifat, Königtum und Verfall: Die politische Theorie Ibn Khalduns* (Munich, 1968), pp. 9ff.

23. Jörg Fisch, "Kausalität und Physiognomik: Zyklische Geschichtsmodelle bei Ibn Khaldun und Oswald Spengler," *Archiv für Kulturgeschichte* 67 (1985): 263–309.

24. Rotraut Wielandt, *Offenbarung und Geschichte im Denken moderner Muslime* (Wiesbaden, 1971), pp. 20ff.

25. Bertold Spuler, "Islamische und abendländische Geschichtsschreibung: Eine Grundsatz-Betrachtung," *Saeculum* 6 (1955): 125–137.

26. Wielandt, *Offenbarung und Geschichte*, pp. 36–37.

27. Rosenthal, *Muslim Historiography*, pp. 205ff.

28. Sivers, *Khalifat, Königtum und Verfall*, p. 39.

29. Bernd Radke, "Das Wirklichkeitsverständnis islamischer Universalhistoriker," *Der Islam* 62 (1985): 59–70.

30. Ludwig Ammann, "Geschichtsdenken und Geschichtsschreibung von Muslimen im Mittelalter," in *Die Vielfalt der Kulturen: Erinnerung, Geschichte, Identität*, ed. Jörn Rüsen, Michael Gottlob, and Achim Mittag (Frankfurt a.M., 1998), vol. 4, pp. 191–216, 201.

31. Franz Rosenthal, trans., *The Muqqadima: An Introduction to History*, 3 vols. (Princeton, 1967), vol. 1, p. 11.

32. Jacob Neusner and Tamara Sonn, *Comparing Religions through Law: Judaism and Islam* (London, 1999), pp. 236–237.

33. Mircea Eliade, *Das Heilige und das Profane: Vom Wesen des Religiösen* (Frankfurt a.M., 1998), pp. 63–64.

34. James R. Lewis, "Some Aspects of Sacred Space and Time in Islam," *Studies in Islam* 29, no. 3 (1982): 167–178.

35. Neusner and Sonn, *Comparing Religions through Law*, pp. 168–169.

36. Louis Gardet, *La cité musulman: Vie sociale et politique* (Paris, 1981), p. 28.

37. Sylvie Anne Goldberg, *La Clepsydre: Essai sur la pluralité des temps dans le judaisme* (Paris, 2000), pp. 309ff.

38. Rémi Brague, *La loi de dieu: Histoire philosophique d'une alliance* (Paris, 2005), pp. 82–83.

39. Nomi Maya Stolzenberg and David N. Myers, "Community, Constitution, and Culture: The Case of the Jewish *Kehilah*," *University of Michigan Journal of Law Reform* 25 (1992), pp. 633–670.

40. Francesco Maiello, *Histoire du calendrier de la liturgie à l'agenda* (Paris, 1993); Dan Diner, "Ubiquitär in Zeit und Raum. Annotationen zum jüdischen Geschichtsbewusstsein," in *Synchrone Welten: Zeiträume jüdischer Geschichte*, ed. Dan Diner (Göttingen, 2005), pp. 13–36.

41. André Neher, *Jewish Thought and the Scientific Revolution: David Gans and His Times* (Oxford, 1986), pp. 216ff.

42. Yosef Hayim Yerushalmi, *Zakhor: Jewish History and Jewish Memory* (Seattle, 1982), pp. 77–105.

43. David N. Myers, *Resisting History: Historicism and the Discontents in German-Jewish Thought* (Princeton, 2003).

44. Shmuel Feiner, *Haskalah and History: The Emergence of a Modern Jewish Historical Consciousness* (Oxford, 2002), pp. 26ff.

45. Leon Wieseltier, "'Etwas über die jüdische Historik': Leopold Zunz and the Inception of Modern Jewish Historiography," *History and Theory* 20 (1984): 135–149.

46. Andreas Gotzmann, *Eigenheit und Einheit: Modernisierungsdiskurse des deutschen Judentums der Emanzipationszeit* (Leiden, 2002), pp. 227–228.

47. Martin Kramer, "Introduction," in *The Jewish Discovery of Islam: Studies in Honor of Bernard Lewis*, ed. Martin Kramer (Tel Aviv, 1999), pp. 1–48.

48. Susannah Heschel, *Abraham Geiger and the Jewish Jesus* (Chicago, 1998), pp. 50–75.

49. Jacob Lassner, "Abraham Geiger: A Nineteenth-Century Jewish Reformer on the Origins of Islam," in *The Jewish Discovery of Islam: Studies in Honor of Bernard Lewis*, ed. Martin Kramer (Tel Aviv, 1999), pp. 103–135, esp. p. 107.

50. Norman Daniel, *Islam and the West: The Making of an Image* (Edinburgh, 1980), pp. 79ff.

51. Róbert Simon, *Ignác Goldziher: His Life and Scholarship as Reflected in His Works and Correspondence* (Budapest, 1986).

52. Martin Kramer, "The Road from Mekka: Muhammad Asad (born Leopold Weiss)," in *The Jewish Discovery of Islam: Studies in Honor of Bernard Lewis*, ed. Martin Kramer (Tel Aviv, 1999), pp. 225–248.

53. Günther Windhager, *Leopold Weiss alias Muhammad Asad: Von Galizien nach Arabien, 1900–1927* (Vienna, 2002).

54. Muhammed Asad, *Der Weg nach Mekka* (Berlin, 1955).

55. Reinhard Schulze, "Anmerkungen zum Islamverständnis von Muhammad Asad (1900–1992)," in *Islamstudien ohne Ende: Festschrift für Werner Ende*, ed. Rainer Brunner et al. (Würzburg, 2002), pp. 429–447.

56. Bernard Lewis, "The Pro-Islamic Jews," in *Islam in History: Ideas, People, and Events in the Middle East*, revised edition (Chicago, 1993), pp. 142–143; Bernard Lewis, "The Study of Islam," in *Islam in History: Ideas, People, and Events in the Middle East*, revised edition (Chicago, 1993), pp. 12–13.

57. Joel L. Kraemer, "The Death of an Orientalist: Paul Kraus from Prague to Cairo," in *The Jewish Discovery of Islam: Studies in Honor of Bernard Lewis*, ed. Martin Kramer (Tel Aviv, 1999), pp. 181–223.

58. Paul Kraus, *Gesammelte Aufsätze: Alchemie, Ketzerei, Apokryphen im frühen Islam*, ed. Rémi Brague (Hildesheim, 1994).

59. Kraemer, "The Death of an Orientalist," pp. 192–193.

60. Rémi Brague, "Leo Strauss and Maimonides," in *Leo Strauss's Thought: Toward a Critical Engagement*, ed. Alan Udoff (Boulder, 1991), pp. 93–114, esp. p. 103.

61. Heinrich Meier, *Das theologisch-politische Problem: Zum Thema Leo Strauss* (Stuttgart, 2003), pp. 11–48.

62. Kenneth Green, *Jew and Philosopher: The Return to Maimonides in the Jewish Thought of Leo Strauss* (New York, 1993), p. 15.

63. Leo Strauss, *Spinoza's Critique of Religion* (Chicago, 1997).

64. Lawrence Berman, "Maimonides, the Disciple of Alfarabi," *Israel Oriental Studies* 4 (1974): 154–178.

65. Green, *Jew and Philosopher*, p. 13.

66. Alfred L. Ivry, "Leo Strauss on Maimonides," in *Leo Strauss's Thought: Toward a Critical Engagement*, ed. Alan Udoff (Boulder, 1991), pp. 75–92, esp. p. 77.

67. Abdurrahman Badawi, *La Transmission de la philosophie grecque au monde arabe* (Paris, 1987).

68. Leo Strauss, *Philosophie und Gesetz—Frühe Schriften*, ed. Wiebke Meier and Heinrich Meier, in Leo Strauss, *Gesammelte Schriften*, ed. Heinrich Meier (Stuttgart, 1997), vol. 2, p. 46. English translation is: Leo Strauss, *Philosophy and Law: Contributions to the Understanding of Maimonides and His Predecessors* (New York, 1995).

69. Harry A. Wolfson, "The Jewish Kalam," *Jewish Quarterly Review* 57 (1967): 544–573; Sarah Stroumsa, "Saadya and Jewish Kalam," in *The Cambridge Companion to Medieval Jewish Philosophy*, ed. Daniel H. Frank and Oliver L. Eaman (Cambridge, 2003), pp. 71–90.

70. Friedrich Niewöhner, "Are the Founders of Religion Imposters?" in *Maimonides and Philosophy*, ed. Shlomo Pines and Yermiyahu Yovel (Dordrecht, 1986), pp. 233–245.

71. Brague, "Strauss und Maimonides," p. 103.

72. Josef Stern, "The Idea of *Hoq* in Maimonides' Explanation of the Law," in *Maimonides and Philosophy*, ed. Shlomo Pines and Yermiyahu Yovel (Dordrecht, 1986), pp. 92–130.

73. Brague, "Strauss and Maimonides," p. 96.

74. Ivry, "Leo Strauss on Maimonides," p. 79.

75. Green, *Jew and Philosopher*, p. 135.

76. Strauss, *Philosophie und Gesetz*, p. 38.

77. Ibid., p. 58.

78. Muhammad Asad, *The Principles of State and Government in Islam* (Berkeley and Los Angeles, 1961).

79. Schulze, "Anmerkungen zum Islamverständnis von Muhammad Asad," pp. 439–440.

80. Abu l'Ala Maududi to Maryam Jameelah, 25 February 1961, in *Jameelah and Maududi Correspondence* (Jeddah, 1992), p. 18.

81. Schulze, "Anmerkungen zum Islamverständnis von Muhammad Asad." p. 440.

82. Shammai Fishman, "Ideological Islam in the United States: 'Ijtihad' in the Thought of Dr. Taha Jabir al-Alwani," trans. Tzemah Yoreh. Online at www.e-prism.org/images/IdeologicalIslam.pdf.

83. Gil Graff, *Separation of Church and State: Dina de-Malkhuta Dina in Jewish Law* (Tuscaloosa, 2003).

84. Iokhanan Petrovskii-Shtern, *Jews in the Russian Army: 1827–1917* (Cambridge 2008).

85. Shammai Fishman, *Fiqh al-Aqalliyyat: A Legal Theory for Muslim Minorities* (Washington, 2006); Barber Johansen, *Contingency in a Sacred Law—Legal and Ethical Norms in the Muslim Fiqh* (Leiden, Bristol, and Cologne, 1999), pp. 1–76.

INDEX OF PROPER NAMES